Fred,

with best wishes from Martin!

CONSTITUTIONALISM 2030

Constitutionalism is in crisis. And the crisis unfolds not only on a national or a regional level. It is a global phenomenon: Democracy is no longer on the rise, the rule of law appears weakened, political cohesion seems to erode. The protection of human rights is being questioned, international criminal law is not broadly recognised, international trade may have lost some of its appeal. Institutional actors find their authority questioned, established political parties are threatened by ever-changing popular movements. But to where does the charted road lead? How will the 'Crisis of Constitutionalism' unfold in the years to come? Nobody knows, of course. But at the same time, nobody is too keen to make an educated guess either. This volume remedies that. By giving nine scholars in law and political science the opportunity to make their predictions as to where the constitutionalist project will stand ten years from now, it creates a forum of deliberation that will not only aim at anticipating the developments in question but at the same time shape academic discourse on constitutionalism alongside it.

Constitutionalism 2030

Edited by
Christoph Bezemek

•HART•
OXFORD • LONDON • NEW YORK • NEW DELHI • SYDNEY

HART PUBLISHING

Bloomsbury Publishing Plc

Kemp House, Chawley Park, Cumnor Hill, Oxford, OX2 9PH, UK

1385 Broadway, New York, NY 10018, USA

29 Earlsfort Terrace, Dublin 2, Ireland

First published in Great Britain 2022

A catalogue record for this book is available from the British Library.

A catalogue record for this book is available from the Library of Congress.

ISBN: HB: 978-1-50994-270-1
ePDF: 978-1-50994-272-5
ePub: 978-1-50994-271-8

Typeset by Compuscript Ltd, Shannon

Also what you omit weaves at the web of all the human future.

Friedrich Nietzsche, Thus Spake Zarathustra

PREFACE

Let us start with a request that might seem a little odd: please close this book. Ok: don't just close it and return it to the shelf. Rather: close it, have a look at the cover and then, please, reopen it.

What did you see?

Some, I guess, would answer: a part of a (even if rather badly damaged) fourteenth century fresco panel. Ambrogio Lorenzetti's 'Allegory on Bad Government',[1] to be specific; a mandatory stop for every tourist visiting the *Sala dei Nove* in Siena's Palazzo Pubblico, even though it may not be the most pleasant sight: Tyranny enthroned in the centre, surrounded by a court of vices: Fraud, Treason and Cruelty to the right, Furor, Division and War to the left, Avarice, Vainglory and Pride above. Justice lying to her feet, bound and beaten. Below that: people in despair, suffering fear, violence, and destruction. At its sides dried up fields and the city in ruins.[2]

There are, to be sure, more agreeable works of art on display in the Palazzo.[3] But then again: Lorenzetti's depiction was not intended to be agreeable,[4] but to serve as a constant reminder of the responsibility the city's magistrates had taken upon them and as a cautionary tale of what would happen, were they to neglect it.[5]

Some, however, in beholding Lorenzetti's mural, would see more than a 700-year-old masterpiece of gothic art: they would see the future. A future bound to happen was Lorenzetti's warning not heeded. A future with the responsibility of government neglected, a future with the (global) constitutionalist project in ruins, its values bound and beaten at the feet of tyranny, a future with people in despair, suffering fear, violence and destruction. Another prophecy of doom? Perhaps. A final outcry that requires drastic action to be taken? Maybe. Who is to say?

But what about our responsibility? Specifically: what about our responsibility as academics? Aren't we to say? Or at the very least: don't we have to try?

[1] As it is typically referred to (until) today, even though the denomination was different before the 18th century – see EC Southard, 'Ambrogio Lorenzetti's Frescoes in the Sala della Pace: A Change of Names', (1980) 24 *Mitteilungen des Kunsthistorischen Institutes in Florenz* 361 and DN Ben-Aryehm, 'War and peace: the description of Ambrogio Lorenzetti's Frescoes in Saint Bernardino's 1425 Siena Sermons' (2001) 15 *Renaissance Studies* 272.

[2] J Polzer, 'Ambrogio Lorenzetti's "War and Peace" Murals Revisited: Contributions to the Meaning of the "Good Government Allegory"' (2002) 23 *Artibus et Historiae* 63 (73).

[3] Such as Simone Martini's glorious *Maestà*.

[4] Differing from the particularly pleasant 'Allegory of Good Government' depicted in the *Sala* which graces the cover of Martin Loughlin's wonderful volumes – *The Idea of Public Law* (Oxford, OUP, 2004) and *Foundations of Public Law*' (Oxford, OUP, 2010). I do admit that this is not a mere coincidence.

[5] N Ferguson, *The Tower and the Square* (London, Penguin Books, 2018) 425.

This book is some of us trying. And to be frank: to do so proved to be eye-opening; and that is thanks to the scholars who joined this somewhat unusual project (most of which I have the privilege to call my friends for quite some time now). Their contributions, unique in their way, breathed life (and knowledge) into what otherwise might easily have been another academic pipe dream. I am grateful for their commitment and their intellectual generosity.

Also, I am grateful to Hart Publishing, to Kate Whetter and Rosie Mearns in particular, who from the very outset shared my enthusiasm for this project und provided continuous support far beyond what is to be expected.

Claudia Namesnik, as usual, was the heart and head in organising everything concerning this project. Finally, I'm grateful to my team of research associates and research assistants who helped to bring all the contributors and their contributions (so, basically, all of this) together: many thanks to Katja Heine, Anja Krasser, Patrik Rako, Dirk Seybold and Raphael Ulbing for their invaluable help. I am confident that in their capable hands constitutionalism may, indeed, be safe in the years to come.

CONTENTS

PART THREE
ACTORS

LIST OF CONTRIBUTORS

Christoph Bezemek, University of Graz, Faculty of Law

Christoph Bezemek is Professor of Law at University of Graz and the Dean of University of Graz Faculty of Law. A graduate from University of Vienna and Yale Law School, he has held numerous visiting teaching appointments at Universities in Europe, Africa, and the Americas. His research focuses on Constitutional Law, Legal and Political Theory and he has published extensively on those topics.

Stefanie Bock, University of Marburg, Faculty of Law

Stefanie Bock is Professor of Law at the Philipps-Universität Marburg for Criminal Law, Criminal Procedure, International Criminal Law and Comparative Law. She also is Acting Director of the International Research and Documentation Centre for War Crimes Trials (ICWC). Her research focuses on Criminal and Criminal Procedure Law in its international dimension. As vice chair of the Criminal Law Commission of the German Women Lawyer's Association, Stefanie Bock also advocates for gender equality in society, work, and family.

Tomas Dumbrovsky, Doha Institute for Graduate Studies

Tomas Dumbrovsky is an Assistant Professor at the Centre for Comparative Law at Charles University in Prague and, currently, a visiting professor at the Doha Institute for Graduate Studies. Having completed his studies in law and political science at Charles University and Yale Law School, he held fellowships at the European University Institute, the University of Amsterdam, Michigan Law School and the Max Planck Institute in Heidelberg. Tomas has published in the fields of EU Law, Comparative Constitutionalism and Constitutional and Democratic Theory.

Stefanie Egidy, Max Planck Institute for Research of Collective Goods, Bonn: Institutions

Stefanie Egidy is a Constitutional Law scholar and Senior Research Fellow at the Max Planck Institute for Research on Collective Goods, in Bonn (Germany). She graduated from the University of Wuerzburg and Yale Law School and is admitted to the bar in Germany and New York. Using interdisciplinary and comparative methods, her scholarship examines how constitutional democracies react to pressure and change with a particular focus on the behaviour of institutions.

Matthias Klatt, University of Graz, Faculty of Law

Matthias Klatt is Professor of Jurisprudence at University of Graz. Previous positions included the Juliana Cuyler Matthews Junior Research Fellowship in Law at New College, Oxford, and an Associate Professorship in Public Law, EU Law, Public International Law and Legal Philosophy at the University of Hamburg. He had also clerked at the German Federal Constitutional Court. He has published widely on both Legal Philosophy and International Constitutional Law.

Antonios Kouroutakis, IE University Madrid, School of Law: Global Trade

Antonios Kouroutakis is an Assistant Professor at IE University in Madrid, Spain where he teaches Constitutional Law and the Regulation of New Technologies. Prior to that he held visiting appointments in Asia, Europe and South America. Antonios received a DPhil in Law from University of Oxford and an LLM from UCLA School of Law. His research focuses on Constitutional Engineering, Public Law and Regulation; he has published widely on these topics.

Andreas T Müller, University of Innsbruck, Faculty of Law

Andreas Müller was educated at University of Innsbruck and Yale Law School. He is Professor of Law at the Department of European Law and Public International Law of the University of Innsbruck. A visiting professor and research fellow at various universities in Europe, and the Americas, his research focuses on International and European Human Rights Law, International Humanitarian Law, International Criminal Law and International and European Migration and Refugee Law.

Bilyana Petkova, University of Graz, Faculty of Law

Bilyana Petkova joined the Faculty of Law at University of Graz in 2020 as a Professor of 'Law and Society in the Digital Age'. Previously, she was a faculty member at HBKU College of Law – Doha and the European and International Law Department of Maastricht University School of Law. A former Visiting Professor at the Georgetown Law Center and at the Melbourne Law School, Bilyana's research probes the intersection of Comparative Public Law and Law and Technology.

Yaniv Roznai, Radzyner School of Law, Interdisciplinary Center (IDC) Herzliya

Yaniv Roznai is an Associate Professor at the Radzyner School of Law, Interdisciplinary Center (IDC) Herzliya. A graduate both from the London School of Economics (LSE) and the IDC, he held numerous (visiting) positions in the US and Europe. Yaniv is the Co-Founding Chair of the Israeli Association of Legislation, an elected member of the Council of The International Society of Public Law. His scholarship focuses on Comparative Constitutional Law, Constitutional Theory, Legisprudence, and Public International Law.

Paulina Starski, University of Freiburg, Faculty of Law

Paulina Starski is Professor of Law at University of Freiburg. Previously she held a professorship in 'Public Law and Global Governance' at University of Graz. Prior to that she was a Senior Research Fellow at the Max Planck Institute for Comparative Public Law and International Law, Heidelberg, a Visiting Professor at the Humboldt-University Berlin and a Hauser Global Fellow at NYU School of Law. A graduate from Bucerius, her research focuses on Public International Law.

Introduction

Constitutionalism 2030: A Prediction

CHRISTOPH BEZEMEK

I. The Crisis

Constitutionalism is in crisis.[1] Everybody, it seems, says so (even if for different reasons):[2] Values once taken for granted seem to be cavalierly discarded.[3] Pictures that remind us of a past many of us do not even remember accompany our daily lives.[4] And whatever is happening at the moment to affirm such a dim view is not just happing elsewhere. It is happening right here or, in any event, somewhere close: in neighbouring countries, across an entire region, on a global scale, as some

[1] Of course, what counts as 'crisis' when it comes to constitutional matters in the first place may well be the subject of debate: just see MJ Gerhardt, 'Crisis and Constitutionalism' (2002) 63 *Montana Law Review* 277, 280–7, or T Khaitan, 'Executive aggrandizement in established democracies: A crisis of liberal democratic constitutionalism' (2019) 17 *International Journal of Constitutional Law* 342, 345–6.

And, certainly, the concept of 'Constitutionalism' is multi-faceted, to say the least. This volume, overall, follows the line of discussion as presented by A O'Donoghue, *Constitutionalism in Global Constitutionalism* (Cambridge, Cambridge University Press, 2014) 15–24 in combining procedural and substantive aspects (in particular, democracy, division of powers, and the rule of law).

Also, readers will soon realise that – while the introduction as well as the chapters may at various points specifically emphasise constitutionalism on the national, the regional or the global level, the volume, overall, does not sharply distinguish 'Global Constitutionalism' from 'Constitutionalism, globally', but rather perceives these levels in their interdependence and interaction. Conceptually thus, if you will, (even if somewhat loosely) the structure underlying the volume at hand builds on the cognitive framework established by scholars such as K Lachmayer, 'The International Constitutional Law Approach: An introduction to a new perspective on constitutional challenges in a globalizing world' (2007) 1 *ICL Journal* 91, or M Kumm, 'The Cosmopolitan Turn in Constitutionalism: An Integrated Conception of Public Law' (2013) 20 *Indiana Journal of Global Legal Studies* 605.

[2] To be sure, there are some optimists who paint the picture of a brave new world to come – see, eg, the while different, overall sanguine accounts of G Friedman, *The Storm Before the Calm* (New York, Doubleday, 2020) or JW Müller, *Democracy Rules* (London, Allen Lane, 2021).

[3] Truth, that is, at the very foundation of the concept, the correspondence of statements and facts, being but one, even if quite prominent, victim – just see D Block, *Post-Truth and Political Discourse* (London, Palgrave Macmillan, 2019).

[4] As this introduction was written in early 2022, this footnote only referred to the attack on the US Capitol about a year earlier. Now, of course, as this book goes to print, war has come to Europe once again and with it all the suffering and despair so aptly depicted in Lorenzetti's 'Allegory'; highlighting alarmingly how futile exercises in prediction may be. Still, even if from a different perspective and with an (interim) outcome that proved beneficial, 6 Jan 2021 was a particularly drastic event. For a scholarly analysis from different perspectives see, ia, A Kydd, 'Decline, radicalization and the attack on the US

of us fear.[5] Ah, and yes: we find ourselves in (what we, once more, hope to be) the aftermath of a pandemic that only made things worse (again: everybody seems to say so too, even if for different reasons).[6]

To emphasise this, runs the risk of stating the obvious;[7] nowadays at least, when every second article, monograph or edited volume in the field seems to lament this fact.[8] Disillusion (if not worse) seems warranted. The edifice of Constitutionalism, the object of wide-spread admiration and firm support in a not too distant past, appears dilapidated.

This condition, it seems, has essentially been brought about by three distinct – even if interdependent – causes.

A. Fading Foundations

First: on the national level, the foundation on which the very concept of Constitutionalism rests has been weakened. In some communities, it seems, democracy has successfully parted ways with liberalism;[9] and those responsible for it are not even ashamed to admit as much.[10] The rule of law is threatened not

Capitol' (2021) 2 *Violence: An International Journal* 3, or DC Rapoport, 'The Capitol Attack and the 5th Terrorism Wave (2021) 33 *Terrorism and Political Violence* 912, or M Rudden, 'Insurrection in the U.S. Capitol: Understanding psychotic, projective and introjective group processes' (2021) 18 *International Journal of Applied Psychoanalytic Studies* 372.

And while the event was drastic in its own right, some scholars perceive it to be far more than a mere isolated incident – see BF Walter, *How Civil Wars Start* (New York, Random House, 2022).

[5] Just see T Snyder, *The Road to Unfreedom* (New York, Tim Duggan, 2018), S Lavitsky and D Ziblatt, *How Democracies Die* (New York, Crown, 2018), Y Mounk, *The People vs Democracy* (Cambridge, Harvard University Press, 2018), or A Applebaum, *Twilight of Democracy: The Seductive Lure of Authoritarianism* (New York, Doubleday, 2020).

[6] See, ia, A Kádár, 'In its Nature – How Stealth Authoritarianism Keeps Stealing Along During the Pandemic, and How Can it be Stopped?' (2020) 12 *Journal of Human Rights Practice* 293, S Thomson and E Ip, 'COVID-19 emergency measures and the impending authoritarian pandemic' (2020) 7 *Journal of Law and the Biosciences* lsaa064, N Kabira and R Kibugi, 'Saving the soul of an African constitution: Learning from Kenya's experience with constitutionalism during COVID-19' (2020) 20 *African Human Rights Law Journal* 436, Y Chang, 'The Post-Pandemic World: between Constitutionalized and Authoritarian Orders – China's Narrative-Power Play in the Pandemic Era' (2021) 26 *Journal of Chinese Political Science* 27, or G Hamlai, 'The Pandemic and Illiberal Constitutional Theories' in K Lachmayer and MC Kettemann (eds), *Pandemocracy in Europe* (Oxford, Hart, 2022).

[7] And, of course, hardly qualifies as a novel claim – just see DJ Hill, 'The Crisis in Constitutionalism' (1913) 198 *The North American Review* 769. Still, that neither makes the current assessment alarmist nor unwarranted.

[8] Just for the latter see, ia, the various contributions in MA Graber, S Levinson and M Tushnet (eds), *Constitutional Democracy in Crisis?* (Oxford, Oxford University Press, 2018), in E Nanopoulos and F Vergis (eds), *The Crisis Behind the Eurocrisis: The Eurocrisis as a Multi-Dimensional Systemic Failure of the EU* (Cambridge, Cambridge University Press, 2019), or in HA García and G Frankenberg (eds), *Authoritarian Constitutionalism: Comparative Analysis and Critique* (Northampton, Edward Elgar, 2019) or see W Sadurski in U Belavusau and A Gliszczyńska-Grabias (eds), *Constitutionalism under stress: Essays in honour of Wojciech Sadurski* (Oxford, Oxford University Press, 2020), F Bignami (ed), *EU Law in Populist Times: Crises and Prospects* (Cambridge, Cambridge University Press, 2020).

[9] That is: classic liberalism. This is where M Klatt, in ch 1, currently perceives a major threat to democracy; urging us to overcome the current crisis of deliberative practice.

[10] For the original discussion of the concept of 'illiberal democracy' see F Zakaria, *The Future of Freedom: Illiberal Democracy at Home and Abroad* (New York, W. W. Norton & Company, 2003). For a

only by political actors who openly call for expedience to take precedence over legality,[11] but also by emerging technologies effectuating a rule by law that would disjoin legality and generality.[12] Power sharing within larger entities seems to have lost its appeal with newly established polities crumbling and century old commonwealths on the brink of dissolution,[13] making way for what appear to be smaller and smaller communities;[14] thereby crushing the hopes of those who thought regional federalisation would pave the way for true global governance.[15]

B. Brittle Blocks

Then again: in a global perspective, the building blocks of Constitutionalism are threatened by corrosion: far too often, and in far too cavalier a manner, human rights are held in disregard if not in disrepute when the going gets tough.[16]

comprehensive take from a contemporary perspective see the various contributions in A Sajó, R Uitz and S Holmes (eds), *Routledge Handbook of Illiberalism* (New York, Routledge, 2021), A Buzogány, 'Illiberal democracy in Hungary: authoritarian diffusion or domestic causation?' (2017) 24 *Democratization* 1307, D Bourchier, *Illiberal Democracy in Indonesia* (Abingdon, Routledge, 2015), R Wodak, 'Entering the 'post-shame era': the rise of illiberal democracy, populism and neo-authoritarianism in Europe' (2019) 9 *Global Discourse* 195, AP Chatterji, TB Hansen and C Jaffrelot (eds), *Majoritarian State: How Hindu Nationalism is Changing India* (Oxford, Oxford Universtiy Press, 2019), W Bartlett and T Prelec, 'UAE: Sultanism meets illiberal democracy' in F Bieber and N Tzifakis (eds), *The Western Balkans in the World: Linkages and Relations with Non-Western Countries* (New York, Routledge, 2020).

[11] For the classical account underpinning what is commonly referred to as the 'neo-Schmittean' Position see E Posner and A Vermeule, *The Executive Unbound: After the Madisonian Republic* (Oxford, Oxford University Press, 2011) but also see, more recently, T Ginsburg and M Versteeg, 'The bound executive: Emergency powers during the pandemic' [2021] *International Journal of Constitutional Law* 1. For another recent take on the topic against the backdrop of the pandemic see P Gragl, 'Lawless Extravagance: The Primacy Claim of Politics and the State of Exception in Times of COVID-19' in K Lachmayer and MC Kettemann (eds), *Pandemocracy in Europe* (Oxford, Hart, 2022).

[12] Thus, Y Roznai in ch 2 sees great technological advancements that support an ever more effective rule *by* law. Advancements, however, that come with a price tag, as this entails to move closer and closer to a formal understanding of rule by law separated (to say the least) from the core values underlying the rule of law.

[13] For a current overall take on the phenomenon of separatism see D Kingsbury, *Separatism and the State* (London, Routledge, 2021). For select case studies see among the vast number of contributions to the field for some of the respective regions: C Borgen, 'From Kosovo to Catalonia: Separatism and Integration in Europe' (2010) 2 *Goettingen Journal of International Law* 997; M Arnold and M LeRiche, *South Sudan: From Revolution to Independence* (Oxford, Oxford University Press, 2013); A McHarg, T Mullen, Page and N Walker (eds), *The Scottish Independence Referendum: Constitutional and Political Implications* (Oxford, Oxford University Press, 2016), J Muñoz and R Tormos, 'Economic expectations and support for secession in Catalonia: between causality and rationalization' (2015) 7 *European Political Science Review* 315, LA Daniels and A Kuo, 'Brexit and Territorial Preferences: Evidence from Scotland and Northern Ireland' (2021) 51 *Publius: The Journal of Federalism*.

[14] Or larger and larger cities and urban networks if B Petkova's prediction in ch 3 of this volume should prove true.

[15] See, ia R Marchetti, 'Global governance or world federalism? A cosmopolitan dispute on institutional models' (2006) 20 *Global Society* 287, Y Blank, 'Federalism, Subsidiarity, and the Role of Local Governments in the Age of Global Multilevel Governance' (2010) 37 *Fordham Urban Law Journal* 509, or M Jachtenfuchs and N Krisch, 'Subsidiarity in Global Governance' (2016) 79 *Law and Contemporary Problems* 1.

[16] Which is why some scholars argue in favour of discarding the concept altogether: see, most notably, E Posner, *The Twilight of Human Rights Law* (Oxford, Oxford University Press, 2014).

The tough then, of course, get going. But they seem to wander further and further from the basic principles of liberty and equality in dignity that traditionally served as the tenets of a 'right to have rights'[17] as it has shaped our understanding of the normative implications of our shared humanity.[18] At the same time, the will and means of the international community to effectively pursue a joint effort to hold those responsible whose deeds caused suffering beyond repair seems to fade;[19] while the nation state extends its jurisdiction.[20] Globalisation in general,[21] and global trade in particular,[22] seem to fall short of the promises made only two decades ago: a world which we were taught to and were used to perceive as becoming smaller and smaller now seems to expand,[23] placing things that seemed within our grasp out of reach.[24]

C. Maintenance Mandated

And finally: those in charge of maintaining (and enlarging) the edifice of Constitutionalism nowadays do not necessarily appear to be up to the job: formal state and inter-state institutions are often tainted by appearing partisan, prejudiced and falling short of effectively pursuing the common good and the promise it holds for the community,[25] no matter its size.[26]

[17] Just see J Isaac, 'A New Guarantee on Earth: Hannah Arendt on Human Dignity and the Politics of Human Rights' (1996) 90 *American Political Science Review* 61.

[18] Which is why, in ch 4, A Müller asks us to meet the multiple challenges that lie ahead by taking human rights seriously in the days to come rather than devising ever 'new' human rights.

[19] For a general assessment just see the various contributions in J Nicholson (ed), *Strengthening the Validity of International Criminal Tribunals* (Leiden, Brill, 2018), or the various aspects discussed by J Powderly, 'International criminal justice in an age of perpetual crisis' (2018) 32 *Leiden Journal of International Law* 1.

[20] Wich according to S Bock in ch 5 will bring about possible overcriminalisation, unjust dual punishments, prosecutorial forum shopping, and legal insecurities resulting from complex and overlapping jurisdictional regimes.

[21] Just see C Crouch, *The Globalization Backlash* (Cambridge, Polity, 2019).

[22] For a representative cross section of the problems at hand see G Sampson, 'Challenges Facing the World Trade Organization: An Overview' (2018) 51 *The Australian Economic Review*, 453–473 or B Hoeckman 'Trade Wars and the World Trade Organization: Causes, Consequences, and Change', (2020) 15 *Asian Economic Policy Review* 98–114.

[23] Against that backdrop, A Kouroutakis in ch 6 predicts the number of free trade agreements to rise and fears that the current (if only temporary) fix to the WTO dispute settlement may prove to be permanent, thus, at the same time proving the vital importance of global trade and its fragility.

[24] Again, the COVID-19 pandemic only added to the challenges ahead – for an outlook see A Madhok, 'Globalization, de-globalization, and re-globalization: Some historical context and the impact of the COVID pandemic' (2021) 24 *Business Research Quarterly* 199–203; J Stiglitz, 'Globalization in the aftermath of the pandemic and Trump' (2021) 43 *Journal of Policy Modelling* 794–804.

[25] Thus, in ch 7 S Egidy argues that institutions will need to work on their resilience in the years to come and suggests multiple ways how to do that.

[26] See, from different perspectives, E Bertsou, 'Rethinking political distrust', (2019) 11 *European Political Science Review* 213–230, F Butzlaff and S Messinger-Zimmer, 'Undermining or defending democracy? The consequences of distrust for democratic attitudes and participation' (2020) 14 *Critical Policy Studies* 249–266 or JW van Prooijen, G Spadaro and H Wang, 'Suspicion of

Political parties, that is: traditional political parties, seem to have lost not only their appeal *to* but also the trust *of* their former adherents[27] who appear just too willing to follow those who either offer easy solutions for complex problems or stand in the way of easy solutions, complicating matters by the fabrications that keep their machinery going.[28] With the trust in parties their ability to serve as a pillar of liberal democracy faded.[29] Ever new popular movements seem on the rise, riding the waves of public opinion only to be washed away by the tide of challenges that seem to change with heightened frequency every now and then.[30]

II. The Task

As gloomy as the picture thus drawn may seem: nothing about this is particularly new. We know that. We have seen it in the news. We have read it in the paper. We have endured it on social media. And all of these phenomena have been subjected to extensive (academic) scrutiny. And to do so yet again may have only minor appeal. But where to does the charted road lead?

After all, we cannot, in good conscience, accept the state of the constitutionalist enterprise – globally, regionally, or nationally – as a given. And we cannot, in good faith, think of it as something that strives toward perfection as a matter of course. Constitutionalism and its effects, on a national, a regional and a global scale, has always been nothing short of an achievement that, if contrasted with the vast part of human history, proved to be truly exceptional in more than one meaning of the

institutions: How distrust and conspiracy theories deteriorate social relationships' (2022) 43 *Current Opinion in Psychology* 65–69.

[27] See, among the more recent contributions, K Heidar and B Wauters (eds), *Do Parties Still Represent?* (London, Routledge, 2019); A Grzymala-Busse, 'The Failure of Europe's Mainstream Parties' (2019) 30 *Journal of Democracy* 35–47 or D Brady, J Ferejohn and A Paparo, 'Are we losing touch?' Mainstream parties' failure to represent their voters on immigration and its electoral consequences' (2020) 50 *Italian political Science Review* 398.

This crisis of representation and legitimacy crisis political parties find themselves in will last until 2030 as P Starski argues in ch 8.

[28] Just see the various contributions in H Tumber and S Waisbrod (eds), *The Routledge Companion to Media Disinformation and Populism* (2021).

[29] Also, of course, hardly a novel claim – see, eg, P Schmitter, 'Political Parties Are Not What They Once Were', in Gunther/Diamond (eds), *Political Parties and Democracy* (Baltimore, Johns Hopkins University Press, 2001) 67–89 and, yet, a matter of growing concerns also, and in particular, as some argue, as parties themselves have become a threat to democracy – see TG Daly and BC Jones, 'Parties versus democracy: Addressing today's political party threats to democratic rule' (2020) 18 *International Journal of Constitutional Law* 509–538.

[30] Lest we forget: The COVID-19 pandemic, again, serving as a major catalyst – see, most recently, the various contributions in Bringel/Pleyers (eds), *Social Movements and Politics in a Global Pandemic Crisis, Solidarity and Change* (Bristol, Bristol University Press, 2022). That, however, does not mean that after the pandemic we will witness a significant change: T Dumbrovsky in ch 9 is positive that we are likely to see a greater concentration of political movements which may well play a major role in an increasingly federalised Europe or in the Arab world.

term; an exceptional achievement that – more often than not – came at the price of struggle, suffering and despair.

And while we may, thus, *analytically*, distinguish select constitutions along all sorts of – typically binary – categories, such as 'flexible' or 'rigid',[31] to refer to only one, even if particularly well-established, take, *politically*, the constitutionalist project as such – no matter its scale – may adequately only be described by a single attribute: it is 'fragile'; ever-dependent on certain conditions to be met and ever-dependent on the will to meet them: 'Constitutionalism', to put it in the words of Dieter Grimm,

> is not guaranteed forever. Just as it emerged at a certain historical moment under certain historical conditions, it can also disappear or change its meaning if these conditions are no longer given or largely modified.[32]

But at the same time: nobody seems keen to make an educated guess either. And that is somewhat surprising. After all, it was Oliver W Holmes Jr who taught us that, studying the law, '[t]he object of our study [...] is prediction'.[33]

So, would we not expect scholars professionally preoccupied with the constitutionalist enterprise in its various forms and on its various levels to predict how events will unfold?

Those familiar with Holmes' work and the influence it exerted on various strands of legal scholarship would interject that the predictions Holmes had in mind, if we in fact were to agree with what Holmes exactly had in mind,[34] were limited in scope when compared to the task of predicting the future development of constitutionalism on a national, regional or global level. That may well be the case. And still, it is not to say that an endeavour on this scale was not worthwhile.[35] It was after all no lesser scholar of constitutionalism than Bruce Ackerman who opened his seminal essay on 'The Rise of Global Constitutionalism' by asking the reader to '[t]urn back the clock sixty years, and glimpse into the future: What were the prospects for constitutionalism as they might have appeared in the late 1930s?'[36]

And so: why not glimpse into the future? Not by looking back on a particular point of history, marvelling at the unexpected turn of events, but by actually looking ahead in an effort to determine the causes and effects of a process that – as matters stand – is bound to bring about a particular outcome.

[31] J Bryce, [1884], 'Flexible and Rigid Constitutions', in *Studies in History and Jurisprudence* (New York, Oxford University Press, 1901) 124–215.

[32] D Grimm, *Constitutionalism: Past, Present, and Future* (Oxford, Oxford University Press, 2019).

[33] OW Holmes Jr, 'The Path of the Law' (1897) 10 *Harvard Law Review* 61.

[34] See C Bezemek, 'Bad for Good – Perspectives on Law and Force', in Bezemek/Ladavac (eds), *The Force of Law Reaffirmed* (Heidelberg, Springer, 2016) 15–26.

[35] Even if, in all honesty, this is not what this volume, in focusing on core concepts and elements of the (global) constitutionalist enterprise, undertakes.

[36] B Ackerman, 'The Rise of World Constitutionalism' (1997) 83 *Virginia Law Review* 771.

This is not a simple task. As the popular saying, attributed variously to Niels Bohr, Mark Twain, and others, goes: it is difficult to make predictions, especially about the future.[37]

And while one should not shy away from a task only because it is difficult, it is important to emphasise that predicting, necessarily, asks for more than to engage in a mere guessing game. It is (for our purpose at least) an endeavour based on law and fact; an endeavour that requires both expertise and experience.[38] Just as it requires an adequate frame of reference for them to be put to somewhat good use.

III. The Frame

Thus, the first task to be accomplished was to create a framework that would allow to comprehensively approach the task at hand. 'Comprehensive' is not to say, however, that such an enterprise would aspire to be exhaustive. What it intends to do is to connect select threads of the phenomenon of a crisis of constitutionalism on its various stages (or what is perceived as such a crisis) to a tightly woven net that may prove to be a sufficiently robust basis for any further discussion of the topic.

The causes for the current state of affairs, as outlined above, offer a good starting point to do so; not least because of their respective point of reference: the way they are arranged, they each focus on different layers of the problem described as the 'crisis of constitutionalism'. These layers may be described for the purpose of our endeavour as 'Aspects', 'Areas', and 'Actors':

- 'Aspects' that focus on select structural principles underlying constitutionalism on the national and on the international level;
- 'Areas' that focus on select fields of international law particularly significant for constitutionalism on a global level and on their influence on national law; and
- 'Actors' that focus on key agents that shape the state of Constitutionalism on the national and on the international level.

The classification thus introduced allows to approach the topic from various angles. This again may serve as the necessary precondition for getting a full(er) picture of the phenomenon at hand to ensure that the layers themselves are subdivided into distinct fields. The Aspects covered in this volume, accordingly, include 'Democracy', the 'Rule of Law' and 'Federal Integration'; addressing legitimacy, legality and (vertical) division of powers as essential moments of the

[37] To be fair: it *is* difficult to make predictions; or, as some argue outright futile when undertaken as an exercise in causal explanation – see D Kahnemann, O Sibony and C Sunstein, *Noise: A Flaw in Human Judgment* (London, William Collins, 2021) 148–158.

[38] Or so we would believe; but see P Tetlock, *Expert Political Judgment: How Good Is It? How Can We Know?* (Princeton, Princeton University Press, 2017), arguing that we should rather rely on 'foxes'

constitutionalist enterprise. The 'Areas' in focus are 'International Human Rights', 'International Criminal Law' and 'Global Trade'; combining representative examples of global constitutionalism. Finally, the 'Actors' put in the spotlight of the investigation at hand are 'Institutions', 'Parties' and 'Popular Movements'; guardians of continuity and drivers of change on the national, regional and global level.

It is evident, that the framework itself as well as its particular subfields may be challenged (or at least questioned in one part or another): After all, why not put an emphasis on 'Limited Executive' rather than on 'Federalism', on 'International Environmental Law' rather than on 'International Criminal Law'?

One may argue that the subfields so defined are widely perceived to be the essential building blocks of the constitutionalist project in a global perspective (putting aside the specific take on this project),[39] addressing concerns such as the status of the individual, the interrelation of legality and legitimacy, the interaction between various political entities (broadly understood), the (global) standards these entities have to meet and the forces that shape the process on various levels.

Still, challenges as to the adequacy of the fields selected may never be met in a perfectly satisfying manner. At the same time: maybe they need not be, as long as the overall impression of the subject thus offered is to be considered insightful. So, while each of the nine fields thus defined may be studied separately in order to allow for a prediction as to its future development, the contrast with the other fields will add to a comprehensive understanding of how the crisis of constitutionalism will (or rather: may) unfold in a global perspective the project strives to achieve.

IV. The Future

Not to be misunderstood: this 'comprehensive understanding' may be completely off. In fact, this is very likely: reality, as indicated before, tends to get in the way of even the best of predictions.[40] But that, *again*, does not make the endeavour a futile effort. On the contrary, it may underline just how important it is. After all: if '[t]hose who cannot remember the past are condemned to repeat it',[41] those that

rather than 'hedgehogs' when making predictions While this may indeed be true, it would certainly take lots of the intellectual fun out of our endeavour. After all: is it not particularly enjoyable to learn about the views, ideas and (yes:) predictions of scholars you admire, even if they are likely wrong?

[39] Just see A Wiener, A F Lang Jr, J Tully, M P Maduro and M Kumm, 'Global constitutionalism: Human rights, democracy and the rule of law' (2012) 1 *Global Constitutionalism* 1.

[40] As indicated above (n 38) whether a prediction is good (and what good a prediction is), may depend on your point of view. To be sure: many (and for sound reasons, starting with the impossibly 'big' questions raised and answered in this volume) among those professionally concerned with the methods of forecasting (and their application) would consider the undertaking at hand naïve – see P Telock and D Garner, *Superforecasting: The Art and Science of Prediction* (London, Random House, 2015). That is: with the exception of S Egidy (ch 7) who goes to some lengths when it comes to this.

[41] G Santayana, 'The Life of Reason: Introduction and Reason' in 'Common Sense' in Wokeck/Coleman (eds), *The Works of Georgs Santayana*, (Cambridge, MIT Press, 2011) 177.

fail to concern themselves with the future are doomed to just let it take its course. And that just does not seem tempting: even those like Jack Balkin who follow in the footsteps of Polybius and Machiavelli by setting out to measure 'Constitutional Time' in recurring cycles freely admit that constitutionalism 'will [not] take care of itself'[42] but is in need of action taken on its behalf. A sober look at the current state of affairs and on how it will evolve, given how matters stand, thus, does not ensure that things will turn out as predicted; particularly if it is well done. Because then, it is more likely that action is taken on its basis; action that, in turn, may prove the prediction wrong.[43] That happening may, indeed, be the most gratifying outcome; that is to say if the outlook presented is grim, in any case.

Still, we must not overrate the effects a modest academic endeavour can possibly yield. Scholarly analysis, for various reasons, is ill-suited to provide a forum for agitation. And yet it can provide a solid foundation for conclusions to be drawn and action to be taken. If that were to be the case – even if to the most negligible extent – this would be no small achievement.

In order to hedge our bets, however, it seemed of great use to the 'comprehensive understanding' to be developed by way of contrast; not to be cast in the same mould by a single individual (no matter his sense of mission) but rather to be compiled by a group of scholars who are offered the flexibility necessary to independently engage in predictions for the respective field over a certain period of time. And 10 years seemed quite reasonable for that (even though 2020 did prove authoritatively that even a single year's course may be quite difficult to predict), which is why in this volume, indeed, we're talking about the state of constitutionalism in 2030.

Of course: the flexibility thus offered has to put up with different methodological approaches as well as with differing emphases. This is not necessarily a weakness. Quite on the contrary: with fields of inquiry so loosely defined, it is inevitable to place an emphasis on particular questions; that is: if the prediction is not to be lost in intangible generalities.

And certainly: the questions before us well-nigh beg to be addressed not only in a doctrinal perspective but to be answered in a transdisciplinary manner; embracing jurisprudence just as political science or lessons to be learned from a governance perspective and thereby, if nothing else, documenting the rich variety of the contemporary discourse on constitutionalism:

Thus, in chapter one Matthias Klatt, a legal philosopher and international constitutional law scholar, discusses the state of democracy in 2030. In chapter two Yaniv Roznai, a comparative constitutional law scholar, takes a look at the rule of law in the years to come. Bilyana Petkova, a scholar in law and society in the digital age, addresses the future of vertical power sharing in chapter three.

[42] J Balkin, *The Cycles of Constitutional Time* (Oxford, Oxford University Press, 2020) 6.

[43] Distinctly not because, *normatively*, this volume purses a certain agenda (for this see, from a progressive perspective, J Balkin and R Siegel (eds), *The Constitution in 2020* (Oxford, Oxford University Press, 2009), but precisely because of its *predictive* approach.

In chapter four Andreas Müller, an international law scholar, discusses the state of human rights in 2030. Stefanie Bock, a criminal law scholar approaches the future of international criminal law in chapter five. Antonios Kouroutakis, a scholar in constitutional law and the regulation of new technologies sets out to discuss the future state of global trade in chapter six. In chapter seven Stefanie Egidy, a scholar specialising in public law and economic analysis focuses on the future of (the role of) institutions. Paulina Starski, a scholar in comparative public law, European and international law, in chapter eight discusses the state (and the importance) of political parties in 2030. Finally, in chapter nine Tomas Dumbrovsky, a scholar in public law and political science addresses the importance popular movements will have in the years to come.

Of course: even a number of scholars and a variety of perspectives will not provide a safeguard against missing the mark. To be sure: we must come to terms with the possibility that some, if not all of the predictions we set out to make today may not fall victim to their own success, but rather prove to be plain wrong.

Still, even then this undertaking must not necessarily be considered a failure. Much rather this would invite us to ask the same questions anew once the answers haven been proven wrong, and to do so again thereafter. Thus, in order to assess the damage they have done, the nine scholars participating in this project thankfully agreed to review (and revise) their predictions after ten years, and then again ten years later; nothing less.

But that is for days to come. For now: let us see what the future holds.

PART ONE

Aspects

1

Democracy in 2030

MATTHIAS KLATT

I. Democracy's Janus-Face

Democracy is one of the fundamental principles which structure the constitutional state. Its conceptual core consists of a tripartite ideal requiring that the people are the sole and ultimate sovereign: the people are the *bearer* of the state's powers (democracy as an authority *by* the people); the *aim* to be pursued by the state's powers is to further the well-being of the people (democracy as authority *for* the people); the *procedures* of both the forming and the execution of the sovereign's will must adhere to the principle of majority rule (democracy as authority according to majoritarian procedure).[1]

These three elements, taken together, require that we can ascribe every exercise of state power to the sovereign: the people themselves. It must be possible to trace every exercise of state power back to the people. The mechanism that must link all exercises of power to the sovereign people is a chain of legitimacy. In the words of the German Federal Constitutional Court (FCC):

> Democratic legitimisation, as required by the constitution, demands a continuous, uninterrupted chain of legitimacy between the people and the authorities and institutions which exercise state powers. However, this legitimisation does not need to happen by an immediate decision of the people in all cases. Therefore, as a general rule, it suffices that the legitimisation can be attributed to the sovereign people qua bearer of the state's authority.[2]

Sometimes, the chain of legitimacy is relatively short: when the officer supervising an election declares the election's final result, only a few intermediate steps lie between this authoritative declaration and the people's voting. More often than not, however, the chain of legitimacy is much longer. This is because numerous intermediate links stand in between the people's voting and, for example, the

[1] W Maihofer, 'Prinzipien freiheitlicher Demokratie' in E Benda (ed), *Handbuch des Verfassungsrechts der Bundesrepublik Deutschland* 2nd edn (Berlin, De Gruyter 1994) 5.

[2] BVerfG *BVerfGE* 47, 253, para 46 (juris).

seizure of a person's bank account to garnish the monetary values required to pay the tax dues the debtor is unwilling to meet.

Irrespective of whether the chain is long or short, to convey the legitimacy to the exercise of public authority, it is not sufficient that formal requirements are met. The formal conception of democracy merely mirrors the far too narrow, positivistic understanding of law as the command of a sovereign ruler, whose function is to settle disputes by authoritative pronouncement.[3] The formal requirement – a majority of votes – is necessary but not sufficient for democratic legitimacy. For a full legitimisation of public authority, material conditions are also required:

> The point of democracy […] is to secure government not only by the people (or their representatives) but to secure it in their collective interest: there must be provision for the advancement of a common good, in recognition of which everyone can, in principle, collaborate by obedience to a legitimate regime of law. For such a regime, only a more thorough-going and substantive equality can serve: each person's treatment must be capable of *justification* by reference to an explicitly articulated conception of the public good, open to uninhibited debate and criticism.[4]

Only fundamental rights allow the people to exercise their voting rights informed, freely, and wisely and to engage in justificatory practices on the question of what substantive notions of equality and liberty require. Democracy, in its whole meaning, is not exhausted by formal majority rule. Instead, it is a limited rule of the formal majority. Fundamental rights must limit formal majority rule. Without such limitation, majority rule would be neither sustainable nor substantially wise in the first place. Fundamental rights, then, are the 'basic ingredients of any liberal democratic polity'; taken together, rights 'afford the individual citizen the security necessary to resist the arbitrary will of officials (elected or otherwise)'.[5] Democracy and fundamental rights do not operate, as we often assume, as conceptually independent.[6] Rather, rights are conceptually interconnected with majority rule.

For this reason, a central tension comes into sight. The principle of democracy is thoroughly kind to fundamental rights *and* also thoroughly hostile to them. Democracy is kind to rights because it requires them in order to operate in full swing. Without fundamental rights such as freedom of speech, assembly, and information, democracy could not fulfil its primary function. Blind, deceived, disinformed, voiceless and frightened citizens cannot successfully legitimise state authority. Therefore, democracy is impossible without fundamental rights.

[3] *cf* HLA Hart, *The Concept of Law* 2nd edn (Oxford, Oxford University Press 1994) 18–78.

[4] TRS Allan, 'Democracy, Legality, and Proportionality' in G Huscroft, BW Miller and GCN Webber (eds), *Proportionality and the Rule of Law: Rights, Justification, Reasoning* (New York, Cambridge University Press 2014) 209.

[5] ibid 210.

[6] *cf* RH Fallon Jr, 'Individual Rights and the Powers of Government' (1993) 27(2) *Georgia Law Review* 343, 344.

At the same time, however, democracy is hostile to rights. Majority decisions tend to infringe or even violate fundamental rights.[7] Positions that deny this downplay the Janus-faced relationship between rights and democracy.[8]

The central tension requires citizens to constantly negotiate and renegotiate between formal majority rule and substantive fundamental rights. Thus, the trade-off must be calibrated and recalibrated time and again. This is the reason why, ultimately, the constitutional principle of democracy requires a particular model of democracy: deliberative democracy.[9]

II. Democracy's Decay

The ideal, normative core of democracy is a political practice of argumentation and deliberation, a game of giving and asking for reasons among free and equal citizens.[10] However, unfortunately, the realities of our democratic institutions fall increasingly short of this ideal.

In 2021, the year I am writing this contribution, a pro-Trump, anti-democratic mob storms the US Capitol in an attempt to disrupt a session of Congress assembled to formalise Joe Biden's victory – and they do this in the name of the people. Authoritarian political parties do not grab power by the means they used to, for example in Latin America of the 1970s, namely by force or military coup.[11] Nowadays, they do it in the people's name: soft authoritarianism does not fight democracy anymore. Instead, it uses democracy for its own, thoroughly undemocratic purposes.[12] Developments in Brazil, India, and the Philippines demonstrate this demise. Right-wing governments in Hungary and Poland use their majority power to damage essential elements of the rule of law employing legislative measures that violate the judiciary's independence – again, in the people's name.[13]

[7] I discuss an example in section IV below.

[8] 'There is, then, no chasm between democracy and basic or human rights [...] they are conceptually 'co-original', though in practice they can of course come into conflict.' R Forst, 'The Rule of Reasons: Three Models of Deliberative Democracy', in *The Right to Justification: Elements of a Constructivist Theory of Justice*. Flynn, Jeffrey (transl.) (New York, Columbia University Press 2007) 186–187.

[9] For a recent forceful defence of deliberative democracy, see C Lafont, *Democracy without Shortcuts: A Participatory Conception of Deliberative Democracy* (Oxford, Oxford University Press 2020).

[10] RB Brandom, *Articulating Reasons: An Introduction to Inferentialism* (Cambridge, Harvard University Press 2000) 189; Forst (n 8) 155–156; Allan (n 4) 210.

[11] Y Roznai and T Hostovsky Brandes, 'Democratic Erosion, Populist Constitutionalism, and the Unconstitutional Constitutional Amendments Doctrine' (2020) 14(1) *The Law & Ethics of Human Rights* 19, 21.

[12] N Bermeo, 'On Democratic Backsliding' (2016) 27(1) *Journal of Democracy* 5; A Kendall-Taylor and E Frantz, 'How Democracies Fall Apart: Why Populism is a Pathway to Autocracy' (2016) www.foreignaffairs.com/articles/2016-12-05/how-democracies-fall-apart.

[13] P Blokker, 'Populism as a constitutional project' (2019) 17(2) *International Journal of Constitutional Law* 536; for Poland specifically, see O Doyle and R Walsh, 'Deliberative Mini-Publics as a Response to Populist Democratic Backsliding' in M Cahill and others (eds), *Constitutional Change and Popular Sovereignty: Populism, Politics and the Law in Ireland* (Comparative constitutional change, London, New York, Routledge, 2021).

The examples all demonstrate how a perverted version of democracy can be abused to destroy the rule of law. This possibility, by the way, helpfully indicates that, when evaluating the status quo of constitutionalism, one must think about the joint status and internal connections among the various constitutional principles to see the complete picture. Thus, a focus on each constitutional principle taken alone will not suffice.

These experiences of the functional decline of democracy are confirmed by theoretical research.[14] Many scholars have provided a rather pessimistic diagnosis in the last decade by demonstrating the various causes and routes of democracy's decay. An overview of recent books on democracy reveals a clear and abundant concern about ongoing processes of democratic deconsolidation: *How Democracies Die*,[15] *Crises of Democracy*,[16] *De-democratization of Democracy*,[17] *How Democracy Ends*,[18] *Against Democracy*,[19] *Authoritarianism in America*,[20] *Post-Democracy*.[21]

Populist and anti-liberal parties around the world abuse democratic processes and erode the democratic order.[22] The label populism reflects the claim of populists to speak in the name of the people, while the people are understood as a unitary, homogenous entity. However, the reality is different. It is different not only because the people are a rich diversity of individuals, characterised by quite different values and pluralism of standpoints, but also because populists – contrary to what the label insinuates – do not even represent a majority of the whole of the people. Instead, populism often is the attempt of small minorities to capture the political agenda under the pretence to represent majorities.

Current challenges to democracy also include the 'rise of incivility, political polarisation, the normalisation of disinformation and the growing appeal of finding simplistic solutions to complex problems'.[23] As dear as democracy is to us – its current ramifications cast doubt upon this political ideal. Or do they? Sometimes, the frantic talk of a 'crisis of democracy' reminds me of political statements delivered in the context of the breakdown of the former Soviet Union and the German Democratic Republic. At that time, many commentators declared that communism and Marxism were dead once and for all. This diagnosis was profoundly

[14] D Landau, 'Abusive Constitutionalism' (2013) 47 *University of California Davis Law Review* 189; TG Daly, 'Democratic Decay: Conceptualising an Emerging Research Field' (2019) 11(1) *Hague Journal on the Rule of Law* 9.

[15] S Levitsky and D Ziblatt, *How Democracies Die* (New York, Crown, 2018).

[16] A Przeworski, *Crises of Democracy* (Cambridge, Cambridge University Press, 2019).

[17] P Manow, *(Ent-)Demokratisierung der Demokratie: Ein Essay* vol 2753 (Berlin, Suhrkamp, 2020).

[18] D Runciman, *How Democracy Ends* (London, Profile Books, 2018).

[19] J Brennan, *Against Democracy* (Princeton, Princeton University Press, 2017).

[20] CR Sunstein, *Can It Happen Here? Authoritarianism in America* (New York, Dey St. an imprint of William Morrow, 2018).

[21] C Crouch, *Post-Democracy* (Cambridge, Polity Press, 2009).

[22] Roznai and Hostovsky Brandes (n 11) 20–21; see also the contributions in T Daly and W Sadurski, 'Democracy 2020: Assessing Constitutional Decay, Breakdown, and Renewal Worldwide' www.iacl-democracy-2020.org/s/Democracy2020-e-book_December-2020-min-ha6p.pdf.

[23] N Curato and others, 'Deliberative Democracy in the Age of Serial Crisis' [2020] *International Political Science Review* 1–12, 2.

mistaken. What had died were certain, quite imperfect, practices and purported realisations of a political idea. Not the idea itself.

In a similar vein, I would like to submit that the current crisis is a crisis not of the principle of democracy per se. Instead, it is a crisis of our abilities to live up to its ideal. The crisis is one of a perverted practice. Some scholars advise us that theory was to blame for this crisis of practice. If that diagnosis was accurate, constitutional theorists must set to work: they must, or so the advice goes, rework the theoretical concept and basic structures of democracy, in the light of the current crisis, to make it better and more robust, or more modern.

We must resist this advice. Our main task is not to improve the theory of democracy. The principle of democracy is robust and capable of coping with all the current dangers. We had better concentrate, not on theory but practice. We need better political education for young people.

Moreover, we need to raise our voices as public intellectuals. We must rise not as scholars but as citizens. We must not improve the theory of deliberation. Instead, we must engage in deliberating more actively.

III. Democracy's Discourse

If we do not live up to the specific challenge which I laid down at the end of the previous section, democracy will die from within. The main dangers currently do not lie outside democracy. They lie inside. The dangers stem from those who dismiss the basic rules of deliberation.

If we look at the foundation of rational discourse, we can rather clearly see that this foundation is under attack. For example, one of the fundamental rules of rational discourse is this: everyone may introduce any assertion into the discourse.[24] Another rule supplements: no speaker may be prevented from exercising this right by any coercion, be it internal or external to discourse.[25]

In our times, rules like these are increasingly violated: not everyone may say everything anymore. Due to the rise of an ideology-laden 'wokeness' and 'cancel culture', our real discourses are now characterised by these rules instead: so-called white people may not introduce assertions regarding people of colour. Men may not introduce assertions regarding women. Highly controversial assertions may not be introduced into the discourse. Instead, they must be cancelled. 'Woke' protagonists claim that certain propositions may not be maintained at all. Instead of discussing them critically, they suggest 'cancelling' them entirely.

This suggestion, however, denies the discursive rights to these people and, therefore, comes close to self-contradiction. This is detrimental since the causes woke protagonists are campaigning for are often highly sensitive and serious

[24] R Alexy, *A Theory of Legal Argumentation: The Theory of Rational Discourse as Theory of Legal Justification* (Oxford, Oxford University Press, 1989) 193.

[25] ibid.

human rights issues that indeed deserve more attention, discursive and otherwise. But these laudable goals cannot justify the means, and this is the reason why it is somewhat ironic that the cancel movement should be labelled as a 'culture'. Given that it runs counter to so many acquisitions the cultural heritage of rationalism, liberalism and enlightenment had achieved, the label cancel 'anti-culture' would be more appropriate.

The most fundamental change cancel 'culture' causes to the rules of rational discourse lay, arguably, in a significant modification of the claim to correctness.[26] Correctness is not attributed anymore to intersubjective, objective rationality. Instead, correctness is being subjectivised. This is one reason why fake news is on the rise. Correctness is what helps the ideology to win. Measured by this yardstick, even utterly incorrect facts can be correct. Discursive correctness is replaced by ideological correctness.

Do not assume that this is far away. I could list numerous examples, but maybe a few illustrations from the world of Universities specifically are insightful. After all, universities are the paradigmatic forum of free and equal deliberation. The ideal of rational discourse is nothing less than their very fundament. Nevertheless, nowadays, the quality of discourse in universities illustrates the crisis of democracy that I identified earlier. I am not talking here about the fact that, due to anti-COVID measures, guards and security agents are patrolling our campus and controlling the access to our free deliberation fora at Universities.[27] This picture is otherwise known only from dystopia and totalitarian states, but it is temporary and justified as an attempt to cope with the pandemic. Instead, I refer to various instances that demonstrate that free discourse is in decline within the institution of free discourse par excellence.

Cancel 'culture' has arrived in our Universities. In October 2019, the founder of a right-wing party in Germany wanted to return to his professorship in Hamburg after losing elections, but he got cancelled. As a result, he could not deliver his lectures; he was shouted down, not with arguments but with hate. In the US, the philosopher Peter Boghossian resigned from his position at Portland State University, citing harassment and a lack of intellectual freedom.[28]

In recognition of her scholarly contributions and services to higher education, the Scottish philosopher Kathleen Stock had been appointed Officer of the Order of the British Empire. Nevertheless, she resigned from her professorship at the University of Sussex. Her views on transgender rights and gender identity had not

[26] On the claim to correctness as fundament of rational (legal) discourse, see R Alexy, 'Law and Correctness' (1998) 51(1) *Current Legal Problems* 205; M Klatt, 'Robert Alexy's Philosophy of Law as System' in M Klatt (ed), *Institutionalized Reason: The Jurisprudence of Robert Alexy* (Oxford, Oxford University Press, 2012) 5–6, 12–13, 15–18; M Klatt, 'Proportionality and Justification' in E Herlin-Karnell and M Klatt (ed), *Constitutionalism Justified: Rainer Forst in Discourse* (Oxford, Oxford University Press, 2019) 170–173, 190–191.

[27] On the various negative impacts of COVID upon liberal education, see M Klatt, 'What COVID-19 Does to Our Universities' (2021) 6(1) *University of Bologna Law Review* 1.

[28] P Boghossian, 'My University Sacrificed Ideas for Ideology. So Today I Quit' (8 September 2021) bariweiss.substack.com/p/my-university-sacrificed-ideas-for.

found the approval of trans activists, and they had agitated against her, celebrating her resignation with the song *Ding-Dong! The Witch is Dead* from the *Wizard of Oz*.[29] Nothing can summarise better what was happening in this case than the twitter commentary by the Oxford historian Timothy Garton Ash:

> Whatever your views on her views on gender and sexual identity, every civilised person must condemn this harassment [and] intimidation of a woman on campus. It is discrimination in the name of anti-discrimination, harassment in the name of anti-harassment.[30]

These are individual cases, to be sure, but taken together, they amount to a worrying picture. As a result, more than 600 professors in Germany recently founded a new association, the Network for Academic Freedom, out of their 'common concern to defend the freedom of research and teaching against ideologically motivated restrictions and contribute to strengthening a liberal academic climate'.[31]

The founding of this network is yet another indicator that the quality of our deliberative practices is on the decline because its foundations are in danger. Even in our universities, a 'particular moralistic imagination' of correct opinions and forms of life is on the rise, prescribing 'a morally pure and fully unified' picture, discrediting any divergent standpoints as morally inferior.[32] A prescribed morality is, however, entirely immoral. Morality requires autonomous decisions taken by free people. Such decisions are hindered by attempts to enforce moral conduct top-down, by administrative regulations or public rumpus intended to shame people. These attempts destroy the very fundament of scholarship and morality alike: rational argumentation. Cancel 'culture' activists intend to replace deliberation with power. They do not realise (or do they?) that they help build a dictatorship of whitewashed thinking and speaking under the disguise of moral principles.

In the realm of universities, an argument pursued by 'woke' people is that the students must be protected from being exposed to certain immoral or otherwise deprecated positions. The best protection, however, is the development of critical thinking by a dispute with such positions. Thus, the argument from protection is dangerous and paternalistic because it denies the competence of the 'protected' students to engage critically with such positions to find their standpoint. Moreover, denying their competence hinders the students from developing such abilities in the first place.

[29] P Neumann, 'Streit um das Geschlecht: Transaktivisten vertreiben eine Philosophieprofessorin von der Universität Sussex' *Die Zeit* (4 November 2021) 75.

[30] Timothy Garton Ash, quoted after H Lambert, 'Kathleen Stock and Sussex University: The War Over Academic Freedom' *New Statesman* (20 October 2021) www.newstatesman.com/politics/feminism/2021/10/kathleen-stock-and-sussex-university-the-war-over-academic-freedom.

[31] Netzwerk Wissenschaftsfreiheit, 'Manifesto' (9 November 2021) www.netzwerk-wissenschaftsfreiheit.de/en/about-us/manifesto/; for a critical view, see A Binder and I Saliba, 'Die Uni ist eine Risikozone: Privilegierte Professoren müssen es aushalten, wenn die jüngere Generation sie angreift' *Die Zeit* (21 October 2021) 41; S Huhnholz, 'Weltschmerz in der Führungsetage' *Frankfurter Allgemeine Zeitung* (14 July 2021) N 3.

[32] *cf* J-W Müller, *What Is Populism?* (Philadelphia, University of Pennsylvania Press, 2016) 20.

In the name of wokeness, minorities develop an extreme grimness that can turn into an utterly illiberal and intolerant ideology at any time. This very possibility belies any potential original justification of their political aims. The president of the Humboldt University in Berlin has just announced his intention to resign by the end of this year to protest against the new Higher Education Act, enacted by a majority of the Berlin legislature. The president pointed to the fact that the new Act deeply infringed upon the internal structures and self-administration of the University in an attempt to secure more permanent jobs for younger scholars.[33] The latter indeed is a laudable political goal – but the means employed are just horrendous The same holds for another example: the introduction of parity regulations in electoral laws, which I will discuss in the next section.

IV. Democracy's Equality

I will now turn to an example that is indicative of the developments I have laid out so far. This example draws on recent constitutional law case from Germany which concerned democracy, more precisely electoral law. Electoral law is of high relevance for the principle of democracy, given that, in an indirect democracy, the sovereign determines its representatives first and foremost by elections. In 2019, the legislators of two German federal states, Thuringia and Brandenburg, changed the laws regulating the elections in their states. Their political aim was to achieve a better gender-balanced representation of the electorate in Parliament. It took their cue from older parity legislation in France, following an amendment of the French Constitution.[34]

A. Parity in Electoral Law

The state legislators enacted a 'parity statute' which introduced a new requirement for the candidates' lists submitted by political parties for election to the state's Parliaments. A specific part of the election, namely the proportional representation generated based on the second vote, is organised based on such lists. Prior to an election, the parties establish a fixed ranking of their candidates. The voters cannot

[33] S Kunst, 'Exzellenz in Gefahr: Warum ich als Präsidentin der Berliner Humboldt-Universität zu Berlin [sic!] zurücktrete' *Die Zeit* (4 November 2021) 57. For a report of an entirely different, yet related attempt to 'govern' the Bavarian Universities from above, see F Evers, 'Wissenschaft in der Lieferkette' *Frankfurter Allgemeine Zeitung* (3 February 2021) N4.

[34] *cf* French Constitution: Art 1 II: 'Statutes shall promote equal access by women and men to elective offices and posts as well as to position of professional and social responsibility.' and Art 4 II: '[Political parties] shall contribute to the implementation of the principle set out in the second paragraph of article 1 as provided for by statute.'

alter this ranking; they vote for an ordered list in its entirety. Depending on how many votes a list can gather, a certain number of listed candidates get a mandate, strictly following the order of the list.

The new requirement introduced in the two states is this: each list submitted by a party must assign ranks alternatingly to men and women.[35] An exception clause was provided for parties who wished to represent people of one gender only. In Thuringia, the opposition called upon the state's constitutional court for abstract judicial review to determine the compatibility of this new regulation with the Basic Law. In Brandenburg, four members of Parliament filed a constitutional complaint. Both constitutional courts declared the new regulations void.

B. Arguments of the Proponents

The political aim of these parity laws is to bring more women into Parliament. A few numbers may illustrate the need to do so. For example, in Thuringia, 51 per cent of the people are women, but women hold only 31 per cent of the seats in Parliament. The proponents of the new legislation see this disproportionate representation of women as clear evidence of structural discrimination in electoral law and want to change this.

Indeed, this is a legitimate aim. The proponents can point to the text of the Constitution itself. Article 3 II 2 Basic Law regulates equality before the law and entails the following positive obligation of the state:

> Men and women shall have equal rights. The state shall promote the actual implementation of equal rights for women and men and take steps to eliminate the disadvantages that now exist.

This is not just political rhetoric and not just a vague goal Parliament was at liberty to ignore. It is binding constitutional law. There is no aim-selecting discretion of the state powers in this regard. This goal must be pursued. The legislator can argue that, by modifying the electoral laws, it wanted to fulfil this obligation. Any aim that is prescribed by the Constitution is by definition legitimate.

The diagnosis provided by the proponents stipulates that women still do not enjoy equal rights to democratic participation. The cause for this situation is not to be found in the voting behaviour of the electorate.[36] The unequal representation of men and women in Parliament is independent of this voting behaviour. Instead, it stems from a different upstream source, namely the nomination lists provided by the political parties. This background is why the proponents blame the internal

[35] Special provisions were made for people of diverse gender; I will not consider them here.

[36] *cf* Landtag Brandenburg, 'Gesetzesentwurf der Fraktion Bündnis 90/Die Grünen: Inklusives Parité-Gesetz – (Drittes Gesetz zur Änderung des Brandenburgischen Landeswahlgesetzes)' (22 February 2018). Drucksache 6/8210, 1.

structures of political parties for being the leading cause of the problem. Internal structures, the proponents argue, privileged male candidates, at least factually.[37] According to them, current electoral law allowed for internal candidature procedures which discriminated against female candidates. This discrimination was proved by statistical data, which showed, in the case of Brandenburg between 2014 and 2019, that the share of seats held by women (39 per cent) was 22 per cent less than the share held by men (61 per cent).[38]

The parity regulation aims to work against this cause to make political decision-making more inclusive. It wants to support the enforcement of the right to equality of the candidates of all political parties and the citizen's right to equal democratic participation and effective influence on Parliament. Furthermore, the parity regulation intends to secure the integrative character of elections by protecting female candidates from structural discrimination.[39]

Another important argument of the proponents is that only gender parity could fully represent the people with their complete plurality of preferences, perspectives, interests, and concerns in Parliament.[40] This plurality should be as broad as possible so that the competing positions could be considered in legislative procedures that are open regarding content. Currently, the gender ratios in Parliament were unbalanced. Consequently, parliamentary decision-making was not open regarding content because one gender had an advantage that could distort deliberation and decision-making in Parliament. Due to the gender imbalance, male dominance excluded relevant female concerns from the parliamentary debate. According to the proponents, equal access to candidature is hindered by 'deep-rooted power structures, prejudice, and work routines'.[41] In contrast, the parity regulation could strengthen the integrative character of elections because it abolishes the dominance of male representatives and brings about more diversity among members of Parliament.

C. Critique

From the perspective of the Constitution, parity laws are problematic because they infringe severely upon several fundamental rights and principles, which are moreover of high abstract weight. Three of these principles shall be considered here. All of them protect the election itself and procedures and acts made in preparing an election, most importantly, the nomination of listed candidates by the political parties.[42]

[37] This diagnosis is reported in VerfGH Weimar *Juristenzeitung* 2021, 352, para 38 (juris).
[38] VerfG Potsdam *Juristenzeitung* 2021, 361, para 102 (juris).
[39] VerfGH Weimar (n 37) para 59 (juris).
[40] VerfG Potsdam (n 38) para 106 (juris).
[41] R Süssmuth et al, 'Es gibt keinen Besitzstandsschutz im Wahlrecht' (21 October 2020) 3 verfassungsblog.de/es-gibt-keinen-besitzstandsschutz-im-wahlrecht/.
[42] VerfGH Weimar (n 37) para 76 (juris).

i. *Electoral Freedom*

The fundamental right to electoral freedom requires that elections be free of any coercion and pressure exercised by the state or societal groups. The forming of the political will of the people must be state-free.[43] Elections must form the people's will in a bottom-up, not in a top-down manner:

> The integrity of the fundamental act of democratic legitimisation, the election of the people's representatives in parliament, must be preserved to an extremely high degree. In elections, the forming of the sovereign's will must take place from the people to the state authorities, not the other way around from the state authorities to the sovereign people. [...] State authorities in their official functions are barred from influencing the forming of the political will in the elections in an attempt to sustain or change the power in government bodies. Furthermore, the constitution forbids state authorities to identify with political parties or electoral candidates and support or combat them using governmental means.[44]

The fundamental right protects both the active and the passive freedom of voters. Parity regulations infringe on active freedom since they hinder the voters from influencing gender distribution in Parliament by voting for a list that registers only or primarily men or women. Instead, the regulation imposes upon the voters a specific gender-related composition of Parliament.[45]

The new legislation attempts to turn the voting process upside-down. The result of the election is prescribed by the current majority concerning a specific attribute, namely gender. In this respect, the result is fixed before the election takes place. Thus, the democratic principle of forming the political will bottom-up is turned into its exact opposite. The legislator establishes which election result and which line-up in Parliament will be 'correct'.

In addition, the active freedom of party members is infringed since they also cannot vote for candidates irrespective of their gender. Furthermore, parity regulations infringe on passive electoral freedom. The requirement that the ranks have to be filled alternatingly with men and women ('zip principle') infringes with the passive freedom of party members running for a specific list position, if this position must be filled, due to the parity regulation, with a candidate of the other gender.

ii. *Electoral Equality*

The fundamental right to electoral equality requires all votes to have the same counter value and success value. However, the parity regulation orders that list which do not rank men and women alternatingly throughout must be disallowed, and they will not participate in the election. Consequently, all votes favouring a

[43] BVerfG *BVerfGE* 103, 111, para 78 (juris).
[44] BVerfG *BVerfGE* 44, 125, para 49 (juris).
[45] VerfGH Weimar (n 37) para 78 (juris).

woman or a man lose their impact on the result completely. Their success value is lost if that specific position had to be filled with a candidate of the other gender.[46] This mechanism infringes the right to active electoral equality.

Furthermore, passive electoral equality requires that all candidates who wish to run for a list position have an equal opportunity of candidature in the party-internal nomination procedure, election campaigns, and voting procedures.[47] Thus, the legislator must not tamper with the existing competitive situation.[48] Parity regulations infringe in precisely this way with passive electoral equality since all candidates cannot run for half of the list positions, for which they could have run without the parity regulation.[49]

iii. Freedom of Political Parties

The German Constitution protects the freedom of political parties in Article 21 I Basic Law. Political parties are free to choose the characteristics defining their identity, shape their political objectives and orient their political programme and agenda.[50] This norm protects the activities of parties, the freedom of their programme and the equality of opportunities.

Parity regulations infringe on all three aspects. The freedom of activities protects the freedom of parties to determine their candidates for elections. First, by forcing the parties to arrange a gender-based list, parties are constrained to determine their candidates based on gender specifically.[51] Second, parity regulation does not force the parties to include specific content in their programme. However, the freedom to shape their political objectives and orient their political programme includes the free choice of the means employed to present the political programme to the electorate. Hence, a political party could underline their programme by a particular gender-specific composition of their electoral list. For example, they may wish to establish a list with a very high or even exclusive rate of candidates of a specific gender. Employing such means is hindered by the parity regulation.

Third, the right of political parties to equal opportunities is infringed by any diverging treatment of the parties, which changes their equal opportunities in the election. One might think that the parity regulation applies to all parties alike and does not pose any problems regarding equality of opportunities. Such an argument draws to the formally equal treatment. The parity regulation does not differentiate in its wording between the parties but establishes its scope in an abstract and general manner. However, even a formally equal treatment can discriminate

[46] ibid 83.
[47] BVerfG *BVerfGE* 71, 81, para 37 (juris).
[48] BVerfG *BVerfGE* 41, 399, para 37 (juris).
[49] VerfGH Weimar (n 37) para 86 (juris).
[50] BVerfG *BVerfGE* 111, 382, para 103 (juris).
[51] VerfGH Weimar (n 37) para 90 (juris).

indirectly in cases where its practical consequences produce inequality caused precisely by the legal arrangement.[52] This is the case here.[53] Parties who have a significantly higher ratio of one gender among their members are facing unequal consequences. They either have to nominate considerably fewer candidates than they could have brought into Parliament or nominate candidates from the smaller ratio of the other gender who are seen as less suitable from the party's perspective.

Furthermore, parties with only a few members are discriminated against indirectly because they will have difficulty filling all list positions. Consequently, they will bring fewer candidates into Parliament than they could have brought without the parity regulation. Lastly, parties who wish to promote people of one gender specifically will want to fill the front positions exclusively with people of that gender. Thus, again, these parties are more severely affected than others by the parity regulation.

iv. Constitutional Justification

That the parity regulations infringe with the rights as outlined above does not render them unconstitutional. Instead, the infringements amount to a violation of these rights only on the condition that they cannot be constitutionally justified. Two constitutional principles are relevant in this regard.

The first is the principle of democracy. The proponents had argued that this principle required the composition of Parliament to mirror the gender rates existing in the electorate. In order to build such a mirror, they argued, the nomination of male and female candidates in party lists must follow gender parity all over.[54] This argument builds upon the diagnosis that until now, as a matter of fact, only men had a democratic advance in all political sectors. Moreover, due to that advance, only men enjoyed real and effective influence upon the state powers.

Already this diagnosis is somewhat astonishing, considering that it is meant to refer to a country like Germany in the twenty-first century. One wonders whether the reality in society, regarding the allocation of political power and the opportunities of people to participate and raise their voice, is adequately described here. Accordingly, the constitutional court of Thuringia stressed in its decision that men and women have, as a matter of fact, equal active and passive electoral rights.[55] Both subpopulations have equal rights to participate in political decision-making. Men do not have more rights than women, and women do not have more rights than men.

Nonetheless, the proponents maintain that, in political practice, women had more often difficulties managing their presence and appointments than men, given that the professional life as a politician was hardly compatible with

[52] BVerfG *BVerfGE* 8, 51, para 64 (juris).
[53] VerfGH Weimar (n 37) paras 95–97 (juris).
[54] *cf* ibid 103.
[55] ibid 109.

family commitments.[56] This argument presupposes an outdated view of the role allocation between men and women. Our social reality as of today is different. Many men engage actively in family work, and when they do, they face exactly the same difficulties with managing their presence and appointments. There is no difference at all between the two genders in that respect. The proponents overlook that they use an undesirable status quo from former times as an argument, thereby cementing it instead of torpedoing it. One could object that it was statistically valid that women still did family work more than men. This is true.

Nevertheless, this fact cannot be invoked as an argument for gender parity. It could only be used to argue for parity between people who engage in family work and those who do not engage in family work, irrespective of which gender these people have. Thus, there is a severe mismatch between argument and conclusion in the proponents' reasoning.

Even if one accepted the proponents' diagnosis of the current state of affairs in society, their 'mirror theory' of democracy must be rejected. Democracy follows a distinct principle of representation.[57] In the words of the Constitutional Court of Thuringia:

> According to the principle of representation, each member of parliament represents the entirety of the people, and they are accountable to them. Members of parliament are not accountable to a state, a constituency, a party, or a section of the people, but to the whole of the people. They represent the people in their entirety, not as individuals [...]. What is condensed in parliament is the party-political preference of the people, not its composition concerning gender, social or any other structure.[58]

In elections, the covenant people create is their unitarian representative body.[59] This understanding renders the proponents model of democratic representation deeply problematic. Their idea of a gender-specific representation, as intuitively plausible as it may seem, is unconvincing. Under German constitutional law, members of Parliament are representatives of all people, of the sovereign in its entirety. They are not representing a group interest, be it gender-based or otherwise. Parliament is not supposed to be a proportionate mirror of all sub-groups as they appear in society. After all, there would be many other sub-groups who could claim to impact the lists. What about the proportions of old and young people? Of intelligent and less intelligent? Of high income and low income? Ill and healthy? Singles and Families? People are many things more than just men and women, and all sorts in between. All these differences matter – should they also be reflected in the lists?

By selecting only one feature, the legislator reduces the complex identities of people, voters and representatives alike to an almost ridiculously shallow personality. It denies the central tenets of modern societies: the diverse structure of

[56] Süssmuth et al (n 41) 2.
[57] BVerfG *BVerfGE* 131, 316, para 72 (juris).
[58] VerfGH Weimar (n 37) para 104 (juris).
[59] BVerfG (n 57) para 72 (juris).

individual identities. The legislator decrees from above which item of the identity of voters and their representatives matters for elections. This imposition is utterly illiberal.

Furthermore, parity laws of this kind are based on an antiquated, backwards-oriented idea of political representation.[60] The underlying claim is that only one's own kind can represent each person. Thus, women must be represented by women, men by men. Public servant by public servant. Blue-collar worker by blue-collar worker. Such a system once was in place. From the medieval ages to early modern Europe, the political system was based on corporative classes. This, however, is hardly a role model for democracy in the twenty-first century.

The proponent's mirror theory is incompatible with the principle of representation as a fundament of democracy. Therefore, the mirror theory cannot justify the infringements.

This also holds for the second argument from democracy pursued by the proponents: They argued that the parity regulation was justified because the election was an integrative process that presupposed the equal opportunity of all citizens to participate. This argument is built upon earlier adjudication of the Federal Constitutional Court, which had used the notion of integration to justify infringements with electoral rights.[61] However, this integration did not regard the integration of men and women, but rather the integration of various political powers.[62] According to the Constitutional Court of Thuringia,

> [it] would be out of touch with everyday life to assume that women and men's subpopulations are 'political powers that must be integrated' in the sense of the justificatory grounds accepted by the Federal Constitutional Court.[63]

Consequently, the integrative function of election is not a good reason to justify focusing the constitutional principle of democracy on gender-groups, rather than on individuals irrespective of their gender.

The second principle that may justify the infringements is the positive obligation to 'promote the actual implementation of equal rights for women and men and take steps to eliminate disadvantages that now exist', Article 3 II 2 Basic Law.[64] The proponents of the parity regulation argue that this norm does allow quota regulations in the by-laws of political parties. This argument neglects that political parties hold a fundamental right to programme design, protecting their right to adjust their internal rules to their political goals.[65] However, this is distinct from

[60] G Lübbe-Wolff, 'Verordnete Identität' *Handelsblatt* (22 September 2020) 12.

[61] *cf* BVerfG *BVerfGE* 135, 259, para 54 (juris).

[62] This becomes clear in BVerfG *BVerfGE* 95, 408, para 46 (juris).

[63] VerfGH Weimar (n 37) para 108 (juris).

[64] The Constitution of Thuringia entails a similar, yet slightly more strict obligation in its Art 2 II 2 which demands not only to 'promote', but also to 'secure' the equal rights. This difference between the two norms poses some problems for the interpretation of the Thuringian norm, which is the relevant normative standard in the Thuringian case. For reasons of simplicity, I will not go deeper into these matters here.

[65] VerfGH Weimar (n 37) para 79 (juris).

the question of whether the legislature can infringe with the citizen's right to electoral freedom by imposing parity quotas. After all, the parity regulation does not aim at allowing parties the freedom to introduce quotas; it forces them to introduce them.

Apart from that, two arguments, in particular, count against a justification. First, the wording of the norm is highly abstract; it does not mention quotas in electoral law specifically. To be sure, the abstractness of the norm's wording precludes such quotas neither. Second, the parity regulation is a means to promote the actual implementation of equal rights. The dissenting opinion in the Thuringia case pointed to this fact, concluding that the norm's wording justifies the infringements:

> The obligation to establish a parity list 'promotes' equal opportunities. Therefore, the wording of the positive obligation readily supports the enactment of the parity regulation.[66]

The dissenting opinion argued further that an explicit allowance of parity regulations was not required since other infringing but justified means were likewise not mentioned explicitly. So, nothing could be derived from the mere lack of an explicit allowance.[67]

The matter, however, is more complicated than that. Due to the vagueness of the wording, the matter boils down to what degree of specificity we request. How specific must the wording be? In this respect, it is essential to note that both the abstract and the concrete weights of the infringed principles are of rather a high degree:

> In light of the number of rights infringed with by the quota regulation (freedom of election, passive freedom of election, electoral equality, passive electoral equality, the party's freedom of activities and programme design, the principle of equality of political parties) and their outstanding importance for the democratic process, as well as in light of the intensity of the infringements, the expressiveness of the wording is too little to provide by itself a justification of the parity regulation.[68]

We can learn a critical standard rule here: *ceteris paribus*, the more severe infringements with fundamental rights are, the more specific the wording of a norm justifying these infringements must be. It is no coincidence that the dissenting opinion denied precisely this standard rule, arguing that the intensity of infringements was not a part of the semantic argument.[69] This artificial separation between the interpretive canons, however, must be rejected. The intensity of infringement may not be part of the semantic argument, but it is an essential element of the interpretation as a whole.

Furthermore, in the Thuringia case, the genetic argument helps to settle the matter: while establishing the new Thuringia Constitution, the issue of including

[66] ibid 155.
[67] ibid.
[68] ibid 131.
[69] ibid 156.

an obligation to parity representation was discussed but, ultimately, rejected. It follows that

> [t]he genesis of this norm compels us to conclude that the *pouvoir constituant* did not want to establish freedom of the *pouvoir constitué* to introduce parity quotas for the authorities and institutions of the State of Thuringia.[70]

The dissenting opinion challenges this argument by pointing out that the rejected proposals had called for a complete parity in all state authorities, not just in Parliament. This challenge presupposes that nothing can be followed from a rejection of a more far-reaching proposal for the less far-reaching parity in the legislature. However, this challenge cannot hide the fact that the Constitution-givers did not agree to include the specific means of a parity clause for Parliament. After all, this would have been a natural line of compromise given the rejection of the more far-reaching proposal. Nevertheless, even this compromise, the less far-reaching means, was not enacted. This is the reason why an argumentum a *maiore ad minus* is convincing in this case.

Lastly, the argument provided by the Thuringia Government, that the Constitution must be interpreted per Article 11, 7, and 4 I CEDAW fails because these norms do not even address the issue of parity quotas in electoral law.[71]

The upshot of the above considerations is that the parity regulations cannot be justified on constitutional grounds. Hence, they had to be declared void by the constitutional courts.[72]

V. Conclusion

Democracy faces many challenges. In this chapter, I have defended the view that these challenges do not regard the solid theoretical fundaments of the constitutional principle of democracy but rather our democratic practices. More precisely, the main challenge currently lies in improving citizens' abilities and willingness to engage in rational discourse. However, unfortunately, in the various instances mentioned throughout this chapter, the roots of deliberation are being increasingly denied by illiberal, autocratic means employed to pursue goals that – on their terms – may be plausible and worthy of praise.

The main challenge of our times is not to rebuild or adjust the theoretical fundament of democracy, its institutions or processes. Instead, we have to learn anew how to communicate and deliberate in a constructive, respectful, tolerant

[70] ibid 136.

[71] ibid 137. Interpreting national laws in accordance with public international law is an instance of system-conforming interpretation; on the latter *cf* the contributions in M Klatt (ed), *Constitutionally Conforming Interpretation. Comparative Perspectives: Volume 1: National Reports* (Hart Studies in Constitutional Theory, Oxford, Hart Publishing 2022 (forthcoming)).

[72] VerfGH Weimar (n 37) para 138 (juris).

way, given the conditions of a pluralistic society.[73] The current 'crisis of democracy' is, first and foremost, a crisis of deliberative practice.[74] In consequence, the remedy lies in strengthening those virtues which are essential to the functioning of democracy. We need to develop the basic techniques of the humanities: listening, questioning, arguing, reflecting, justifying.[75] We need to nurture our ethos of critical thinking.[76]

This ethos requires avoiding the simplistic reflex of cancelling cancel 'anti-culture'. Declaring that some position was discursively impossible in a sweeping shortcut way is no solution to our problem. To the extent that populist and cancelling propositions contain a core of rational argument behind their ideological facade, we need to attend to it observantly and curiously. Rationalist culture requires us to interrogate these positions accordingly. Labelling something as ideology and committing it to the waste-paper basket will likewise destroy the fundaments of deliberation and, ultimately, democracy.

According to a famous dictum by Böckenförde, '[t]he liberal and secularised state is sustained by conditions it cannot itself guarantee'.[77] Thus, democracy requires citizens to endorse the idea of rational discourse and engage in deliberation and justificatory practices precisely when this practice gets messy, chaotic, complex, strenuous, and disheartening.

The most critical challenges the current crisis of democracy confronts us with are not for constitutional theorists to work upon. But instead for citizens. It is practice that matters most in the current situation, not theory. The good news is that the theory of the constitutional principle of deliberative democracy is robust, comprehensive, integrating and powerful.

Can we say the same of us?

[73] JD Inazu, *Confident Pluralism: Surviving and Thriving through Deep Difference* (Chicago, University of Chicago Press, 2018); Gegen Vergessen – Für Demokratie eV (ed), *Konstruktive Kommunikation in der Demokratie: Ein Baustein in der Politischen Bildung* (Berlin, 2020); M-L Frick, 'Streitkompetenz als demokratische Qualität: Vom Wert des Widerspruchs' (2020) 70(12-13) *Aus Politik und Zeitgeschichte* 28.

[74] JS Dryzek and others, 'The Crisis of Democracy and the Science of Deliberation' (2019) 363(6432) *Science* 1144; *cf* the debate on the potential of deliberative mini-publics, M Böker and S Elstub, 'The Possibility of Critical Mini-Publics: Realpolitik and Normative Cycles in Democratic Theory' (2015) 51(1) *Representation* 125; Doyle and Walsh (n 13).

[75] *cf* SA Ercan, CM Hendriks and JS Dryzek, 'Public Deliberation in an Era of Communicative Plenty' (2019) 47(1) *Policy & Politics* 19.

[76] See also B Kempen, 'Universität als Risikozone' *Frankfurter Allgemeine Zeitung* (20 July 2021) 6. Habermas recently urged us to strengthen the subjective conditions for public deliberation in J Habermas, 'Überlegungen und Hypothesen zu einem erneuten Strukturwandel der politischen Öffentlichkeit' in M Seeliger and S Sevignani (eds), *Ein neuer Strukturwandel der Öffentlichkeit?: Sonderband Leviathan 37* (Baden-Baden, Nomos, 2021) 471, 492–499.

[77] E-W Böckenförde, 'The Rise of the State as a Process of Secularization [1967]' in M Künkler, T Stein and E-W Böckenförde (eds), *Religion, Law, and Democracy: Selected Writings* (Oxford Constitutional Theory vol 2, Oxford, Oxford University Press, 2020) 167.

2

The Rule of Law in 2030

YANIV ROZNAI*

I. Introduction

Attempting to predict what the Rule of Law will be in 2030 is a challenging task. Of course, predicting the future in general is a challenging task, but predicting what the rule of law concept will be in the future is especially challenging by the mere fact that even now – in 2021, not 2030 – the rule of law is considered a contested concept, and it has been such for a while.[1]

As I shall elaborate in this chapter, in jurisprudential writing, the rule of law is comprised of a number of formal, procedural and substantive aspects, concerning the way in which a community is governed. The formal principles usually concern the generality, clarity, publicity, stability, and prospectivity of the legal norms that govern a society. The procedural aspect usually concerns the processes by which legal norms are created and administered, and the judicial and regulatory institutions that enforce the law. Finally, for some, the rule of law must include a focus on the content of law and thus also includes certain substantive aspects, such as fundamental rights, justice, proportionality, political accountability or democracy.[2] For obvious reasons, the latter aspects are more contentious. These varied – and often conflicting – aspects of the rule of law make it a complex and contested concept.

What seems to be the core of the rule of law is that it is not the arbitrary – and maybe repressive – rule of men, in the sense that legal rules exist, that everyone is bound by them and that these rules are equally enforced. As Jeremy Waldron writes:

> The most important demand of the Rule of Law is that people in positions of authority should exercise their power within a constraining framework of well-established public

* I wish to thank Noy Rousso and Gal Maor for a very useful research assistance, the participants of the Graz Constitutionalism 2030 Conference, Suzie Navot and Christoph Bezemek for excellent comments.

[1] J Waldron, 'Is the Rule of Law an Essentially Contested Concept (In Florida)?' (2002) 21 *Law and Philosophy* 137; RH Fallon, "The Rule of Law' as a Concept in Constitutional Discourse' (1997) 97 *Columbia Law Review* 8.

[2] See, eg, T Bingham, *The Rule of Law* (London, Penguine, 2010); P Craig, 'Formal and substantive conceptions of the rule of law: an analytical framework' (1997) 21 *Public Law* 467.

> norms rather than in an arbitrary, *ad hoc*, or purely discretionary manner on the basis of their own preferences or ideology. It insists that the government should operate within a framework of law in everything it does, and that it should be accountable through law when there is a suggestion of unauthorized action by those in power.[3]

The rule of law means, in its more general form, 'that government officials and citizens are bound by and abide by the law'.[4] It is a government by law rather than by individuals.

This chapter will highlight the various aspects of the rule of law: its procedural, formal and substantive aspects. It will then explore three movements that will significantly influence how the rule of law concept will be conceived in 2030: first, a move from rule *of* law to rule *by* law, in which laws are used as a government tool; second, a move from substantive aspects of the rule of law that emphasise democracy and rights to its formal aspects; and third, a move from general laws to more personalised legislation. The first two trends are the product of the populist wave that has eroded democracies around the world in recent years. The third trend is the product of technological innovations, such as artificial intelligence and big data. Taken together, these three trends will transform the concept of the rule of law, as we knew it in 2020.

II. The Various Aspects of the Rule of Law Concept

A. The Procedural Aspect

The rule of law has long historical origins, going back to Greek thought and to Aristotle's formulation that 'the rule of law … is preferable to that of any individual'.[5] It has since been developed to incorporate various different (and often vague) meanings, often dissimilar to the correlative continental concepts of the German *Rechtsstaat*, the Italian *Stato di diritto*, the French *État de droit* or the Spanish *Estado de derecho* etc', according to which the state is the source of law but is also subject of law and acts only by means of law.[6]

[3] J Waldron, 'The Rule of Law', *Stanford Encyclopedia of Philosophy*, www.plato.stanford.edu/entries/rule-of-law/.

[4] BZ Tamanaha, 'The History and elements of the Rule of Law' [2012] *Singapore Journal of Legal Studies* 232, 233. Of course, the law itself may provide exceptions to this idea. See Adam Shinar, 'One rule to rule them all? Rules of law against the rule of law' (2017) 2 *The Theory and Practice of Legislation* 149.

[5] BZ Tamanaha, *On the Rule of Law: History, Politics, Theory* (Cambridge, Cambridge University Press, 2004) 9.

[6] It is not my intention in this chapter to review the historical development of the concept. For a brief historical overview, see P Alvazzi Del Frate and A Torini, 'Rule of Law between the Seventeenth and Nineteenth Centuries', in G Amato, B Barbison and C Pinelli (eds), *Rule of Law vs Majoritarian Democracy* (Oxford, Hart Publishing, 2021) 11–23; M Loughlin, *Foundations of Public Law* (Oxford, Oxford University Press, 2010) 313–324. For an elaborated study, see the doctoral thesis of F Neuman, *The Governance of The Rule of Law – An Investigation into the Relationship Between the Political Theories, The Legal System, and The Social Background in The Competitive Society* (1936), www.etheses.lse.ac.uk/668/.

One of the classical earliest formulations of the rule of law was provided by AV Dicey for whom, as provided in his *Introduction to the Study of The Law of the Constitution*,[7] the rule of law is built on three main conceptions: *First*, 'that no man is punishable or can lawfully be made to suffer in body or goods except for a distinct breach of law established in the ordinary legal manner before the ordinary courts of the land'.[8] In other words, individuals should not be subject to arbitrary powers. *Second*, everyone is equally subject to the law and no one is above the law:

> not only that with us no man is above the law, but (what is a different thing) that here every man, whatever be his rank or condition, is subject to the ordinary law of the realm and amenable to the jurisdiction of the ordinary tribunals. … With us every official, from the Prime Minister down to a constable or a collector of taxes, is under the same responsibility for every act done without legal justification as any other citizen.[9]

Third, a bit more ambiguous in terms, is that 'the general principles of the constitution (as for example the right to personal liberty, or the right of public meeting) are with us the result of judicial decisions determining the rights of private persons in particular cases brought before the courts …'.[10] Of course, Dicey's formulation is connected to the English Constitution's understanding of parliamentary sovereignty and the common law's tradition of rights protection through judge-made law.[11]

Underlying Dicey's conception of the rule of law, Jeffrey Jowell has claimed that there are some core values of legality, certainty, consistency, accountability, efficiency, due process and access to justice. These values now call for substantive fairness, natural justice, and justification for restricting rights and liberties.[12]

What seems to be clear, or at least rather accepted, is that the procedural account of the rule of law basically circles around two aspects: the enforcement and supremacy of law. In this 'procedural' sense, the rule of law means that there will be a predetermined legal framework according to which the state must act. The state must be a rule-by-law state, and everyone is subject to law. It is manifested by the famous statement of Henry de Bracton that 'The king must not be under man but under God and under the law.'[13] Everyone is subject to the law, that ought to be enforced equally.[14]

[7] AV Dicey, *Introduction to the Study of The Law of the Constitution*, 8th edn (London, Macmillan, 1915). For an elaboration, see MD Walters, 'the Spirit of Legality: A V Dicey and the Rule of Law', in J Meierhenrich and M Loughlin (eds), *The Cambridge Companion to the Rule of Law* (Cambridge, Cambridge University Press, 2021) 153–170.

[8] Dicey, ibid 110.

[9] ibid 114.

[10] ibid 115.

[11] See MD Walters, *A V Dicey and The Common Law Constitutional Tradition – a Legal Turn of Mind* (Cambridge, Cambridge University Press, 2020) 226–231.

[12] See, notably, J Jowell, 'The Rule of Law and its underlying values', in J Jowell and D Oliver (eds), *The Changing Constitution* 6th edn (Oxford, Oxford University Press, 2007) 5, 9–13.

[13] H de Bracton, *On the Laws and Customs of England* [1258] GE Woodbine (ed), SE Thorne (trns) (Cambridge, Belknap Press, 1968) 33.

[14] On the importance of enforcement to the rule of law, see JJ Spigelman, 'The Rule of Law and Enforcement' (2003) 26 *University of New South Wales Law Journal* 200.

So, to conclude this aspect, the rule of law, in its narrow sense, means 'a general framework of rules under which all – including rulers – are obliged to live'.[15]

B. Formal Aspects

The procedural account seemed necessary for the rule of law but also inadequate. What if a law is not promulgated? Or established a prohibition but is incomprehensible? Or a system of laws in which the laws constantly change on a daily basis and contradict each other? In such a system, it is extremely difficult to obey the law, to follow it or to enforce it.

Consequently, various theorists regard the rule of law as embodying some further formal requirements – a set of intrinsic qualities that make law a general framework to which the government is subject. Joseph Raz, for example, referred to clarity, prospectively, stability, openness, and access to an impartial judiciary, as formal qualities law ought to comply with.[16] John Rawls claimed that rule of law precepts are: that the act imposed by law be reasonably expected to be carried out; that the law is the result of the action of legislative, executive and judicial authorities, which operate in good faith; the fulfilment of equal treatment – that similar cases will be treated similarly, so that people can plan their actions accordingly; there is no offence without law; the law should be known and public; retroactivity is prohibited; law should be clear and understandable; and the rules of natural justice must be observed.[17] Other thinkers provided other similar requirements, with some minor differences.[18]

A classical formulation is proposed by Lon Fuller, in his list of requirements of legality – minimum requirements without which a legal system cannot exist, which he described as 'The inner morality of law.'[19] These are: the generality of law, in the sense that there must be rules (however fair or unfair; as opposed to on an ad hoc basis); promulgation and publication of laws; prospectively of law, as retroactive laws cannot guide conduct;[20] laws must be clear and understandable; laws must be stable without frequent changes; consistency as to eliminate contradictions in the laws; laws should not require the impossible; and there should be

[15] M Loughlin, *Swords & Scales – An Examination of the Relationship between Law and Politics* (Oxford, Hart Publishing, 2000) 184–185.

[16] J Raz, 'The Rule of Law and Its Virtue' (1977) 93 *Law Quarterly Review* 195, 198–202.

[17] J Rawls, *A Theory of Justice* (Cambridge, The Belknap Press of Harvard University Press, 1971) 236–239.

[18] See, eg, FA Hayek, *The Constitution of Liberty* (London, Routledge, 1960) ch 10; L Solum, 'Equity and the Rule of Law', in I Shapiro (ed), *The Rule of Law: Nomos XXXVI* (New York, New York University Press, 1994) 120, 121–123.

[19] L Fuller, *The Morality of Law* (New Heaven, Yale University Press, 1969) ch 2. Much has been written about Fuller's account. For a recent textual analysis of Fuller's writings, see K Rundle, *Forms Liberate – Reclaiming the Jurisprudence of Lon L Fuller* (Oxford, Hart Publishing, 2012).

[20] For Fuller, 'a retroactive law is truly a monstrosity … To speak of governing or directing conduct today by rules that will be enacted tomorrow is to talk in blank prose' ibid 53.

congruence between official action and the declared rules.[21] Fuller created these functional or formal criteria in light of his understanding of law as 'the enterprise of subjecting human conduct to the governance of rules'.[22]

A total failure in any one of these directions, Fuller claimed, 'does not simply result in a bad system of law; it results in something that is not properly called a legal system at all'.[23] This is because such a total failure would make it impossible to subject people's conduct to these rules, making them functionally useless in guiding conduct. Of course, even Fuller understood that in various legal systems not all his conditions are fully respected; so, for example, he writes that where all these conditions are met there is a 'utopia of legality'.[24]

C. Substantive Aspects

The formal and procedural aspects, which are strongly connected, seemed insufficient as they neglect the substance of the law – its content. And accordingly, as Judith Shklar wrote, 'Fuller's inwardly moral law not only may, but has been, perfectly compatible with governments of the most repressive and irrational sort.'[25] As a result of the totalitarian experience of the twentieth century and the horrors of WWII, the rule of law concept has been revisited. The new approach to the concept deviated from the formalistic or procedural models of the rule of law to a broader concept strongly connected to human rights protection – now, human rights were put under the protection of the rule of law.[26] Thus, modern studies emphasise the rule of law not merely in its formal and procedural aspects, but also as a concept that expresses some fundamental legal values that a modern government must adhere to (often strongly connected to liberal democracy).[27] This sense thus shifts the focus to the content of laws.

In light of this criticism voiced towards the formal and procedural aspects, some were opposed to the notion that extremely harsh and unjust laws conform to the notion of rule of law. Ronald Dworkin, for example, criticised the formal conception of the rule of law (which he described as a 'rule-book' conception) and argued instead that legal rules must contain inherent moral content, which he terms 'rights' conception. This conception

> 'assumes that citizens have moral rights and duties with respect to one another, and political rights against the state as a whole. It insists that these moral and political rights

[21] ibid ch 2.
[22] ibid 106.
[23] ibid 39.
[24] ibid 41.
[25] JN Shklar, 'Political Theory and the Rule of Law', in JN Shklar and S Hoffmann (eds) *Political Thought and Political Thinkers* (Chicago, The University of Chicago Press, 1998) 21, 33.
[26] L Lacche, 'Rule of Law Metamorphoses in the Twentieth Century', in Amato, Barbisan and Pinelli (n 6) 25, 37; Del Frate and Alberto Torini (n 6).
[27] D Dyzenhous, *Recrafting the Rule of Law: The Limits of Legal Order* (Oxford, Hart Publishing, 1999).

> be recognized in positive law, so that they may be enforced upon the demand of individual citizens through court or other judicial institutions …'[28]

Dworkin's conception does not make any distinction between 'substantive justice' and the 'rule of law'. Just the opposite: the rule book should 'capture and enforce moral rights'.[29]

Others suggested different substantive standards for the rule of law. Guillermo O'Donnell, for example, claimed that

> What is needed, rather, is a truly *democratic* rule of law that ensures political rights, civil liberties, and mechanisms of accountability which in turn affirm the political equality of all citizens and constrain potential abuses of state power.[30]

Aharon Barak, former President of the Israeli Supreme Court, argued that in order for the rule of law to exist, law must show a due balance between the individual and the society:

> The human being and human rights underlie this substantive perception of the rule of law, with a proper balance among the different rights and between human rights and the proper need of society. The substantive rule of law 'is the rule of proper law, which balances the needs of society and the individual.'[31]

This emphasis on proportionality and balancing places a large amount of responsibility on the judiciary.

The thicker, substantive aspect of the rule of law, is expressed in the 2020 Rule of Law Report of the European Commission: 'Under the rule of law, all public powers always act within the constraints set out by law, in accordance with the values of democracy and fundamental rights, and under the control of independent and impartial courts.'[32]

D. The Multifaced Character of the Rule of Law

Surely, the more substantive aspects one infuses to the term rule of law, the vaguer and more ambiguous it becomes. In constitutional discourse, Carl Schmitt argued, the concept of *Rechtstaat* eventually comes down to this: 'Law should above all be what I and my friends value.'[33] Accordingly, due to its multifaced character, the rule of law has become a rhetoric tool, often for competing claims. Martin Krygier

[28] R Dworkin, *A Matter of Principle* (Oxford, Clarendon Press, 1985) 11.

[29] ibid 12.

[30] G O'Donnell, 'The Quality of Democracy – Why the Rule of Law Matters' (2004) 12 *Journal of Democracy* 32.

[31] A Barak, *The Judge in a Democracy: The Role of a Supreme Court in a Democracy* (Princeton, Princeton University Press, 2006) 55–56.

[32] 2020 Rule of Law Report, 'The rule of law situation in the European Union', www.eur-lex.europa.eu/legal-content/EN/TXT/PDF/?uri=CELEX:52020DC0580&from=EN.

[33] C Schmitt, *Legality and Legitimacy* (Durham, Duke University Press, 2004) 14.

writes that 'the rule of law is today the beneficiary, sometimes the victim, of enormous rhetorical enthusiasm. No one is against.'[34]

Consider, for example, the saga surrounding former Prime Minister of Israel, Benjamin Netanyahu, who, during his term, was under a criminal indictment based on bribery, fraud, and breach of trust and his criminal trial is currently being conducted in the Jerusalem District Court. Notwithstanding these criminal charges, Netanyahu did not resign from office, and had no intention of doing so. But does not serving as Prime Minister while facing criminal charges confront the rule of law? That is a challenging question, as 'Basic Law: The Government' (from 2001), the constitutional statute that regulates the structure, authorities and activities of the executive, does not seem to prohibit this state of affairs. In contrast, it actually makes clear that a sitting Prime Minister can be indicted. It only provides that a Prime Minister, convicted with an offence involving moral turpitude, can be removed from office, and will be automatically removed if such conviction is final.[35] Prima facie, then, the basic law indeed allows a Prime Minister to remain in office notwithstanding criminal indictments until the criminal trial is finalised. So, from the formal rule of law perspective, the law seemed clear.

On the other hand, there was no precedent for such behaviour. All past Prime Ministers who were suspected of criminal offenses stepped down before being indicted. Moreover, there were various judicial decisions in which the Supreme Court has held that even without an explicit statutory provision to that effect, the Prime Minister must remove from office a minister or a deputy minister, who was indicted for charges of corruption or fraud, and also ordered the removal of mayors who had been indicted for corruption.[36] So, a minister would have to resign and the Prime Minister would not have to resign? Allowing Netanyahu to form a government and serve as Prime Minister, experts from the Israeli Democracy Institute claimed, would result in a negative and irreversible precedent for the rule of law.[37] Thus, from a substantive point of view of the rule law, that emphasises accountability, arguably a Prime Minister under criminal indictment must resign. The rule of law versus the rule by law. Eventually, the Supreme Court did not intervene, holding that there are no grounds for the Prime Minister's removal notwithstanding the 'difficulty' of having an office holder who is accused of grave crimes.[38]

So, from this story, one of many others, it seems clear why Shklar has argued that 'It would not be very difficult to show that the phrase 'the Rule of Law' has

[34] M Krugier, 'On the Rule of Law. History, Politics, Theory by Brian Z. Tamanaha' (2005) 32 *Journal of Law and Society* 657.

[35] For a review see E Chachko, 'Indicting a Sitting Prime Minister: The Israeli Constitutional Framework' Lawfare, www.lawfareblog.com/indicting-sitting-prime-minister-israeli-constitutional-framework.

[36] On these cases, see Y Dotan, 'Impeachment by Judicial Review: Israel's Odd System of Checks and Balances' (2018) 19 *Theoretical Inquiries in Law* 705. See also R Weill, 'Is the Judicial Impeachment of the Israeli Prime Minister Constitutional?', United Kingdom Constitutional Law Blog, www.ukconstitutionallaw.org.

[37] See, eg, Press Release 'PM Under Indictment – A Dangerous Precedent', www.en.idi.org.il/articles/31477.

[38] HCJ 2592/20 *Movement for Quality Government v Attorney General* (6.5.2020).

become meaningless thanks to ideological abuse and general over-use ….'[39] Due to its multifaced character, every side to a political controversy may use (or abuse) the rule of law concept to support his argument.

The thicker version of the rule of law, that includes substantive aspects, carries the disadvantages of undermining conceptual coherence as well as the support of societies who might reject the rule of law notion due to its connection to broader democratic or human rights requirements.[40] On the other hand, insisting on a completely morally neutral understanding of the concept, carries the adverse risk of the instrumental use of the law for extreme repressive means, as described earlier by Shklar or Bingham, which seems unsatisfying. Thus, perhaps a better path would be to conceive the rule of law in 'a more nuanced elaboration of the thin account' – or vice versa in a more nuanced lessening of the thick account, one that focuses on the concept's autonomous moral value of respecting human beings' rational autonomy as well as its close relation to other democratic values.[41]

Now, once we have an idea regarding the various aspects of the rule of law concept, we may proceed to evaluate how the rule of law will look like in 2030. In the next section, I suggest three trends or movements that will affect the rule of law concept in the coming decade: the move from 'rule of law' to 'rule by law'; the move from substantive aspects to formal aspects of the rule of law, and finally, the move from general to personalised laws.

III. How the Rule of Law will Look in 2030

Three main movements will have a significant influence on how 'the rule of law' would be conceived in 2030. These movements, elaborated below, are formed in light of two tectonic events that shape our modern democratic lives: the era of populism of democratic erosion (or backsliding) and the emergence of new technologies.

A. From the 'Rule of Law' (back) to the 'Rule by Law'

The first one is the move from 'the rule of law' to 'the rule by law'.

In its most basic formulation, the rule of law means rule of the law. It is the rule by law and not by men, the supremacy of regular as opposed to arbitrary power: 'the rule of law is a law of rules'.[42] The government, as an instituted organ, possesses only

[39] Shklar (n 25) 1.

[40] See J Tasioulas, 'The Rule of Law', in J Tasioulas (ed), *The Cambridge Companion to the Philosophy of Law* (Cambridge, Cambridge University Press, 2020) 117.

[41] ibid.

[42] A Scalia, 'The Rule of Law as a Law of Rules' (1989) 56 *University of Chicago Law Review* 1175, 1187.

power given to it by law. Law is the central means for governance. The understanding of the rule of law as 'rule by law', is of course a thin and narrow account of the relationship between state and law: the administration and governmental power must act according to law and be subject to legislative authority. This account of the 'legislative state' is equivalent to the French term of '*L'etat legal*'. But it is very different from the understanding of '*L'etat de droit*' or 'rule of law', that is much wider and emphasises also that the exercise of legislative power itself is conditioned by certain authoritative norms.[43] Such a narrow account might not even correspond with the thin formal concept of the rule of law. This is because if the 'rule of law' concept is reduced to its narrow version of 'rule by law', then it is almost empty of meaning. The government would act according to the rule of law, even if it acted in an arbitrary or discriminatory manner, as long as its actions are accompanied by law.

Accordingly, some theorists distinguish between the rule of law and the rule by law.[44] The distinction seems clear; the rule of law is supposed to place law above politics. The very basic idea that every person and agency are subject to the law. Law limits governmental authority. Rule by law, in contrast, means the instrumental use of law as a tool of political power. It means that instead of law as the controlling state authority, the state uses law to control its citizens or other organs. This narrow notion is becoming central in the era of populism and the crisis of democratic erosion.

Constitutional Democracies around the world are in a crisis.[45] The 2021 Freedom House report shows that 2020 marked a serious crisis of democracy and recorded the 15th consecutive year of decline in global freedoms. Moreover, the proportion of 'not free countries' is now the highest it has been in the past 15 years.[46] Even European countries that were considered, until recently, stable democracies, are facing 'democratic backsliding' or 'democratic erosion'.[47]

Democratic erosion, as defined by Tom Ginsburg and Aziz Huq, is as a 'process of incremental, but ultimately still substantial, decay in three basic predicates of democracy – competitive election, liberal rights to speech and association, and the rule of law'.[48] It is not my intention to fully analyse the tools used by populists to

[43] Loughlin (n 6) 322–323 (discussing this distinction in the writings of Carre de Malberg, among others).

[44] See, eg, Tamanaha (n 5) 3.

[45] See, eg, MA Graber, S Levinson and M Tushnet (eds), *Constitutional Democracy in Crisis?* (Oxford, Oxford University Press, 2018); S Levitsky and D Ziblatt, *How Democracies Die* (New York, Penguin Random, 2018); D Runciman, *How Democracy Ends* (New York, Basic Books, 2018); Y Mounk, *The People vs. Democracy: Why Our Freedom Is in Danger and How to Save It* (Cambridge, Harvard University Press, 2018).

[46] Freedom in the World 2021 – Democracy Under Siege, www.freedomhouse.org/sites/default/files/2021-02/FIW2021_World_02252021_FINAL-web-upload.pdf.

[47] See, eg, P Blokker, *New Democracies in Crisis?: A Comparative Constitutional Study of the Czech Republic, Hungary, Poland, Romania and Slovakia* (Abingdon, Routledge, 2013); A Jakab and D Kochenov (eds) *The Enforcement of EU Law and Values – Ensuring Member States' Compliance* (Oxford, Oxford University Press, 2017); AL Pap, *Democratic Decline in Hungary: Law and Society in an Illiberal Democracy* (Abingdon, Routledge, 2018); W Sadurski, *Poland's Constitutional Breakdown* (Oxford, Oxford University Press, 2019). For a conceptual account, see TG Daly, 'Democratic Decay: Conceptualizing an Emerging Research Field' (2019) 11 *Hague Journal of Rule of Law* 9.

[48] T Ginsburg and AZ Huq, *How to Save a Constitutional Democracy* (Chicago, University of Chicago Press, 2018) 45.

erode the democratic order, but merely to emphasise one such tool and that is the instrumental use of law for achieving the populist goals. Without elaborating on the concept of populism, which is challenging by itself, I shall only use Adamidis' concise definition that populism 'is a predominantly ideational phenomenon, which advocates an extreme majoritarian vision of democracy by claiming absolute, unlimited sovereignty for the morally pure people …'.[49] Populism, he notes, instrumentalises concepts of rule of law, giving them new meanings, and rejecting the idea that the political majority is subject to various legal or constitutional constraints.[50]

Various recent studies have described how in numerous populist regimes, the rule of law was subverted and harmed by populists' abuse of rule of law instruments to undermine checks and balances and to authorise systematic arbitrariness, that eventually lead to a deep democratic decay. These has been called 'abusive constitutionalism', 'stealth authoritarianism', 'constitutional coups', or 'legal and constitutional hypocrisy'.[51] Kim Lane Scheppele uses the term 'autocratic legalism' to describe populist leaders' use of legal tools in the service of an illiberal agenda: reforming checks on executive power, weaken challenges to their rule, and undermine accountability institutions, all by legal and constitutional methods.[52]

Consider the situation in Hungary. In 2010, a dramatic shift in the political landscape took place, when a government led by Prime Minister Viktor Orbán was elected with the support of a two-thirds majority in Parliament. This majority allowed the government to amend the Constitution at will; and indeed, within 19 months, the 1989 Constitution was amended 12 times, for partisan and political purposes. Sonja Priebus describes this constitutional manipulation as playing 'with, and not by the rules'.[53] Indeed, for Adamidis, populists aim to rule by law, and use legal means to undermine other institutions, or remove various checks on their powers, based on the argument that the laws enacted by them (the governmental majority) are the words of the 'sovereign people'. Thus: 'populism, as extreme majoritarianism, is possibly the 'rule by law' system par excellence …'.[54]

This manipulation corresponds with what Paul Blokker identified as the populists' instrumental approach to law: 'The practical approach of populists to the law is an instrumental one, which mobilizes the law in the name of a collectivist

[49] V Adamidis, 'Democracy, populism, and the rule of law: A reconsideration of their interconnectedness' [2021] *Politics* 6. For conceptual elaborations see M Tushnet and B Bugaric, *Power to the People: Constitutionalism in the Age of Populism* (Oxford, Oxford University Press, 2022) ch. 2; C Mudde, 'The Populist Zeitgeist' (2004) 39 *Government and Opposition* 541, 543; JW Muller, *What Is Populism?* (London, Penguin, 2016).

[50] ibid.

[51] D Landau, 'Abusive Constitutionalism' (2013) 47 *University of California Davis Law Review* 189; OO Varol, 'Stealth Authoritarianism' (2015) 100 *Iowa Law Review* 1673. 1673–1742; KL Scheppele, 'Constitutional Coups in EU Law', in M Adams, A Meuwese and EH Ballin (eds), *Constitutionalism and the Rule of Law: Bridging Idealism and Realism* (Cambridge, Cambridge University Press, 2017) 446.

[52] KL Scheppele, 'Autocratic Legalism' (2018) 85 *University of Chicago Law Review* 545, 547–548.

[53] S Priebus, 'Hungary', in A Fruhstorfer and M Hein (eds), *Constitutional Politics in Central and Eastern Europe* (Heidelberg, Springer, 2016) 101, 103.

[54] Adamidis (n 49) 9.

project.'[55] Populists frequently change the law and the constitution for instrumental, narrow, political interests. Frequency is important here. The rule of law becomes the rule of more and more laws. The more legal rules are shaped as putty in the government's hands, the more the government becomes less subordinate to legal rules and undermines the predictability or transparency of the legal rules. Very often, the frequent changes in laws are taking place through temporary legislation, and indeed studies show an increased use of temporary laws, a governance tool that allows the government to overcome parliamentary opposition.[56] And when the frequent legal changes occur in the constitutional sphere, it collapses the distinction between constitutional politics and everyday politics. All in all, such instrumental uses of law advance the arbitrary character of the government.

Such an instrumental use, I argue, not only transforms the concept of the 'rule of law' to its thin origins of 'rule by law', but also undermines the very idea of objecting arbitrary rule. This is why Blokker is correct in his claim that the populist constitutional project 'leads to a rule of law crisis and heightens the arbitrary nature of the political regime'.[57] Nicola Lacey thus appropriately argues that 'this amounts to a corruption of the rule of law: what we might call rule by law rather than the rule of law'.[58] And so, the rule of law becomes a 'weapon' or a tool,[59] in the hands of the populist leaders for achieving their ends. The rule of law, in the populist era, then becomes the 'rule of my law' – the law of the leader, arguably speaking on behalf of the people. If this trend continues, the rule of law will be increasingly treated in its narrow, thin, concept of 'rule by law', and abused as a façade to mask arbitrariness as legality. As András Sajó describes,

> Illiberal democracies do not respect the RoL as a value but still prefer to rule by law. … for a number of reasons the leader does not wish to be above the law, and prefers to use the advantages of a compromised and unprincipled RoL …. instead of simply replacing the law with his naked will … he will bend the law and set new rules in his favor and in favor of the needs of the regime. Hence the need for constant cheating.[60]

If the rule of law, as an idea, elevates law above politics, portraying law as constraining political power, rule by law expresses the instrumental use of law at the hands of political actors. Instead of regarding law as controlling state authorities, we

[55] P Blokker, 'Populism as a Constitutional Project' (2019) 17 *International Journal of Constitutional Law* 535, 545.

[56] See I Bar-Siman-Tov, 'Temporary Legislation's Finest Hour: The Rise of Temporary Legislation in Israel and Principles for Its Improvement' (2018) 41 *Tel Aviv University Law Review* 539. And more generally I Bar-Siman-Tov, 'Temporary legislation, better regulation, and experimentalist governance: An empirical study' (2018) 12 *Regulation & Governance* 192.

[57] Blokker (n 55) 546.

[58] N Lacey, 'Populism and the Rule of Law' (2019) 28 London School of Economics Working paper, www.eprints.lse.ac.uk/101867/1/Lacey_populism_and_the_rule_of_law_wp28.pdf.

[59] JM Maravall, 'The Rule of Law as a Political Weapon', in JM Maravall and A Przeworski (eds), *Democracy and the Rule of Law* (Cambridge, Cambridge University Press, 2003) 261–301.

[60] A Sajó, *Ruling by Cheating – Governance in Illiberal Democracy* (Cambridge, Cambridge University Press, 2021) 252–3.

shall increasingly witness how state authorities use law to control citizens and to promote narrow political interests.

This, however, undermines the very raison d'etre of rule of law. In its core, the rule of law was meant to limit the arbitrary use of political power. But if now, law itself is used in an arbitrary manner by the government, as a tool for achieving narrow political goals, for capturing state institutions, and for eliminating limitations on power, how is it that the government is subject to law? Law is only used (or abused) for governmental purposes, often in a temporary and ad hoc manner.[61] 'Law is used as an instrument to govern, while the state is not willing to submit itself to the law … consequently, arbitrariness is not ruled out.'[62] This move empties the concept of rule of law from its content.

B. From Substantive (back) to Formal Aspects of the Rule of Law

The rule of law concept arose as a creation of the formation of the modern state. Hence, it has strong connections to rights:

> Human liberty arises from the modern and antidominial conception of power, and it is tied to the notion of social contract and to a conception of rights as law. Rights are guaranteed by the form of the state.[63]

As mentioned in the previous section concerning the distinction between rule *of* law and rule *by* law (or between *l'Etat de droit* and *L'Etat legal*), the former was meant to displace the latter, based on the principle that 'law exists to protect individual rights'.[64] According to such an understanding of the rule of law, the rule of law means not only that the government must exercise it powers by – and be subject to – general legislation rather than arbitrary rule of 'irregular decrees and ad hominem proclamations', but more than that; it may also require that the law 'contain, or at least not violate, certain substantive principles and rights'.[65]

Accordingly, Tom Bingham, for example, argued that

> a state which savagely represses or prosecutes sections of its people cannot in my view be regarded as observing the rule of law, even if the transport of the persecuted minority to the concentration camp or the compulsory exposure of female children

[61] On this, see also Y Roznai, 'Clownstitutionalism: How to Make a Joke of the Constitution?', in R Albert and J Neo (eds), *Constitutional Amendment and Legitimacy: When is a Constitutional Amendment Illegitimate?* (forthcoming).

[62] D Grimm, 'Rule of Law and Democracy' in Amato, Barbisan and Pinelli (n 6) 43, 52.

[63] B Kriegel, *The State and the Rule of Law*, MA Le Pain and JC Cohen (trns) (Princeton, Princeton University Press, 1995) 42.

[64] Loughlin (n 6) 322.

[65] J Ferejohn and P Pasquino, 'Rule of Democracy and Rule of Law', in Marvall and Przeworski (n 59) 242.

> on the mountainside is the subject of detailed laws duly enacted and scrupulously observed.[66]

Rule of law without due respect for rights is not rule of law. This is an expression of the substantive aspects of the rule of law highlighted previously.

However, a current trend is *the weakening of substantive aspects* of the rule of law, such as democracy and human rights – which are evidently more contentious. Like the previous move, this move is the product of populist politics and democratic erosion. Correlating to the move to rule *by* law, there is a move of rejecting substantive aspects of rule of law, particularly those connect to liberalism, in favour of formal and procedural aspects of the rule of law.[67] 'Populism' Adamidis rightly claims, 'gives precedence to an absolute popular sovereignty and opts to instrumentalize a thin, formal version of the rule of law to serve that end'.[68]

This is a similar, and correlative, trend to the rejection of substantive or liberal aspects of democracy itself, in favour of what some call procedural, formal or illiberal democracy[69] as occurred in Hungary, for example. In a 2014 public speech, the Hungarian Prime Minister, Victor Orbán declared: 'the new state that we are constructing in Hungary is an illiberal state, a non-liberal state. It does not reject the fundamental principles of liberalism such as freedom … but instead includes a different, special, national approach.'[70] Thus, the transformation from a liberal democracy to an illiberal state, with weakened checks and balances and rights protection, seems to have been an explicit goal of the regime.[71]

This challenge to a liberal notion of democracy is not unique to Hungary. In various countries, liberal or substantive notions of democracy are under attack in the name of a purely procedural or majoritarian version of democracy, according to which the political majority represents the sovereign and is thus omnipotent.[72]

[66] T Bingham, *The Rule of Law* (London, Penguin Books, 2010) 7.

[67] On illiberal democracies and the rule of law, see G Palombella, 'Illiberal, Democratic and Non-Arbitrary? Epicentre and Circumstances of a Rule of Law Crisis' (2018) 10 *Hague Journal on the Rule of Law* 5.

[68] Adamidis (n 49) 9.

[69] On the concept of illiberal democracy see F Zakaria, 'The Rise of Illiberal Democracy' (1997) 76 *Foreign Affairs* 22.

[70] Office of the Prime Minister, Prime Minister Viktor Orbán's Speech at the 25th Bálványos Summer Free University and Student Camp, 26 July 2014, www.kormany.hu/en/the-prime-minister/the-prime-minister-s-speeches/prime-minister-viktor-orban-s-speech-at-the-25th-balvanyos-summer-free-university-and-student-camp.

[71] On this transformation, see, eg, G Halmai, 'An Illiberal Constitutional System in the Middle of Europe' [2014] *European Yearbook of Human Rights* 497; K Kovács and GA Tóth, 'Hungary's Constitutional Transformation' (2011) 7 *European Constitutional Law Review* 183; M Bánkuti, G Halmai and KL Scheppele, 'From Separation of Powers to a Government without Checks: Hungary's Old and New Constitutions', in GA Tóth (ed), *Constitution for a Disunited Nation* (Budapest, CEU Press, 2012) 237; R Uitz, 'Can You Tell When an Illiberal Democracy is in the Making?' (2015) 13 *International Journal for Constitutional Law* 279, 280–81.

[72] See N Urbinati, 'The Populist Phenomenon' (2013) 51 *Raisons Politiques* 137, 139, 146–153; N Urbinati, 'Populism and The Principle of Majority', in CR Kaltwasser, P Taggart, PO Espejo and P Ostiguy (eds), *The Oxford Handbook of Populism* (Oxford, Oxford University Press, 2017) 571, 572.

Thus, for example, in Israel, according to some political and public views, democracy is fulfilled through elections and the decision-making process reflecting the majority's will, and no more. Such notion focuses on the formal or procedural aspects of democracy. It considers democracy as purely procedural – a system of self-government in which citizens can make majority collective decisions.[73] So, as part of the populist project, there is a move from liberal democracy to illiberal democracy, Orbán style, or from Aharon Barak's notion of substantive democracy to formal democracy à la the Israeli, conservative right-wing approach. Likewise, discussions of 'substantive' aspects of the rule of law are regarded as political means by detached liberal elites and courts to impose their own liberal and universal world-view upon 'the real national people'.

Populism emphasised the unity of the people; if the populist leader is meant to speak on behalf of the people, as if the people speak in one voice – *vox popoli*, then a liberal understanding of the rule of law that stresses individualism may be regarded as hindrance for the political or collective unity. As Blokker explains:

> the liberal rule of law erodes unity, because it divides the polity …, it weakens its decision-making powers (through a hierarchy of legal rules and constraints), and through its opening up of the polity to international influence …. Liberal individualism promotes a view of the demos as the basis of the democratic polity, which is rejected by populists, in order to be replaced by a collectivist view which emphasizes the belonging of the individual to a larger community, the ethnos.[74]

An example for such a move, from a thick substantive notion of the rule of law, to a formal and thin understanding, has recently appeared in Israel, where a new pedagogic instructions guide attached to the programme of civic studies in the national school system had removed the mention of human rights from the topic of the rule of law, emphasising the autonomy of the latter from any substantive values.

According to the guide to the rule of law:

> some thinkers have emphasized that the rule of law includes another aspect – a substantive aspect, which is the requirement that laws must conform with justice, morality and human rights. Others argue that the rule of law is distinct from the human rights principle.

In another paragraph, it is simply stated that 'the rule of law is separate from the principle of human rights, and even exists in tension with it'.[75] And so, instead of emphasising how the two aspects of rule of law complement and balance each

[73] I elaborate on this process elsewhere. See Y Roznai, 'Who will Save the Redheads? Towards an Anti-Bully Theory of Judicial Review and Protection of Democracy' (2021) 29 *William & Mary Bill of Rights Journal* 327; Y Roznai, 'Israel – A Crisis of Liberal Democracy?', in Graber, Levinson and Tushnet (n 45) 355; N Mordechay and Y Roznai, 'Jewish and (Declining) Democratic State? Constitutional Retrogression in Israel' (2017) 77 *Maryland Law Review* 244.

[74] Blokker (n 55) 550.

[75] Or Kashti, 'A New Guide for Citizenship Studies: Rule of Law Does Not Include Human Rights', www.haaretz.co.il/news/education/.premium-1.8025077; see also Y Yfrach, 'Taking Away Civics: Left-wing Organizations Against the Minister of Education', www.makorrishon.co.il/nrg/online/1/ART2/893/792.html.

other, the new pedagogic guide for civic studies emphasises how they are separate and opposing. These new guidelines for civic studies resulted in harsh criticism upon its publication. In an editorial article, *Haaretz* criticised this move, labelling it an 'Anti-democratic Guide for the Teacher':

> Although part of the guide is written carelessly and sloppily, the message is clear: the rule of law does not include human rights, and there is 'tension' between the two. The guide also ignores the existence of judicial review of laws that infringe on fundamental rights.[76]

The scepticism expressed by the teacher's guide in the substantive aspects of the rule of law can be compared to the previous textbook on citizenship, which emphasised its two meanings – the formal and substantive. According to the old book, the latter aspect refers to 'the content of the law and the degree to which it conforms to the values of democracy':

> A law that is consistent with democratic values is the proper law. The proper law protects human and civil rights and the rights of the minority, prevents the tyranny of the government and allows a balance to be created between the needs of the individual and the needs of the general public.

This older version was deleted and completely revised.[77] The message of the Ministry of Education seems clear: the nature of the laws does not have to be just and moral, and the government can enact laws that violate fundamental rights, democratic values and principles and still abide by the rule of law.

In response, the chairman of the Citizenship Profession Committee, Assaf Malach, argued that

> in the early 2000s there was an ultra-liberal trend in civic studies, which emphasized only the 'substantive rule of law'. The new guide emphasizes the classical rule of law, which is based on the importance of obeying clear and well-known pre-established rules – and not about changing decisions, the result of the interpretation of people as wise as they may be. The subject of human rights is comprehensively discussed in the curriculum and textbooks. No one is questioning it, but the principle of the rule of law is intended to add another aspect of democracy, which is often in tension with human rights.[78]

In a lengthy op-ed he dedicated to the criticism expressed towards this move,[79] Malach responded that the 'substantive rule of law' basically means 'rule of human rights', and that this 'amorphous view' should be of concern to anyone who values the democratic character of Israel, because the modern democracy produces a stable mechanism for the coexistence of human beings who do not necessarily

[76] Editorial, 'Anti-democratic Guide for the Teacher', www.haaretz.co.il/opinions/editorial-articles/.premium-1.8028653.

[77] ibid.

[78] ibid.

[79] A Malach, 'Why The Guide for Civic Studies Was Modified', www.haaretz.co.il/opinions/.premium-1.8062387.

agree on the desired manner for fulfilling rights. The concept 'formal rule of law' misses the way by which it expresses equality and liberty; this principle, together with the majoritarian rule-making principle are in tension with the positions of each individual, who is required to uphold the law passed by a majority decision even if it contradicts his or her personal position. These, Malach claimed, are the basic insights that must be taught and memorised in the context of civic studies in a democratic state. There is no way to have a democratic society without the fundamental principles of majority rule and without emphasising the basic elements of the rule of law.

Malach criticized the situation that has taken root in civic studies in the last two decades, 'as a reflection of the constitutional revolution from the seminary of Supreme Court President Aharon Barak and inspired by it', which for him

> has blurred the most fundamental values of democracy. They are embedded within the important and vital idea of human rights, which with all its vitality has no viability per se. For example, the term 'rule of law' was interpreted almost exclusively in its 'substantive' sense. This interpretation is not acceptable to prominent theorists in the field of law in the world, and pedagogically it is a repetition of the principle of human rights, which in the past and today is studied extensively and systematically as a separate chapter in the citizenship curriculum. The modification made in the latest Teachers Guide is intended to return the weight to the foundations of modern democracy, which are the main guarantee for the continued stability of the democratic regime in Israel.[80]

Elsewhere, he wrote that the concept of the 'rule of law' is a good example of how basic legal concepts have been redesigned by the judiciary and its supporters:

> This is a classic idea, rooted in Aristotle's writing, that any proper regime deserves to be governed by laws rather than human beings. The generality of the law, the clarity of the law and the publicity of the law are intended to reduce as much as possible the power of local considerations arising in concrete events. Only in this way can the natural bias that exists in each individual or group be exploited to take advantage of specific occurrences in favor of their interests and preferences.
>
> In Israel, however, the concept of the rule of law is presented by supporters of the 'Constitutional Revolution' as a need for 'substantive rule of law,' that is, one that protects human rights, in light of an unwritten balancing act known only to jurists, especially Supreme Court judges. Controversial laws are therefore presented as a 'violation of the rule of law,' and the court is required to intervene and overturn them.
>
> This conceptual revolution, which does not conform to the idea of the original rule of law, even disrupts and undermines the rule of law. For from now on the system has ceased to function in accordance with clear and predetermined rules. Through vague concepts such as 'reasonableness', 'proportionality' and 'proper purpose' any legal adviser or judge can thwart lengthy legislative processes or complex action of the executive, in a way that cannot be foreseen. In many cases there is no reason to assume that this frustration is free from the political interests and personal worldviews of the

[80] ibid.

> jurist himself. The 'substantive rule of law' established in the courtroom by knowledgeable jurists is the exact opposite of a clear and public law that has the power to guide human beings at the time of the act.[81]

This approach, manifests in the change in civic studies to focus on formal aspects of the rule of law, instead of substantive aspects that express commitment to human rights and democratic principles, as appeared in earlier versions, correlates with the more general trends in civic studies in Israel, as identified by Ben-Rafael Galanti, Carmel and Levkowitz:

> over the last 20 years, leading rightist and Religious Zionist forces have demanded the reduction of liberal teachings in curricula and a strengthening of Jewish and Zionist values .... That trend peaked under Benjamin Netanyahu's fourth government (2015–2020), when civics education underwent changes of an 'ethno-nationalist' and 'majoritarian' character – changes so fundamental that commentators have described them as an 'earthquake'.[82]

They note that since 2015, Assaf Malach, the newly appointed chair of the Ministry of Education Civics Studies Committee, issued new conservative guidelines and curricula, that minimised liberalism and individualism, and emphasised majoritarian rule rather than liberal models of democracy.[83] Similarly, Dan Avnon argues that the new guidelines for civic studies eliminate aspects of pluralism in democracy while emphasising the principle of majority rule, as the foundation of democratic government in Israel.[84]

If such a trend exists in other countries, and I suspect that with the era of populism and democratic decline this approach finds much appeal,[85] this disattachment of the rule of law from rights will have great implications for how the concept will be conceived in a decade's time.

From a liberal point of view, this trend is problematic because this separation between the two aspects (rule of law and rights) to a narrower formulation of the concept takes us, in a way, many steps backwards in our understanding of the rule of law. Such an understanding of the rule of law (not only in theory) makes

[81] A Malach, 'Making Law for Themselves: The Problems of the Legal System in Israel', www.heb.hartman.org.il/the-problems-at-the-israeli-legal-system/; see also A Malach, 'Rule of law: Tragedy in three acts', www.israelhayom.co.il/opinion/626259 (elaborating why the rule of law concept was distorted in Israeli democracy, mostly by the powerful judiciary that decided cases based upon vague principles as reasonableness and proportionality).

[82] S Ben-Rafael Galanti, P Carmel and A Levkowitz, 'Innovations in Israel's Civics Textbooks – Enlightening Tends in Non-Western Democracies' (2020) 35 *Israel Studies Review* 52, 55–56.

[83] ibid 63, 65.

[84] D Avnon, 'The New Civic: Ethnic, National, Majoritarian' (2016) 10 *Gilui Daat: Interdisciplinary. Journal in Education, Society and Culture* 165, 168.

[85] I am not making any empirical arguments here, although I believe it would be extremely interesting to explore this trend in a comparative empirical perspective. Just as studies on the cultural sphere show how culture subsidiaries have been abused by various regimes in order to entrench governmental powers, it might also be similar in the education sphere. On the former, see A Shinar, 'Democratic Backsliding, Subsidized Speech, and the New Majoritarian Entrenchment' (2021) 69 *The American Journal of Comparative Law* 335.

it perfectly compatible with dictatorships and autocratic regimes – 'even under a highly repressive dictatorship a form of rule of law is possible'.[86]

C. From General to Personalised Law

The third wave that would affect the nature of the rule of law is primarily related to emerging technologies. The future of law would be shaped to a great extent by technological innovations, such as artificial intelligence and big data.[87] This is true for the legal education and practice,[88] for the court system,[89] the administration and enforcement of law,[90] and also to law-making, which I claim, would have significant effects on the rule of law. Technological innovations lead to the third move, which is the weakening of formal aspects such as *generality* and *stability* towards *personalised 'tailor-made' and adaptive law-making*. This move will be accompanied by a correlative strengthening of *publicity* and *enforcement* of the law.

Nowadays, with the assistance of data science, it is much easier to create personalised legal rules tailored to specific circumstances or individuals. For example, technology can assist law enforcers detect patterns and future misconduct based on past data and statistics. While such personalisation of law may carry great efficiency benefits, it would also significantly undermine the rule of law, as a general set of norms to be equally applied. Also, new applications of artificial intelligence and machine learning may assist law to more quickly adapt to changing circumstances, thereby undermining the stability of law.

One of the main features of the rule of law is generality. Christoph Busch writes that 'Legal norms usually formulate impersonal and abstract rules that are supposed to cover a large number of individual cases: To legislate means to generalize.'[91] And so, he explains, consumer law, for instance, would not generally take into account the informational needs of specific individual consumers but

[86] See, eg, R Barros, 'Dictatorship and the Rule of Law: Rules and Military Power in Pinochet's Chile', in Maravall and Przeworski (n 59) 188, 215 (although the author notes there, at 190–192, that many dictatorships also deviate from this narrow concept of rule of law, for instance by exercising wide discretionary emergency powers etc).

[87] B Alarie, A Niblett and AH Yoon, 'Law in the Future' (2016) 66 *University of Toronto Law Journal* 423.

[88] See, eg, R Susskind, *The Future of Law: Facing the Challenges of Information Technology* (Oxford, Clarendon Press, 1998); D Dervanovic, 'Inhuman Lawyer: Developing Artificial Intelligence in the Legal Profession', in M Corrales, M Fenwick and N Forgo (eds), *Robotics, AI and the Future of Law* (Singapore, Springer, 2018) 209.

[89] See Z Loebl, *Designing Online Courts: The Future of Justice is Open to All* (London, Wolters Kluwer, 2019); R Sussking, *Online Courts and the Future of Justice* (Oxford, Oxford University Press, 2021); T Sourdin, *Judges, Technology and Artificial Intelligence: The Artificial Judge* (Camberley, Edward Elgar Publishing, 2021).

[90] H Surden, 'Artificial Intelligence and Law An Overview' (2019) 35 *Georgia State University Law Review* 1305.

[91] C Busch, 'Implementing Personalized Law: Personalized Disclosures in Consumer Law and Date Privacy Law' (2019) 86 *The University of Chicago Law Review* 309, 313.

would be based on 'a fictional model of the average consumer'.[92] Similarly, negligence law focuses on the 'reasonable person' standard, and so on.

However, the development of innovative algorithmic and big data measures, machine learning and artificial intelligence as tools of personalised legal design, mean that legal rules can (and probably would) be tailored to individual persons and particular situations.[93] Such personalisation requires massive quantities of data, but modern trends in data-gathering and data-analysis provide a solid ground for the suggestion that in the near future well-resourced lawmakers will be able to technically shape laws and regulations to particular individual characteristics and circumstances.

Hence, Casey and Niblett suggest that technological developments in data gathering and processing provide the possibility for law to move from more traditional forms of rules and standards to what they term 'microdirectives' that update and change in real time according to the changing individual circumstances.[94] Consider, for example, a changing speed limit according to the weather or road conditions in a given time and given part of the road, that takes into consideration also the data regarding the specific driver's accident history.[95]

And so, to provide some recent examples, Ban-Shahar and Porat have suggested abandoning the objective reasonable person standard in negligence law, and instead adopting a new type of negligence law that is based on a personalised subjective standard of care.[96] Likewise, Libson and Parchomovsky have explored the possibilities of personalised copyright law:

> The existence of big data regarding the characteristics of copyright users can fundamentally transform copyright law by significantly decreasing its social cost. Big data can facilitate the personalization of copyright law via differentiating between paying users … and inframarginal users … Copyright law could differentiate between the penalties that would be imposed on different types of users who infringe copyrights, imposing high penalties on the paying user and low penalties on the inframarginal user. Such personalization is welfare enhancing, compared to the existing regime, as it will increase the use of copyrighted content.[97]

Indeed, there is an emerging body of work concerning the personaliation of law in various areas, such as contract law,[98] tax law,[99] or personalised default rules

[92] ibid.

[93] M Auer, 'Granular Norms and the Concept of Law: A Critique', in C Busch and A De Franceschi (eds), *Algorithmic Regulation and Personlized Law* (London, Bloomsbury Publishing, 2020) 137.

[94] AJ Casey and A Niblett, 'The Death of Rules and Standards' (2017) 92 *Indiana Law Journal* 1401.

[95] See, eg, AJ Casey and A Niblett, 'Self-Driving Laws' (2016) 66 *University of Toronto Law Journal* 429, 431.

[96] O Ben-Shahar and A Porat, 'Personalizing Negligence Law' (2016) 91 *New York University Law Review* 627.

[97] A Libson and G Parchomovsky, 'Toward the Personalization of Copyright Law' (2019) 86 *The University of Chicago Law Review* 527, 528.

[98] O Ben-Shahar and A Porat, 'Personalizing Mandatory Rules in Contract Law' (2019) 86 *The University of Chicago Law Review* 255.

[99] B Alarie, 'The Path of the Law: Towards Legal Singularity' (2016) 66 *University of Toronto Law Journal* 443.

and disclosure in the law.[100] Technological progress makes it possible even for lawmakers to tailor laws to the needs and preferences of specific individuals and circumstances. If current laws that govern human governmental and human actions are uniform, this will change by personalised legal rules that would vary from person to person.[101]

Of course, such tailored-law-making faces various challenges such as the quality of the data the legislators possess, how to avoid discriminatory behaviour and biases, lack of transparency and more.[102] Moreover, if personalised law requires the mastering of big-data technology, one may pose the question is it not the case that private law actors are then better positioned to take a greater role in the enforcement of personalised law.[103]

All these challenges have crucial implications to various rule of law aspects. Most fundamentally, as Marietta Auer notes, a central aspect of the rule of law is its generality – 'the undiscriminating design and application of legal rules regardless of personal differences of the legal subject'.[104] It is this central element of the rule of law that is most severely challenged by personalised laws. Of course, the modern legislator, equipped with advanced technologies may decide to create a new form of law in the form of tailor-made laws. However, Auer rightly claims

> such path-taking may ultimately lead to a point where the entire concept of law – and according of the rule of law – is transformed from a well-established system of general norms to govern social matters and conflicts into an increasingly 'fine-grained' system of personal control of each and any aspect of everyday life.[105]

According to Auer, there are many arguments in favour of personalised law, but it is necessary to keep in mind that an extreme version of personal legislation may lead to a 'somewhat totalitarian bureaucratic society that control its members by personal and paternalistic regulation of every personal aspect … that replaces the rule of law with pervasive technocratic and bureaucratic mechanisms of

[100] A Porat and LJ Stranhilevitz 'Personalizing Default Rules and Disclosure with Big Data' (2014) 12 *Michigan Law Review* 1417; P Hacker, 'Personalizing EU Private Law: From Disclosures to Nudges and Mandates' (2017) 25 *European Review for Private Law* 651. See also Busch (n 91): 'the example of personalized disclosures shows how advances in information technology could increase the granularity of legal rules in other areas of the legal system. From this perspective, many impersonal and standardized rules can be seen as an answer to an information problem – a concession to the bounded capacity of human information-processing. If this is correct, artificial intelligence and superhuman information processing capabilities could redefine the optimal complexity of legal rules and refine them, for example, the content of disclosures to a hitherto unachievable level of granularity.'

[101] For a general discussion on personalised law, its advantages and disadvantages, and its possible application in different areas of law such as torts, consumer law, and even criminal law, see O Ben-Shahar and A Porat, *Personalized Law – Different Rules for Different People* (Oxford, Oxford University Press, 2021).

[102] For a discussion see A J Casey and A Niblett, 'A Framework for the New Personalization of Law' [2019] *The University of Chicago Law Review* 333.

[103] A Verstein, 'Privatizing Personalized Law' (2019) 86 *University of Chicago Law Review* 551.

[104] Auer (n 93) 150.

[105] ibid.

social governance'.[106] This may well be a new form of legal system but it might be one that lacks the inner morality of law, in Fuller's sense. In that respect, technology can challenge the very conceptual foundation of law.[107]

The other side of the weakening of the generality requirement may well be the strengthening of the publicity requirement, abiding by the law and its enforcement. For instance, access to legislation would be fundamentally better.[108] Frequent updates and freely accessible databases of laws and regulations, written in plain language and accompanied by explanatory notes and videos can be available online. 'Siri', special apps and other technological means would assist the people in better accessing and understanding the law that applies to them. In other words, while undermining generality, important advantages of personalised law are that it may be better at informing individuals about their legal obligations. If Fuller was eventually interested in a system to guide human behaviour, then emerging technology that can allow for what Casey and Niblett call 'microdirectives' and tailor-made laws, would come close to an ideal of directing individuals, instructing them on the law that applies to them.[109] Future advanced technological communications will enable not only the ability to tailor microdirectives to each and every individual in real time, but also to communicate the rules, in an easy, accessible and understandable manner. Accordingly, this adaptable legal system would provide every citizen with clear instructions on how to comply with the law in each and every situation. Simultaneously, the existence of big data regarding what people do – whether online, through street cameras, with facial recognition etc, would also fundamentally transform the procedural aspect of the rule of law by significantly decreasing the costs of enforcement of law.

IV. Conclusion: Future Rule of Law

At the 70th session of the UN General Assembly, on 25 September 2015, the Member States adopted a new development agenda titled 'Transforming our world: the 2030 Agenda for Sustainable Development'. The agenda places the rule of law principle together with human rights, justice, equality and non-discrimination, and holding that the rule of law, together with democracy and good governance are vital for sustainable development and peaceful societies.[110] Notwithstanding such aspirations for the rule of law, this chapter claims that the future of the rule of law is grimmer.

[106] ibid.

[107] B Sheppard, 'Warming up to Inscrutability: How Technology Could Challenge Our Concept of Law' (2018) 68 *University of Toronto Law Journal* 36.

[108] On trends of improving access to legislation, see Y Roznai and N Mordechay, 'Access to Justice 2.0: Access to Legislation and Beyond' (2015) 3 *The Theory and Practice of Legislation* 333.

[109] Casey and Niblett (n 94).

[110] www.sdgs.un.org/2030agenda; see N Arajarvi, 'The Rule of Law in the 2030 Agenda' (2018) *Hague Journal on the Rule of Law* 187, 206.

Populism and democratic erosion processes have shrunk the concept to its narrow procedural elements, turning the 'rule *of* law' to a 'rule *by* law' in which governments instrumentalise law for narrow political aims and to entrench their power, and stripping it from any substantive notions strongly connected to democracy and fundamental rights. Thus, such instrumentalisation of law may well 'be a rule of law success story in formal terms, while systematically violating the underlying values of the rule of law'.[111] At the same time, technological developments of machine-learning, artificial intelligence and big data will change the general nature of law to personalised legislation. Such a development may advance public legal awareness, abiding by the law and its enforcement. Nonetheless alongside more effective law-making and law-enforcement, the rule of law in 2030 will be rather remote from the idea of a general law for all people.

[111] M Krygier, 'The potential for resilience of institutions to sustain the rule of law' (2020) 12 *Hague Journal on the Rule of Law* 205.

3

Federalism in 2030

BILYANA PETKOVA*

A somewhat romanticised, somewhat accurate picture of twenty-first century Londoners is that they are 'humorous and irreverent humanists', and of their city – of a place where 'the sin was not to risk upsetting someone but to be boring'.[1] Londoners' wittiness is invariably helped by the city's financial power that forms part and parcel of London's political identity to which, much as in the case of other global cities, technology and the law add yet extra layers. As I will argue elsewhere at length, federalism in the digital age faces a set of interesting challenges and perhaps opportunities that we might see unfolding in the years to come that arguably strengthen and forge urban identities.[2] This chapter looks in detail at some of the issues, starting out by discussing contemporary challenges to federalism as we know it. First, I ask whether federalism is in decline (section I). I show that power sharing within larger, quasi-federated entities has indeed lost much of its appeal (or at least momentum). This trend is then juxtaposed to the emerging rise of urbanism (section II). Next, I present some sociological findings and legal doctrine as they relate to cities in the US and the EU. In section III, the reader can find empirical examples of cities' growing role as global actors. Finally, I conclude by rephrasing the question asked at the outset: are the outlined challenges signs of a shift within federalism itself rather than a crisis of federalism? I argue that the power-sharing vacuum that opens as a result of the failure of vertical federalism allows cities (and urban networks) to grow in prominence on a global stage.

* I am grateful to Christoph Bezemek for inviting me to contribute to his project and for his unwavering trust. This chapter would not have been possible without the excellent research assistance of David Gruber and Laura Papasodaro. All errors are mine.

[1] M Bevir, 'London: a City of Humanism and Power' [2021] *Critical Review of International Social and Political Philosophy* 1, 3.

[2] B Petkova, *Privacy and the City: How Data Shapes City Identities* (NYU Press, forthcoming). See also IS Rubinstein and B Petkova, 'Governing Privacy in the Datafied City' (2020) (47) *Fordham Urb. Law Journal* 755.

I. Federalism in Decline?

A. Federalism as a Principle of Constitutionalism

Federalism, broadly understood as a principle of separation of powers and territorial decentralisation both below and above the state is a fundamental principle of constitutionalism. Robert Schütze theorises three distinct federalist traditions: first, the classic tradition, whereby 'the dogma of State sovereignty relegates the federal principle to purely international and contractual relations between sovereign States' and '(Con)federal Unions are conceived as international organizations'.[3] Second, the American Tradition, which 'placed the federal idea on the middle ground between international and national law'. Sovereignty 'was seen as delegated and divided between two levels of government', implying 'dual government, dual sovereignty and also dual citizenship'. Lastly, the European tradition that rejects this duality of sovereignty, stating that sovereignty could either 'lie with the States, in which case the [European] Union (EU) was a voluntary international organization', or it could 'lie with the [European] Union, in which case the Union was a "State"'. Consequently, a European understanding of federalism 'refer[s] to the constitutional devolution of power within a sovereign nation'.[4] Schütze's repudiation of dual federalism and the turn to cooperative federalism he observes empirically and espouses normatively for both the US and the EU leaves the sovereignty puzzle unsolved.

While also leaving the sovereignty question at the heart of theoretical debates on federalism unanswered for the purposes of this chapter, I want to point out one of the defining values of federalism being 'the framework it creates for … ongoing negotiation of disagreements large and small'.[5] Federalism, both cooperative and at times uncooperative, is thus a mechanism that ideally serves in a checks-and-balances sort of fashion to prevent tyranny and secure liberty. In making space for conflicts to unravel on the (sub)-state level, be that after a centralised solution has been adopted or before one has emerged, federalism provides both institutionalised spaces for contestation and facilitates integration in heterogeneous polities.[6] In this sense, I theorise federalism as having broad purchase and as a constitutional principle akin (though going beyond) that of the separation of powers. Whereas territorial decentralisation is often pertinent to the federal principle, it is arguably not its sole expression for the sake of comparative law studies like the present endeavour. Fully-fledged federations might in fact regularly function as unitary states. Similarly, decentralised states are 'federations but in name' or

[3] R Schütze, *From Dual to Cooperative Federalism* (Oxford, Oxford University Press, 2009) 15.

[4] ibid 31.

[5] CM Rodriguez, 'Negotiating Conflict Through Federalism: Institutional and Popular Perspectives' (2014) 123 *Yale Law Journal* 2094, 2097.

[6] B Petkova, 'Domesticating the 'Foreign' in Making Transatlantic Data Privacy Law' (2017) 15(4) *International Journal of Constitutional Law* 1066.

'non-institutional federations'[7] while other entities that embody federal elements like the EU perhaps best merit a 'quasi-federal' qualification. Decentralisation and centralisation are a key component of the practice of (quasi)federal arrangements, although the allocation of powers between centre and constitutive units has been understood to mean different things in different federal and (quasi)-federal settings over time. For instance, currently federalism in the US is often evoked in favour of more autonomy for the constitutive states, while at the founding of the US federation and later during the New Deal era it was conversely interpreted to mean more power for the federal unit.[8]

However, while a tug of war between centre and constitutive units might be taken to signify a healthy federal dynamic of constant renegotiation of competences and policies, the current situation is different for two main reasons. First, today in the US but also elsewhere in the world cities are growing. Urban population is rising. When it comes to governance, the city is thus gaining more importance and weight. And yet, in constitutional terms, it still lacks gravity.[9] In federalist terms moreover, the City – an important locus of power and social interaction- remains hardly conceptualised. Second, rather than the familiar tug of war, say on power allocation in the US or other dynamics that could qualify as internal to federalism (say, that of differentiated integration in the EU),[10] certain recent patterns of dissociation both below and above the state make the question pertinent: once a central tenet of constitutionalism, is federalism going to be abandoned in the twenty-first century?

B. Federalism Threats

The rise of populist movements in both America as well as in Europe next to the crisis of the rule of law in the EU, have made scholars question the viability of constitutional democracy as such and of constitutionalism altogether.[11] Granted, identifying a decline in federalism as a building block and defining feature of constitutionalism is not a new idea. In fact, in the US such conclusions date back to the Rehnquist Court that under the banner of a federalist revival rolled back constitutional rights and construed narrowly Congressional power.[12]

[7] A Dowling, 'A Tale of Two Cities: Barcelona and Madrid in Spain', in A Cole and R Payre (eds), *Cities as Political Objects: Historical Evolution, Analytical Categorizations and Institutional Challenges of Metropolitanization* (Cheltenham, Edward Elgar, 2016) 81.

[8] For a helpful chronological summary, see RE Barnett and H Gerken, 'Article I, Sec. 8: Federalism and the Overall Scope of Federal Power', constitutioncenter.org/interactive-constitution/interpretation/article-i/section/8712.

[9] R Hirschl, *City, State* (Oxford, Oxford University Press, 2020).

[10] See Enhanced cooperation, Art 326 et seq TFEU. Differentiated integration in the EU has been understood and conceptualised differently. See R Bellamy, Flexible Europe: Differentiated Integration, Fairness and democracy (Bristol, Bristol University Press, 2022).

[11] See C Bezemek, Introduction in this volume.

[12] C Massey, 'Federalism and the Rehnquist Court' (2002) 53 *Hastings Law Journal* 431(2002).

Without attempting to revisit the legacy of this debate as it unfolded in the US, this section identifies and analyses current tensions in European federalism. Albeit more complex, the examples in Europe include separatism understood as encompassing national separatist tendencies (Catalonia, Scotland) as well as the voluntary departure from a supranational organisation of a key Member State (Brexit) and the ongoing debates about the prospects of Poland as a departing EU Member State (Polexit). By trying to reverse (quasi)-federal integration both below and above the state, these case studies demonstrate how federalism is put to the test.

i. Brexit and Polexit

Recently in Europe, Brexit established a precedent shaking the constitutional foundations of the EU, the supranational organisation that has shaped developments on the continent for the past 50 plus years. The cause of the British referendum that eventually led the UK to leave the EU was to a large extent internal, yet its consequences had a significant bearing on international and European law. Following the 2016 referendum's results, the UK was set on a track to leave the EU. Changing this course was legally possible, both from the perspective of UK law[13] as well as EU law.[14] However, such an action would have inevitably been accused of being undemocratic. After all 52 per cent of the UK had voted 'leave'. However, if we look into the distribution of votes within the UK, only England (53 per cent) and Wales (52.5 per cent) voted 'leave', whereas both Scotland and Northern Ireland resoundingly chose to remain in the EU (62 per cent of Scots and 55.8 per cent of Northern Irish voters casted their vote in favour of remaining). Importantly, even within England itself, the Brexit referendum showed a striking divide between rural and urban. Unsurprisingly, the highly interconnected and vastly internationalised London overwhelmingly voted to remain in the EU (59.9 per cent).[15] The 2010 austerity measures taken in the UK in the aftermath of the global 2007-8 financial crisis had had a big impact on tilting the vote in favour of the 'Leave' campaign.[16] The Conservative Government's spending cuts hit rural workers in remote parts of the country worse, further exacerbating the already

[13] On a national level, the Brexit referendum was merely advisory and did therefore not result in a legal obligation for the UK to leave the EU, see *R (on the application of Miller) v The Prime Minister; Cherry and Others v Advocate General for Scotland* [2019] UKSC 41, s 7.

[14] From the perspective of EU law as well, the *fait* was far from being *accompli*, as the UK's notification of withdrawal was 'neither definitive nor irrevocable', CJEU Case C-621/18 *Wightman and Others* s 49 (ECLI:EU:C:2018:999), following the Opinion of AG Sánchez-Bordona, ss 86 et seq. Since the Withdrawal Agreement entered into force on the 31 January 2020, it could be said that until that date a unilateral revocation of the notification was still possible, *Wightman and Others* s 69.

[15] Greater London Authority, 'EU Referendum Results', data.london.gov.uk/dataset/eu-referendum-results; The Electoral Commission, 'EU referendum results by region: London', www.electoralcommission.org.uk/who-we-are-and-what-we-do/elections-and-referendums/past-elections-and-referendums/eu-referendum/results-and-turnout-eu-referendum/eu-referendum-results-region-london.

[16] T Fetzer, 'Did Austerity Cause Brexit?' (2019) 109(11) *American Economic Review* 3849.

existing cleavages.[17] The informed reader would remember the now anecdotal 'leave' slogan promising £350 million per week (of UK funds allegedly paid to the EU) being freed up for the National Health Service in the event of Brexit. As such, the 2016 UK referendum was both (mis-)interpreted as a referendum on austerity and revealed the growing dissatisfaction of rural England with the pre-eminence of London. In his election campaign for Prime Minister, former Mayor of London, Boris Johnson moreover emphasised his intention to shift financial resources away from London to the benefit of the countryside.[18] Some years later, one would be discouraged to search for such a shift.

This dissociation of one of the key members of the EU's predecessor communities brings with it various implications for the future development of supranational federalism and European integration. The procedure of withdrawing from the EU was only laid down in 2007 with the Lisbon Treaty (Article 50 TEU). Notably, this provision also stipulates that a former Member State that decides to re-join the EU must pass through the same procedure as all other non-EU members (Article 50(5) TEU). Whether Brexit created a precedent inspiring other EU Member States to withdraw, or whether it might be perceived as an example effectively deterring further withdrawals is yet to be seen. However, the very fact that the EU now for the first time has a Member State that decided to abandon the project calls into question the foundational myth of an 'ever-closer union'[19] as well as the experience of the last decades of an 'ever-growing union'. The pattern of dissolution is reinforced by other developments, such as the Polish defiance of the EU fundamental value of the rule of law and its reluctance to adhere to decisions of the CJEU.[20] The Polish Constitutional Court has moreover unambiguously rejected the primacy of EU law.[21] Even though Poland has not voluntarily triggered the Article 50 TEU process like the UK did, it might be that there is an imperative on the EU institutions themselves to force 'Polexit', lest the whole edifice of European law starts to be ridiculed for being a dead letter.[22] Whereas previous national efforts to contest

[17] ibid 3883 et seq.

[18] S Murphy, 'Boris Johnson pledges £3.6bn boost for deprived towns: In first major speech, PM seeks to take spotlight off Brexit with plan to 'turbocharge' regions' *The Guardian* (London 27 July 2019) www.theguardian.com/politics/2019/jul/27/critics-doubt-boris-johnson-can-deliver-new-rail-route-pledge.

[19] Preamble of the TEU, Recital 13 'RESOLVED to continue the process of creating an ever closer union among the peoples of Europe, in which decisions are taken as closely as possible to the citizen in accordance with the principle of subsidiarity'; Preamble of the TFEU, Recital 1, 'DETERMINED to lay the foundations of an ever closer union among the peoples of Europe'; Art 1 TEU 'This Treaty marks a new stage in the process of creating an ever closer union among the peoples of Europe, in which decisions are taken as openly as possible and as closely as possible to the citizen.' Case 26/62 *Van Gend en Loos*, ECLI:EU:C:1963:1.

[20] *Commission v Poland* (C-204/21 R, EU:C:2021:593). Poland has just been sentenced to a periodic penalty payment of €1 million per day until it complies with its legal obligations.

[21] Polish Constitutional Tribunal, 7 Oct 2021, decision K3/21. For an official English translation see: trybunal.gov.pl/en/hearings/judgments/art/11662-ocena-zgodnosci-z-konstytucja-rp-wybranych-przepisow-traktatu-o-unii-europejskiej.

[22] H Hofmann, *Sealed, Stamped and Delivered: The Publication of the Polish Constitutional Court's Judgment on EU Law Primacy as Notification of Intent to Withdraw under Art. 50 TEU?* (VerfBlog, 13 October 2021) verfassungsblog.de/sealed-stamped-and-delivered/.

EU primacy like the *Solange* saga[23] of the German Federal Constitutional Court actually led to increased harmonisation in the area of fundamental rights protection at its best, the Polish case is less likely to exert benevolent influence on EU integration.[24] And while the EU still relies on its unbroken attractiveness to other smaller (and poorer) eastern European countries that are formally on the path of becoming EU Member States, overcoming long-lasting historical differences on the Balkans seems a hard nut to crack. One could think of the continuous implicit Greek veto on North Macedonia's EU membership prospects that would seem to have been recently overcome with the consensus on a new name for that country only to be threatened again by Bulgaria's argument (and potential new veto on North Macedonia's EU membership) based on recognition of Bulgarian as an official language in the EU and of Northern Macedonian as its dialect only.[25]

ii. *Scottish and Catalonian Separatism*

If we look at federal arrangements below the state in Europe, Scottish and Catalonian separatism seem easily inflammable too, showing the same trend of dissolution or precariousness at the level of sovereign states that have a quasi-federated structure. During the Scottish independence referendum in 2014, continued EU membership was a key selling point for the Scots to remain in the UK, since Scotland would have needed to apply to re-enter the EU under Article 49 TEU, thereby temporarily losing its status as an EU Member State along with privileged access to the internal market for Scottish businesses and the enjoyment of EU citizenship status for Scottish citizens.[26] In a head nod to the Scottish separatists, more powers were devolved to Scotland in the aftermath of the 2014 referendum (Scotland Act 2016). Following the Brexit referendum in 2016, in which as noted both Northern Ireland and Scotland voted to remain in the EU, a core issue of sub-national power-sharing arose: when sub-entities overwhelmingly vote to decide differently than the entirety of the federation/quasi-federated state,

[23] See BVerfG 22 October 1986, *Solange II* (BVerfGE 73, 339).

[24] See, eg, S Biernat and E Łętowska, 'This Was Not Just Another Ultra Vires Judgment!: Commentary to the statement of retired judges of the Constitutional Tribunal', (VerfBlog, 27 October 2021), verfassungsblog.de/this-was-not-just-another-ultra-vires-judgment/, ('the judgments of the constitutional courts of other Member States have generally served to raise the level of protection of citizens, whereas the judgment in case K 3/21 lowers that level'); F Bárd and A Bodnar, 'The end of an era: The Polish Constitutional Court's judgment on the primacy of EU law and its effects on mutual trust' No 2021-15 *CEPS Policy Insights*, 4, www.ceps.eu/ceps-publications/the-end-of-an-era/, ('Contrary to often-voiced claims, this judgment cannot be compared to any ruling of other apex courts (such as the German Federal Constitutional Court) on the relation between EU and national laws, for various reasons, most notably because the PCT is not independent').

[25] A Brezar, 'Could North Macedonia be the graveyard of the EU's ideals?', (*Euronews*, 20 July 2021) www.euronews.com/2021/07/20/could-north-macedonia-be-the-graveyard-of-the-eu-s-ideals.

[26] Gl Campbell, 'Scottish independence: How Brexit has changed the debate over EU membership' (*bbc.com*, 3 February 2020) www.bbc.com/news/uk-scotland-scotland-politics-51357050; Martin Currie, 'Scottish independence: Would Scotland be in the EU after a Yes vote?' (*bbc.com*, 29 April 2014) www.bbc.com/news/uk-scotland-scotland-politics-51357050.

their perceived representation arguably gets lost, fuelling already existing secession calls. On the issue of the role for the devolved administrations in Scotland and Northern Ireland in negotiating Brexit, the UK Supreme Court moreover found no legally enforceable right for either to participate in negotiating the withdrawal agreement, only an unenforceable political convention to be consulted by the Westminster Government.[27]

The growing political rift between the English and Scottish Governments post-Brexit, with continued EU membership no longer an incentive for the Scots to remain a part of the UK now make pertinent the question of another Scottish independence referendum. Under the Scotland Act of 1998, reserved matters fall outside of the competences devolved to Scotland (Section 29(2) Scotland Act *e contrario*). Notably, the list of reserved matters does not include the organisation of referenda in general. '[A]spects of the constitution', on the other hand, 'are reserved matters, that is [...] (b) the Union of the Kingdoms of Scotland and England' (Schedule 5 Part I Scotland Act). The question is thus whether the organisation of an independence referendum polling Scots' opinion with potential repercussions for the future of the Union of the Kingdoms falls under such a reserved matter or not. As some have argued, merely asking the Scottish citizens about their opinion on Scottish governance should not fall under Westminster competence.[28] Conversely, others contend that the purpose of a referendum that relates to the future of the Union of the Kingdoms as a whole necessarily falls under reserved competence.[29] At the time of the first Scottish referendum, the constitutional question was circumvented through political cooperation in the form of a governmental agreement between Westminster and Holyrood (2012 Edinburgh Agreement). The Scotland Act was temporarily amended to enable Scotland to hold an ad hoc referendum (Section 30 Order). The sunset clause in the temporary amendment, however, forecloses any possibility of reusing it for future independence referenda, thereby leaving the competence question open. Or as Andrew Tickell puts it: 'This represents an uneasy kind of constitutional truce. Perhaps this is how it should be.'[30]

Catalonian separatists based their claim on the 'right to decide' found in the so-called *plan Ibarretxe*, which in turn has its origins in the right to self-determination under international law.[31] There is no right to self-determination

[27] *R (on the application of Miller and another) v Secretary of State for Exiting the European Union* [2017] UKSC 5.

[28] As the Scottish Government explained, the purpose of the referendum was to find out 'the views of people in Scotland on a proposal about the way Scotland is governed.', The Scottish Government, 'Your Scotland, Your Referendum' (Consultation Paper, 2012), www.webarchive.org.uk/wayback/archive/20170703123959/http://www.gov.scot/Publications/2012/01/1006.

[29] A Tickell, 'The Technical Jekyll and the Political Hyde: The Constitutional Law and Politics of Scotland's Independence 'Neverendum'' in A McHarg et al (eds), *The Scottish Independence Referendum: Constitutional and Political Implications* (Oxford, Oxford University Press, 2016) 334 et seq.

[30] ibid 345.

[31] A López-Basaguren, 'Claims for Secession in Catalonia, Rule of Law, Democratic Principle and Federal Alternative', in A López-Basaguren and L Escajedo San-Epifanio (eds), *Claims for Secession and Federalism: A Comparative Study with a Special Focus on Spain* (Cham, Springer, 2019) 369.

under the Spanish Constitution, something unsurprising given that most states emphasise their territorial indivisibility, with a few exceptions only that give an explicit right to secession to their regions.[32] The Catalonian referendum was thus proclaimed illegal,[33] due to the fact that there was no space for it under Spanish constitutional law. This in turn propelled a question like the one that surfaced in the Scottish-English debate: should an independence referendum be posed to Catalonians only or to all Spanish citizens? Article 92 of the Spanish Constitution moreover makes clear that: 'Political decisions of special importance may be submitted to *all* citizens in a consultative referendum.'[34] Although in Spain, as was the case in the UK, the 'need for reform of territorial autonomy appears to be an indisputable necessity',[35] it is far from undisputed what such reform should look like.[36] Ironically, a constitutional reform reworking Spanish 'non-institutional federalism' would most likely be subject to a referendum under Article 168 of the Spanish Constitution.

Separatism as a challenge to federalism in a nation-state setting seems to have been tackled through constitutional reform in Italy. In the 1990s the Lega Nord party promoted the independence of Padania (a term used for an agglomeration of northern regions in Italy, together with some central ones).[37] The secession attempt of the Lega was partially abandoned in favour of a devolution project aiming to achieve the transfer of an important part of legislative and administrative powers from the centre to the regions. A first reform of the Constitution towards greater autonomy for the regions was approved in 2001. A second reform partly along these lines was rejected in a nation-wide, constitutional referendum in 2006 but eventually succeeded in 2011. However, with Matteo Salvini's leadership of the

[32] J Tornos Mas, 'Secession and Federalism. The Spanish Case', in A López-Basaguren and L Escajedo San-Epifanio (eds), *Claims for Secession and Federalism: A Comparative Study with a Special Focus on Spain* (Cham, Springer, 2019) 398.

[33] JM Castellá Andreu, 'Constitution and Referendum on Secession in Catalonia', in A López-Basaguren and L Escajedo San-Epifanio (eds), *Claims for Secession and Federalism: A Comparative Study with a Special Focus on Spain* (Cham, Springer, 2019) 406.

[34] Emphasis added by the author. See further, Tornos Mas (n 32) 396.

[35] López-Basaguren (n 31) 384.

[36] For example, Tornos Mas argues for increased focus on a pluri-national federalist state. See, Tornos Mas (n 31) 396.

[37] On 15 September 1996 the leader of Lega Nord Umberto Bossi, declared independence and sovereignty for Padania. See 'Dichiarazione di Indipendenza e Sovranità della Padania', web.archive.org/web/20130512030148/http://www.giovanipadani.leganord.org/dichiarazione.asp. The independence had no legal effect and was never recognised by any state. Only the Lega dei Ticinesi, a Swiss political party that shared most of Lega Nord's ideologies, supported the movement. Following the declaration of Padania's independence, judicial enquiries were opened in Venice, Turin, Mantua and Pordenone for attempts to disrupt the unity and territorial integrity of the Italian state, and there were physical clashes between Lega Nord militants and the police in Milan. One year later, a referendum was organised by the northern regions posing the question: 'Do you want Padania to become an independent and sovereign federal republic?'. Almost 5 million people voted and 97% of them voted 'yes'. See 'Cronistoria Della Lega Nord – Dalle Origini ad Oggi, Terza Parte 1996–1998' www.leganord.org/phocadownload/ilmovimento/storia_ln/03_lega_nord_storia96_98.pdf.

Lega Nord, the independence of Padania has been set aside, leaving place for more initiatives seeking further regional autonomy.[38]

II. The Rise of Urbanism and an Open Question on Constitutive Units

Considering Brexit, it seems fair to say that inserting a protocol on subsidiarity to the Maastricht Treaty in favour of devolving more powers to the local authorities in the EU[39] did not help preserve the (quasi-)federal arrangement intact. True, secession attempts on the national level have been avoided by indeed allowing further powers to be devolved to the constitutive units in the UK, Spain and Italy. However, the question becomes who are the constitutive units? In the EU, it was undisputed that these are the Member States. Subsidiarity – although a principle evoked to allow powers to be devolved to the local level in order to be as close as possible to those affected by the legislative act[40] – took the shape of devolution to the national parliaments which are specifically called upon to police the principle of subsidiarity as enshrined in European law.[41] However, as demonstrated in the previous section, in many of the EU Member States the regions are of importance and it might be that the regional parliaments do not necessarily express the view of the national parliament. Furthermore, in each of these regions there are big urban centres that might rival the capital city in economic or cultural terms. One could think of Glasgow and Edinburgh in Scotland, Barcelona in Catalonia and at least Venice and Florence in Northern Italy. Moreover, empirical research has recently shown that the bulk of preliminary references – the instrument of EU law through which usually national lower court judges allow EU nationals to claim rights based on the four freedoms under EU law, come from the EU's major urban hubs.[42]

The rise of urbanism, or as Richard Schragger emphatically puts it 'city power',[43] is a trend sociologists and urban geographers have long observed. Urbanisation is here to stay, with 68 per cent of the world population projected to live in urban

[38] See 'Che fine ha fatto il referendum per l'indipendenza della Padania' *Today* (Rome, 2 October 2017), www.today.it/politica/indipendenza-padania.html.

[39] Protocol (No 2) on the application of the principles of subsidiarity and proportionality, [2008] OJ C115/206.

[40] M Jachtenfuchs and N Krisch, 'Subsidiarity in Global Governance' (2016) 79(2) *Law and Contemporary Problems* 1.

[41] Art 5.3 TEU; Protocol (No 2) on the application of the principles of subsidiarity and proportionality, (n 39).

[42] T Pavone, 'Putting European Constitutionalism in its Place: The Spatial Foundations of the Judicial Construction of Europe' (2020) 16(4) *European Constitutional Law Review* 669.

[43] RC Schragger, *City power: Urban governance in a global age* (Oxford, Oxford University Press, 2016).

areas by 2050.[44] Although surely the pandemic has had an effect,[45] it has done little to reverse things. As urbanites take their laptops to the countryside, it is easy to see that they also carry to less populated and demographically more homogeneous areas their lattes, demand for dock-less bikes or God forbid – scooters: altogether an urban ethos. This means we are likely to witness more, not less, urbanisation even in the emerging post-COVID-19 world. Modern sociologists like Saskia Sassen first entered the fray by setting definitions and describing the phenomenon. A global city, for Sassen, is an urban agglomeration where 'the location of transnational firms' command functions and related activities play an important role in the global economic order'.[46] According to her, the Global City takes on four new economic roles additional to historic city functions. They are 'command points in the organization of the world economy', 'key locations for finance and specialized service firms', 'sites of production, including the production of innovations', and 'markets for the products and innovations produced'.[47] Global Cities 'engage in the global directly, often bypassing the national'.[48] The emphasis on the concentration of financial capital as a defining feature of a global city is somewhat challenged by the work of Richard Florida, another contemporary sociologist. Florida wrote the 'Rise of the Creative Class'[49] emphasising diversity and what another American sociologist, Jane Jacobs, dubbed 'human capital'.[50] For Richard Florida, therefore, human capital rather than, let us call it, capital capital, is both the defining feature of a global city and the decisive factor for its success. Of course, capital and human capital are not mutually exclusive, so the question that urbanists already face in 2020, but would have to grapple with even more so in 2030, is should policies and the law be oriented towards attracting big multinationals or, say, towards attracting a talented working force?

In any event, lawyers have only joined this debate as of late, pointing to the tension that city power might exert on the sovereign state, on the one hand, and on reimagining familiar categories under international law, on the other.[51] In a sense, cities are re-gaining their own identities and global 'centrality' that was once taken away from them in the seventeenth and eighteenth centuries by the emerging nation state.[52] Habitually thought of as 'a creation of their states', to quote the

[44] UN Department of Economic and Social Affairs, *2018 Revision of World Urbanization Prospects*, population.un.org/wup/Publications/Files/WUP2018-Report.pdf.

[45] R Florida et al, 'Cities in a post-COVID world' [2021] *Urban Studies* 1–23.

[46] S Sassen, *The global city: New York, London, Tokyo*, 2nd edn (Princeton, Princeton University Press, 2001) 5.

[47] ibid 3 et seq.

[48] S Sassen, *A Sociology of Globalization* (New York, Norton, 2007) 102.

[49] R Florida, *The Rise of the Creative Class: And How It's Transforming Work, Leisure, Community, and Everyday Life* (New York, Basic Books, 2003).

[50] J Jacobs, *The Death and Life of Great American Cities* (New York, Vintage Books, 1992).

[51] HP Aust, 'Shining Cities on the Hill? The Global City, Climate Change, and International Law' (2015) 26(1) *European Journal of International Law* 255.

[52] E Arban, 'Constitutional Law, Federalism and the City as a Unique Socio-economic and Political Space' in E Hirsch Ballin et al (eds), *European Yearbook of Constitutional Law 2020: The City in Constitutional Law* (The Hague, Asser Press, 2021), 327.

US Supreme Court in *Hunter* v *City of Pittsburgh*,[53] North American cities have gradually emancipated themselves under an ever-expanding variation of what is known as 'home rule' in the US – a provision inserted in the state constitutions, not the federal one – that allows cities to have more autonomy from their state. Back in Europe, German municipalities can enjoy significant autonomy, including fiscal, but only if they are granted such by the Länder or the sub-state[54] (though Berlin, Hamburg, and Bremen are exceptionally granted Länder status). This is not too different to say, Italy or Spain. In Italy, however, the metropolitan cities are explicitly mentioned in the Italian Constitution[55] and with the constitutional reform of 2001, discussed above, Article 118.4 introduced a provision known as 'horizontal subsidiarity'.[56] The provision spearheaded a multitude of local initiatives under what became referred to as a Co-City framework,[57] including a municipal ordinance on the collaborative governance of urban commons in Bologna that was later replicated in over 100 other Italian towns and cities.[58] The constitutional instrument of 'horizontal subsidiarity' indicates that the entirety of decentralised organs of the state, including the municipal tier, are required to cooperate in the devolution of powers 'all the way down'.[59]

In the European vertical or top-down federalism context, devolution has worked best so far in preserving the federal arrangement of power-sharing in various nation-states. The Italian example can be distinguished from the Catalonian and the Scottish case based on the different historical and political circumstances that obtained there on the brink of separatism.[60] However, the Italian crisis, like

[53] *Hunter v Pittsburgh*, 207 U.S. 161 (1907).

[54] D Ehlers, 'Die verfassungsrechtliche Garantie der kommunalen Selbstverwaltung' in D Ehlers and W Krebs (eds), *Grundfragen des Verwaltungsrechts und des Kommunalrechts* (Berlin, de Gruyter, 2000); J Dietlein and SD Peters, *Kommunale Selbstverwaltung im Föderalstaat: Verfassungsrechtliche und verfassungsprozessuale Grundfragen der kommunalen Selbstverwaltung im föderalen System des Grundgesetzes* (Nomos, 2017).

[55] Still, cities have no original powers beyond these of the region, see Art 118.3 of the Italian Constitution.

[56] 'The State, regions, *metropolitan cities*, provinces and municipalities shall promote the autonomous initiatives of citizens, both as individuals and as members of associations, relating to activities of general interest, on the basis of the principle of subsidiarity.'(Art 118(4) Italian Constitution, emphasis mine.

[57] SR Foster and C Ioiane, *Co-Cities: Innovative Transitions Toward Just and Self-Sustaining Communities* (Cambridge MA, MIT Press, Forthcoming 2022).

[58] See generally, commoning.city/co-bologna/;.

[59] Heather Gerken spelled out the normative case for local autonomy as 'federalism all the way down' meaning 'choice, competition, participation, experimentation, and the diffusion of power' Richard Briffault adds on that the US Supreme Court's normative concerns with responsiveness to diverse needs in a heterogeneous society, innovation and experimentation and citizen involvement in democratic processes apply even more to local governments than to states. Certainly, the net that Gerken and Briffault are casting is a broader one – federalism all the way down goes to granting autonomy to school boards and in Briffault's account localities are not limited to cities but on both accounts cities fit in. See, HK Gerken, 'Our Federalism(s)' (2012) 53 *William & Mary Law Review* 1549; HK Gerken, 'The Supreme Court 2009 Term – Foreword: Federalism All the Way Down' (2010) 124 *Harvard Law Review* 4, 8; R Briffault, 'The Challenge of the New Preemption' (2018) 70 *Stanford Law Review* 1995.

[60] Unlike in Scotland and Catalonia where arguably the secession calls were based on years of political struggle for independence and the divisions cut deep along cultural lines, the Italian movement

the Catalonian and Scottish ones, was – at least until now – overcome by mainstreaming federalist claims in the political debate and making devolution an uncontroversial part of both main political parties' platforms. What is more, the current technocratic government backed by the centre-left has recently acknowledged the centrality of cities in the light of Article 118.4 of the Italian Constitution holding that 'Mayors … will be at the heart of the season ahead' and that

> There is a need for cooperation between all levels of administration in the investment, planning and implementation phases [of the National Recovery and Resilience Plan]. This effort must involve everyone: municipalities, regions, ministries.[61]

The question of who the constitutive units are in the national as much as in the European supranational context, however, remains open. Much like in other areas of the law, causality is hard to prove in constitutional and federalism discussions. In any event, insistence on the Member States as a touchstone[62] of the EU's quasi-federal vertical arrangement does not seem to have helped legal mechanisms like subsidiarity to effectively achieve a workable devolution of powers in the EU. In turn, if overstepping the historical importance of cities is replaced with recognition of their role under EU law does not help reverse the current trend toward dissolution, it most certainly would not exacerbate it beyond the status quo.

III. Some (Urban) Empirics on the Rise of City Networks

In the political science and sociology debates, global 'cityscapes' are seen as a result of 'competition between elite enclaves striving for economic command and control'.[63] And while competitive federalism is certainly used as a lens in the internal US legal federalism discourse, the emergent picture of horizontal federalism on a global plane based on city networks is also one of cooperation. Populous cities sometimes boosting the GDP of entire states are entering into horizontal

was motivated by economic reasons only and stirred up by opportunists in the right-wing party. See 'La nuova Lega e la vecchia Lega' *Il Post* (Milan, 4 August 2020) www.ilpost.it/2020/08/04/lega-nord-lega-salvini-premier/; C Bozza, 'Umberto Bossi, anima della Lega, compie 80 anni: la secessione, l'asse con Berlusconi, la malattia' *Corriere della Serra* (Milan, 19 September 2021) www.corriere.it/politica/cards/umberto-bossi-anima-lega-compie-80-anni-secessione-l-asse-berlusconi-malattia/convegno-contro-roma-ladrona.shtml. I am grateful to my colleague and friend of many years, Dr. Alessandro Corda, for helpful discussion on this point.

[61] Mario Draghi further recalled that: 'municipalities and metropolitan cities will have to administer almost EUR 50 billion as implementers of the National Recovery and Resilience Plan.' N Cottone, 'Draghi ai sindaci: 'Successo Pnrr nelle vostre mani'. Gentiloni: 'Preoccupa possibile ritardo'' *Il Sole 24 Ore* (Milan, 11 November 2021) www.ilsole24ore.com/art/draghi-sindaci-il-successo-pnnr-e-vostre-mani-AEtsDHw#U40710946729xIG.

[62] Art 4.2 TEU; see also Case 247/85 *Commission v Belgium* ECLI:EU:C:1987:339.

[63] J Beaverstock et al, 'A Roster of World Cities' (1999) 16(6) *Cities* 445; J Beaverstock et al, 'A New Metageography in World Cities Research' (2000) 90(1) *Annals of the Association of American Geographers* 123.

cooperation through city networks – think of C40 and the environment – and in the US even before the Biden administration committed to enforcing the Kyoto protocol at the federal level,[64] a similar pact to enforce the Paris agreement existed at the city level.[65] Recently, also mayors and city councils are trying to coordinate the regulation of the shared economy (think of Uber and Airbnb). Cities have also started declaring aspirations in becoming major players when it comes to human rights – examples include considerations of equity in construction projects and the idea of contributing to the design of mixed neighbourhoods and shared public spaces. To better illustrate the possibilities for global city action, this section will engage in three case studies on how cities connect in the areas of environmental policy, regulating the shared economy and human rights.

A. City Networks and the Environment

First conceived of and initiated by a former mayor of London, the C40 network is a conglomeration of 97 megacities, representing a total population of over 7,000 million. With a cooperative platform of such size – outnumbering the US and EU population – the C40 network has agreed on several environmental action plans, such as Deadline 2020 and Inclusive Climate Action.[66] The modus operandi of C40 generally consists of member cities pledging to reach certain self-imposed goals in reducing carbon emissions, increasing the production of sustainable energy and other means of facilitating an urban-driven transition towards sustainability. The network itself provides research, technical assistance and supports inter-city exchange that facilitates the spread of best practices.[67] Among other resources, C40 keeps a vast database of case studies of cities around the globe that have taken part in experimental climate action. Interesting to observe is also the reach of C40's regulatory action: instead of only regulating CO_2 city emissions, cities attempt to regulate consumption. Leveraging high consumption in urban settings allows C40 members to exert extraterritorial regulatory influence (or arguably work toward imposing a 'gold standard' in environmental protection), since

[64] See, S Roesler, 'Federalism and Local Environmental Regulation' (2015) 48 *UC Davis Law Review* 1111; arguing for federal pre-emption of state laws that limit local laws furthering environmental action.

[65] J Resnik et al, 'Ratifying Kyoto at the Local Level: Sovereintism, Federalism, and Translocal Organizations of Government Actors (TOGAs)' (2008) (50) *Arizona Law Review* 709.

[66] C40, 'Inclusive Climate Action (ICA) Programme Overview' c40-production-images.s3.amazonaws.com/other_uploads/images/1911_ICA_Programme_Overview_%281%29.original.pdf?1535734552; C40, 'The Future of Urban Consumption in a 1.5°C World – Headline Report' c40-production-images.s3.amazonaws.com/other_uploads/images/2270_C40_CBE_MainReport_250719.original.pdf?1564075036. Other examples of city to city cooperation are shown by networks like (among others) the International Urban Cooperation, a database providing technical expertise for cities willing to develop more sustainably iuc.eu/solutions/); the URBACT program, a city network active on environment as well as other topics urbact.eu/urbact-glance); or EUROCITIES, a network of more than 200 cities active also on environmental topics (eurocities.eu/latest/mayors-unite-for-climate/).

[67] C40, 'Inclusive Climate Action (ICA) Programme Overview', (n 66).

85 per cent of consumption-based emissions in cities stem from production sites outside the city itself.[68] In 2019, within the framework of C40, London adopted an Ultra Low Emissions Zone, an area operating in the city centre 24 hours a day, 365 days a year, pricing access for vehicles that do not have the highest emissions standards. London has now announced the expansion of the area beyond the confines of the city centre, thus becoming the biggest limited traffic zone in Europe.[69] Although C40 adopts a flat hierarchy for its members, the leadership of London in various stages of the network's existence remains palpable.

B. City Networks and the Shared Economy

Another field where cities have started to network and coordinate their efforts is the regulation of the shared economy. An example of European cities acting together is the joint open letter written by ten cities and addressed to the Court of Justice of the European Union in order to express a desire to regulate housing and rentals at the local level.[70] The context was a case before the CJEU where one of the questions was about whether Airbnb should have an obligation to disclose rental data to the local governments or not.[71] The cities jointly argued that they:

> must protect the public interest and eliminate the adverse effects of short-term holiday rental in various ways. (…) Therefore (local) governments should have the possibility to introduce their own regulations depending on the local situation. For this, we need strong legal obligations for platforms to cooperate with us in registration schemes and in supplying rental data per house that is advertised on their platforms.[72]

As noted, cities do not have a direct route to connect to EU law, so the letter remained purely declaratory.

Other examples are the Sharing Cities Action, a network of 70 cities 'working together [on research studies] to develop specific actions to deal with the challenges and opportunities of the platform economy'[73] as well as the EU funded project Sharing Cities.[74] In the context of Sharing Cities, London offers the

[68] C40, 'The Future of Urban Consumption in a 1.5°C World – Headline Report', (n 66).

[69] 'London's Ultra Low Emission Zone expanded to include inner London' (*Intelligent Transport*, 25 October 2021) www.intelligenttransport.com/transport-news/129378/london-ultra-low-emission-zone-expanded/.

[70] The ten cities Amsterdam, Barcelona, Berlin, Bordeaux, Brussels, Krakow, Munich, Paris, Valencia and Vienna have published this open letter as a Joint Press Release. For the full text, see, eg, Gemeente Amsterdam, 'Press release 'Cities alarmed about European protection of holiday rental'' (19 June 2019) www.amsterdam.nl/nieuwsarchief/persberichten/2019/persberichten-laurens-ivens/press-release-cities-alarmed-about/.

[71] Case C-390/18 *Airbnb Ireland* ECLI:EU:C:2019:1112. The press release explicitly refers to the Opinion of AG Szpunar ECLI:EU:C:2019:336.

[72] Joint Press release (n 70).

[73] Sharing Cities Action, 'Sharing Cities Action task force: a network of global cities' www.sharingcitiesaction.net/cities-task-force/sharing-cities-action-task-force-a-network-of-global-cities/.

[74] See generally, Sharing Cities, 'About Sharing Cities: A New Framework for Citizen Engagement' www.sharingcities.eu/sharingcities/about.

opportunity to exploit and replicate its Funding London Model, an investment programme developed in 2004 by the city of London with the purpose of providing and administering venture capital and loans to London-based small and medium enterprises. This model should help Sharing Cities leaders to take steps in raising funds that support smart city developments and stimulate high-growth potential SMEs.[75]

C. City Networks and Human Rights

Still on a declaratory level, cities have also started developing initiatives related to the protection of human rights. For instance, the 'Human Rights Cities' initiative launched back in the 1990's 'is based on the premise that, for international human rights norms and standards to be effective, citizens of all countries need to learn and understand human rights as a framework for sustainable development of their communities'.[76] Today the network encompasses over 40 human rights cities, Graz being the first European one to take part. In May 2014, The World Human Rights Cities Forum adopted 'Principles for a Human Rights City',[77] while a 'European Charter for the Safeguarding of Human Rights in the City' at present has been signed by more than 400 cities.[78] More recently, the Human Rights Cities Network aims to support cities and decision-makers in implementing human rights in urban settings. The objectives of the Network are to create a community of human rights cities where best practices can be shared, key actors can connect, principles and models proposed and propagated, and human rights solutions provided.[79] The European Union Agency for Fundamental Rights has also released a new report proposing a 'framework for becoming and functioning as a 'Human Rights City' in the EU'.[80]

IV. Concluding Remarks

The sheer numbers of urban growth are daunting, they project city power and might. By the same token however, bigness results in certain weakness in terms

[75] Sharing Cities, 'Deliverable 7.8: 'Funding London' Model' (5 January 2017) nws.eurocities.eu/MediaShell/media/FundingLondonModel.pdf.

[76] SP Marks et al, *Human Rights Cities: Civic Engagement for Societal Development* (Washington, Sextant Publishing, 2008) 64.

[77] 'Gwangju Guiding Principles for a Human Rights City' (2014 World Human Rights Cities Forum, 15-18 May 2014) www.hlrn.org/img/documents/Gwangju%20Guiding%20Principles%20for%20Human%20Rights%20City%20adopted%20-%202014.pdf.

[78] United Cities and Local Governments, 'European Charter for the Safeguarding of Human Rights in the City' (2011) uclg-cisdp.org/sites/default/files/documents/files/2021-06/CISDP%20Carta%20Europea%20Sencera_b aixa_3.pdf.

[79] Human Rights Cities Network, 'Who we are' humanrightscities.net/who-we-are/.

[80] European Union Agency for Fundamental Rights, *Human Rights Cities in the EU: A Framework for reinforcing rights locally* (2021).

of governability and city network initiatives remain confined largely to soft law. Whether it is post-Brexit London flexing its muscle to maintain an influential status or – subject to perhaps another chapter – the megapolis in China and the Middle East built from scratch that aspire to become new financial, sports and technological hubs, the era of complete, planetary urbanisation that Lefebvre[81] predicted might not be bestowed upon us as just yet. Some would contend that might be a good thing while others would lament it. However, the shift in demographics of the past decades is evident and it is undisputable that it has led cities to bear the brunt by taking up additional tasks in building new infrastructure without acquiring additional streams of revenue on the one hand,[82] and without having competence commensurate to their growing significance for democracy, on the other.[83] So far, vertical federal constitutional ordering along the lines of nation-states has somewhat successfully managed to keep the precarious pre-existent constitutional arrangement intact by devolving powers to the regions but it is actually cities that are taking centre-stage in an economic, social, cultural and to some degree, political sense. And while devolving healthcare and local policing have been controversial enough in 2020, managing migration flows, usually concentrated in big cities, would be the challenge par excellence for federalism in 2030. The question of constitutive units remains open and is especially poignant for the EU considering the silence of the Treaties with regards to cities but also in view of Article 50. Partly conceived of as an exit procedure for authoritarian governments to be kept at bay,[84] that Article might have been (mis)used in the context of Brexit whereas in view of the continuous crisis of the rule of law in Poland, its merits perhaps lie elsewhere.

The impasse of the nation state has been the usual suspect of all possible crises at least since Anne-Marie Slaughter published one of her seminal books.[85] However, the present situation might carry yet a different overtone – the decline of vertical or top-down federalism. Collective action problems have moved away from the traditional avoidance of conventional welfare (the main raison d'etre of the EU and of the Westphalian state before it as prime examples of vertical federal arrangements). Also, technology diminishes the role geographical proximity used

[81] H Lefebvre, *The Urban Revolution* (Minnesota, University of Minnesota Press, 2003 [1970]).

[82] E Scharff, 'Cities on Their Own: Local Revenue When Federalism Fails' (2021) 48 *Fordham Urban Law Journal* 919; National League of Cities, 'Principles of Home Rule for the 21st Century' (2020) www.nlc.org/wp-content/uploads/2020/02/Home-RulePrinciples-ReportWEB-2-1.pdf [https://perma.cc/7J2N-RN6L].

[83] See section II above.

[84] At the time of drafting of Art 50, the rise of the Austrian far-right politician, Jörg Haider was a big worry for mainstream EU leaders. Since some southern EU states had returned to democracy only in recent years and the reputation of accession eastern European states was equally in question, the hope was that Art 50 would be used to prevent democratic backsliding in that direction. Lord Kerr stated, he 'didn't have UK in mind', see A Gray 'Article 50 author Lord Kerr: I didn't have UK in mind: The EU's divorce clause was designed amid concerns about a 'dictatorial regime.'' *Politico* (Brussels, 28 March 2017) www.politico.eu/article/brexit-article-50-lord-kerr-john-kerr/.

[85] A-M Slaughter, *New World Order* (Princeton, Princeton University Press, 2005).

to play. Moreover, coping with a global pandemic in an ever-more interconnected world might make decentralisation seem the problem rather than the solution to collective action for some. If 2030 is therefore to see constitutionalism survive altogether, then federalism – one of constitutionalism's indispensable elements – must either reconsider what the constitutive units are to which powers can be devolved from the centre in a vertical federal setting; or enhance further the constitutional character of the emerging shift to horizontal federal forms of cooperation.

PART TWO

Areas

4

International Human Rights in 2030

ANDREAS T MÜLLER*

I. Eulogy of Crisis and Eulogy of Ambition

Crisis has shown to be the concept around which the present volume's reasoning revolves. As the introductory remarks correctly point out, '[g]lobal constitutionalism is in crisis'[1] and without doubt, international human rights are in crisis, too.[2]

Yet, this chapter does not seek to deliver a eulogy of crisis. As is well known, the etymological root of 'crisis', the Greek word *κρίνειν*, refers to the activity of reflecting, distinguishing and judging.[3] In that sense, times of crisis call for thorough reflection and sound decision-making. It is well plausible to claim that today we stand indeed at a critical juncture. Our next steps may be decisive for whether we preserve and promote the project of international human rights or whether we fail to protect it against the great many risks and dangers it is facing.

In that sense, crisis promises to be an analytical lens fit for the occasion that has triggered and motivated the present volume. The eulogy in which this chapter wants to engage is different, however. It is the eulogy of ambition. It shall take us back to the 1990s. This was a decade of ambition indeed in the international human rights project, comparable only to its foundational period in the second half of the 1940s. By first turning to this period of human rights ambition and contrasting it with a number of subsequent developments commonly deemed to be debilitating or even destructive to the human rights agenda (II), we shall be able to identify and evaluate major dynamics currently at play in the international human rights project (III).

It would not be difficult to offer an extensive list of relevant developments in the vast field of international human rights law. For reasons of clarity and brevity, however, the following considerations will take the volume's structure as a model

* The author warmly thanks Mag Lukas Baumgartner for his support with proofreading and referencing this contribution.

[1] C Bezemek, Introduction in this volume.

[2] See, for instance, M Mutua, 'Is the Age of Human Rights Over?', in S McClennen and A Schulthesis Moore (eds), *The Routledge Companion to Literature and Human Rights* (London, Routledge, 2016) 450–458; S Moyn, 'How the Human Rights Movement Failed', www.nytimes.com/2018/04/23/opinion/human-rights-movement-failed.html.

[3] www.etymonline.com/word/crisis – etymonline_v_361.

and condense the complexity and intricacy of the actual dynamics from three angles, ie the substance of human rights (III.A), their scope of application *ratione personae* and *ratione materiae* (III.B) as well as the institutional level (III.C), with each of them containing three sub perspectives. Against the background of these nine spotlights, as it were, on current dynamics in international human rights law, the chapter will conclude by a brief outlook taking up the idea again that it is not the time to deplore the crisis of the international human rights project, but to call and gather for its protection and further development (IV).

II. The 1990s … and What Came Afterwards

It is a truism that a global endeavour such as that of international human rights does not operate in a geopolitical vacuum. This was the case in 1945 when the Charter of the United Nations (UN Charter)[4] was adopted by the victorious powers of World War II[5] 'to save succeeding generations from the scourge of war, which twice in our lifetime has brought untold sorrow to mankind'[6] and 'to reaffirm faith in fundamental human rights [and] in the dignity and worth of the human person'.[7] The Universal Declaration of Human Rights (UDHR) of 10 December 1948[8] declared that it constituted an answer to the experience of 'disregard and contempt for human rights hav[ing] resulted in barbarous acts which have outraged the conscience of mankind'.[9] Against this background, it famously proclaimed: 'All human beings are born free and equal in dignity and rights. They are endowed with reason and conscience and should act towards one another in a spirit of brotherhood.'[10] The contemporaneous Genocide Convention, adopted only one day before the UDHR, ie on 9 December 1948, reflected the shared conviction that it was necessary 'to liberate mankind from such an odious scourge'.[11]

[4] Charter of the United Nations (San Francisco, 26 June 1945).

[5] The term 'United Nations' dates back to the Declaration by the United Nations of 1942 in which the signatories pledged not to conclude a separate peace with the Axis powers, ie 'United Nations' was at the time a collective term designating the powers allied against the Axis powers. For their part, the Axis powers were referred to as 'enemy states' in the UN Charter (see Arts 53, 77, and 107). It is worth noting, however, that these provisions were declared obsolete in the *Report of the Special Committee on the Charter of the United Nations and the Strengthening of the Role of the Organization*, UNGA Res 50/52 (15 December 1995) and in the *2005 World Summit Outcome* UNGA Res 60/1 (16 September 2005), para 177, thus eventually making the term 'United Nations' a genuinely universal concept.

[6] Preambular paragraph 1 UN Charter. For peace as the paramount objective of the United Nations see Art 1(1) UN Charter referring to 'maintain[ing] international peace and security' as the first purpose of the United Nations.

[7] Preambular paragraph 1 UN Charter; see further the (albeit rather ephemeral) references to human rights in Arts 1(3), 13(2), 55(3), 62(2), 68 and 76(3) UN Charter.

[8] *Universal Declaration of Human Rights* (adopted 10 December 1948) UNGA Res 217A(III) (hereinafter 'UDHR').

[9] Preambular paragraph 2 UDHR.

[10] Art 1 UDHR.

[11] Preambular paragraph 3 Convention on the Prevention and Punishment of the Crime of Genocide (adopted 9 December 1948, entered into force 12 January 1951) 18 UNTS 277.

And then came the Cold War. It massively delayed the high aspirations of the '*droits-de-l'hommistes*'[12] of the immediate post-war period. In particular, the initial attempts to recast the non-binding UDHR into a binding human rights instrument failed amidst the heightened political and military tensions between the Western and the Eastern hemispheres.[13] Only western Europe as a relatively homogeneous region in ideological terms succeeded in adopting the 1950 European Human Rights Convention (ECHR)[14] as a binding human rights treaty guaranteeing mostly civil and to some extent also political rights.[15]

While the easing of the Cold War from the 1970s onwards made further progress of the international human rights agenda possible – just to mention the Helsinki Final Act of 1975 which accepted human rights as one of the guiding principles of international relations[16] – it was the end of the confrontation between East and West in 1989/90 that heralded the advent of another formidable rise of the international human rights project. The disappearance of the antagonism between the two ideological blocks augured to unleash dynamics towards a new 'age of human rights' under the auspices of the benevolent hegemon in the West, thus promising the 'end of history'.[17] In that sense, global human rights became a positive collateral effect of the *pax Americana*.[18]

Throughout the 1990s, a significant boost for international human rights could be observed in at least four dimensions: in terms of: 1) proliferation of human rights instruments; 2) expansion of membership in these instruments; 3) strengthening institutional protection, and 4) increasing cross-sectional impact.

First, many new international human rights instruments were launched and adopted, seeking to extend particular protection, for instance, to children,[19] persons with disabilities[20] and victims of enforced disappearance,[21] as well as

[12] The neologism 'droit-de-l'hommisme' was created by Alain Pellet to denote the mindset of human rights militants, ie 'human rightist'; see A Pellet, 'Droits-de-l'hommisme et droit international' (2001) 1 *Droits fondamentaux* 2001, 167, 179; idem, '"Human Rightism" and International Law' [2000] *Italian Yearbook of International Law* 10.

[13] This only became possible half a generation later with the adoption on 16 December 1966, on the one hand, of the International Covenant on Economic, Social and Cultural Rights (adopted 16 December 1966, entered into force 3 January 1976) 993 UNTS 3 (ICESCR), and on the other, of the International Covenant on Civil and Political Rights (adopted 16 December 1966, entered into force 23 March 1976) 999 UNTS 171 (ICCPR).

[14] Convention for the Protection of Human Rights and Fundamental Freedoms (Rome, 4 November 1950).

[15] As regards the latter see notably Art 1(3) of the First Additional Protocol to the ECHR (COE, entered into force 18 May 1984).

[16] Nr VII Declaration on Principles Guiding Relations between Participating States (Helsinki, 1 August 1975).

[17] For this – multifaceted and often misused – concept see F Fukuyama, *The End of History and the Last Man* (New York, Free Press, 1992).

[18] See also N Bobbio, *The Age of Rights* (Oxford, Polity, 1991).

[19] Convention on the Rights of the Child (adopted 20 November 1989, entered into force 2 September 1990) 1577 UNTS 3 (CRC).

[20] Convention on the Rights of Persons with Disabilities (adopted 24 January 2007, UNGA Res 61/106) (CRPD).

[21] International Convention for the Protection of All Persons from Enforced Disappearance (adopted 13 December 2006, entered into force 3 May 2008) 2515 UNTS 3.

intensifying the fight against acts entailing systematic human rights violations in a transnational context, notably with respect to human trafficking, smuggling of migrants and illicit manufacturing of and trafficking in firearms.[22]

Second, states heavily engaged in ratifying human rights conventions.[23] This became particularly manifest for the ECHR whose membership virtually doubled after 1990.[24] However, also at the universal level, the major human rights instruments managed to gain substantial additional membership in the last decade of the twentieth century.[25]

Third, and in particular in the wake of the 1993 Vienna World Conference of Human Rights,[26] major developments in the international human rights protection system took place, notably the creation of the position of UN High Commissioner of Human Rights[27] as well as – in a longer perspective – the replacement in 2006 of the Human Rights Commission by the Human Rights Council as the paramount human rights body within the UN system.[28] One may also mention in this context the adoption of the 1993 Paris Principles on National Institutions[29] which testify to the growing awareness of the subsidiary character of the international human rights system and therefore the need for national and international human right bodies to interact and complement each other. In addition, the very creation of the

[22] UN Convention against Transnational Organized Crime (adopted 15 November 2000, entered into force 29 September 2003) 2225 UNTS 209 and its protocols; see Protocol to Prevent, Suppress and Punish Trafficking in Persons, Especially Women and Children (adopted 15 November 2020, entered into force 25 December 2003) 2237 UNTS 319; Protocol against the Smuggling of Migrants by Land, Sea and Air (adopted 15 November 2000, entered into force 28 January 2004) 2241 UNTS 507; Protocol against the Illicit Manufacturing of and Trafficking in Firearms, Their Parts and Components and Ammunition (adopted 31 May 2001, entered into force 3 July 2005) 2326 UNTS 208.

[23] See www.indicators.ohchr.org/.

[24] After the collapse of the Soviet Union and the eastern bloc, many central and eastern European countries joined the Council of Europe, including Hungary (1990), Poland (1991), Bulgaria (1992), Estonia, Lithuania, Slovenia, Romania (1993), the Czech Republic, Slovakia (1993), Moldova, Albania, Ukraine, North Macedonia (1995), Russian Federation, Croatia, Georgia (1999), Armenia, Azerbaijan (2001), Bosnia and Herzegovina (2002), Serbia and Montenegro (2003); see www.coe.int/en/web/about-us/our-member-states.

[25] See, for instance, with respect to the International Covenant on Civil and Political Rights (ICCPR), Albania 1991, Angola 1992, Armenia 1993, Azerbaijan 1992, Belize 1996, Benin 1992, Bosnia and Herzegovina 1993, Brazil 1992, Burkina Faso 1999, Burundi 1990, Cambodia 1992, Cape Verde 1993, Chad 1995, Côte d'Ivoire 1992, Croatia 1992, Czech Republic 1993, Dominica 1993, Estonia 1991, Ethiopia 1993, Georgia 1994, Grenada 1991, Guatemala 1992, Haiti 1991, Honduras 1997, Israel 1991, South Korea 1990, Kuwait 1996, Kyrgyzstan 1994, Latvia 1992, Lithuania 1991, North Macedonia 1994, Malawi 1993, Malta 1990, Moldova 1993, Monaco 1997, Mozambique 1993, Namibia 1994, Nepal 1991, Nigeria 1993, Paraguay 1992, Seychelles 1992, Sierra Leone 1996, Slovakia 1993, Slovenia 1994, Somalia 1990, South Africa 1998, Switzerland 1992, Tajikistan 1999, Thailand 1996, Turkmenistan 1997, Uganda 1995, United States 1992, Uzbekistan 1995, Zimbabwe 1991.

[26] Vienna Declaration and Programme of Action, 25 June 1993, UNGA A/CONF 157/23 (Vienna Declaration).

[27] See ibid, para 17 where '[t]he World Conference on Human Rights recognizes the necessity for a continuing adaptation of the United Nations human rights machinery to the current and future needs in the promotion and protection of human rights' and recommends, in this context, the 'establishment of a High Commissioner for Human Rights for the promotion and protection of all human rights' (ibid, para 18).

[28] UNGA, Human Rights Council (15 March 2006) A/Res 60/251.

[29] UNGA, National institutions for the promotion and protection of human rights (4 March 1994) A/Res 48/134.

International Criminal Court in 1998 with its mandate of combating impunity for 'the most serious crimes of concern to the international community as a whole'[30] deserves to be acknowledged as an additional layer of institutionally protecting human rights at the global level.

Fourth, and most interestingly in terms of structural development, the 1990s represent the decade of international human rights' '*spill over*'[31] into other fields. This can be observed vertically in the reform of existing national constitutions or the creation of wholly new ones under the aegis of international human rights law.[32] This also becomes manifest in a horizontal perspective in terms of cross-fertilisation of other branches of international law, be it international humanitarian law,[33] international criminal law,[34] international environmental law,[35] international trade[36] and investment law[37] and even general international law.[38]

[30] Rome Statute of the International Criminal Court (adopted on 17 July 1998, entered into force 1 July 2002) 2187 UNTS 3 Art 5 (ICC Statute).

[31] For this concept, which is 'borrowed' from the theory of European integration, see, eg, E Haas, *The Uniting of Europe: Political, Social and Economic Forces 1950–1957* (Stanford, Stanford University Press, 1958) 283.

[32] For instance, more than 40 constitutions expressly refer, in their preambular or operative provisions, to the UDHR, 25 of which date from after 1990; see www.constituteproject.org.

[33] See, eg, T Meron, 'The Humanization of Humanitarian Law' [2000] *American Journal of International Law* 239, 278; R Provost, *International Human Rights and Humanitarian Law* (Cambridge, Cambridge University Press, 2002); R Arnold and N Quénivet (eds), *International Humanitarian Law and Human Rights Law. Towards a New Merger in International Law* (Boston, Brill, 2008).

[34] See in particular Art 21(3) of the ICC Statute on 'applicable law': 'The application and interpretation of law pursuant to this article must be consistent with internationally recognized human rights, and be without any adverse distinction founded on grounds such as gender as defined in article 7, paragraph 3, age, race, colour, language, religion or belief, political or other opinion, national, ethnic or social origin, wealth, birth or other status.' See further W Schabas, 'Synergy or Fragmentation? International Criminal Law and the European Convention on Human Rights' [2011] *Journal of International Criminal Justice* 609, 632; A Clapham, 'Human Rights and International Criminal Law', in W Schabas (ed), *The Cambridge Companion to International Criminal Law* (Cambridge, Cambridge University Press, 2012).

[35] See, eg, D McGoldrick, 'Sustainable Development and Human Rights: An Integrated Conception' (1996) 45 *International and Comparative Law Quarterly* 796, 818; F Francioni, 'International Human Rights in an Environmental Horizon' (2010) 21 *European Journal of International Law* 41, 53.

[36] See, eg, E-U Petersmann, 'From 'Negative' to 'Positive' Integration in the WTO: Time for 'Mainstreaming Human Rights' into WTO Law?' (2000) 37 *Common Market Law Review* 1363, 1382; FM Abbott, C Breining-Kaufmann and T Cottier (eds) *International Trade and Human Rights. Foundations and Conceptual Issues* (World Trade Forum, 2005); E-U Petersmann, 'Human Rights, International Economic Law and "Constitutional Justice"', (2008) 19 *European Journal of International Law* 769–798.

[37] See, eg, PM Dupuy, EU Petersmann and F Francioni (eds), *Human Rights in International Investment Law and Arbitration* (Oxford, Oxford University Press, 2009); B Simma and T Kill, 'Harmonizing Investment Protection and International Human Rights: First Steps Towards a Methodology', in C Binder, U Kriebaum, A Reinisch and S Wittich (eds), *International Investment Law for the 21st Century: Essays in Honour of Christoph Schreuer* (Oxford, Oxford University Press, 2009) 678, 695; A Al Faruque, 'Mapping the Relationship between Investment Protection and Human Rights' (2010) 11 *Journal of World Investment & Trade* 539, 560; N Klein, 'Human Rights and International Investment Law: Investment Protection as Human Right' (2012) 4 *Goettingen Journal of International Law* 179, 196.

[38] See only MT Kamminga and M Scheinin (eds), *The Impact of Human Rights Law on General International Law* (Oxford, Oxford University Press, 2009); N Weiß and JM Toucenin (eds), *The Influence of Human Rights on International Law* (Heidelberg, Springer, 2015).

The afore-mentioned 1993 World Conference on Human Rights,[39] the 1995 Beijing Conference on Women[40] as well as the 2000 Millennium Declaration[41] stand for the call to mainstream human rights into all policy areas. In the legal context, the principle of systematic integration as enshrined in Article 31(3)(c) of the Vienna Convention on the Law of Treaties[42] triggered the inclusion of human rights concerns in judicial and arbitral decision-making in fields that used to be considered remote from human rights protection. In the view of many scholars at the time, these various achievements testified to an ongoing 'humanisation' of international law[43] – representing the major building block in the even more momentous project of constitutionalisation of international law.[44] Such a powerful cosmopolitan vision nourished hopes for the entrenchment of human rights, hand in hand with democracy and the rule of law, into domestic constitutional theory and practice.

Our situation today seems to be a far cry from the aspirations of a quarter of a century ago. Again, the geopolitical situation has markedly changed. Predictions of American unipolarism have long gone and have been replaced by the narratives of the rivalry of China in all relevant fields, the renaissance of Russia as well as the rise of other major powers,[45] to the detriment of the 'West' and notably to Europe's relative share of global power. The dynamics unleashed by the end of the Cold War and its containing forces have given rise to various secessionist movements, civil wars and outright international wars in all four corners of the world,[46] resulting in the breaking-apart of existing states, situations of occupation and the emergence of 'failed states'.[47] 9/11 and the ensuing 'war on terrorism' have massively undermined the hopes that the twenty-first century will become a new era of cosmopolitanism and human rights. Having all this in mind, it is en vogue

[39] See n 26 above.

[40] Beijing Declaration and Platform for Action (Beijing, 15 September 1995).

[41] United Nations Millennium Declaration (adopted on 8 September 2000, UNGA Res 55/2), in particular Nr 24 and 25.

[42] For a differentiated account see A Rachovitsa, 'The Principle of Systematic Integration in Human Rights Law' (2017) 66 *International and Comparative Law Quarterly* 557–588.

[43] See, eg, T Meron, *The Humanization of International Law* (Leiden, Brill Academic Publishers, 2006).

[44] See, for instance, J Klabbers, A Peters and G Ulfstein (eds), *The Constitutionalization of International Law* (Oxford, Oxford University Press, 2009).

[45] This is, for instance, illustrated by the relative loss in relevance of the 'Group of Seven' (G7) format, which brings together the world's largest advanced economies (ie Canada, France, Germany, Italy, Japan, the UK and the US), vis-à-vis the 'Group of Twenty' (G20), an intergovernmental forum of the world's largest economies (including both industrialised and developing nations), and BRICS, the cooperation framework of the five major emerging economies (ie Brazil, Russia, India, China and South Africa).

[46] See, eg, the 'Conflict Barometer' annually published by the Heidelberg Institute for International Conflict Research (HIIK); www.hiik.de/?lang=en.

[47] Only to mention in alphabetical order (and without assigning the following countries to one of these scenarios, as several ones qualify under more than one of them) Afghanistan, Georgia, Iraq, Libya, Moldova, Somalia, Syria and Ukraine.

now to observe, or forecast, the end of the human rights age.[48] This is the narrative of international human rights facing an existential crisis. But is this narrative convincing?

III. The Current Dynamics at Play in the International Human Rights Arena

This calls for an effort of identifying and evaluating the current dynamics at play in the international human rights area. As announced before, the vast field lying before us shall be explored by selecting three times three, ie nine perspectives out of the many more that would deserve to be addressed to do justice to the intricate and multifaceted nature of international human rights. So let me proceed by addressing in turn (A) three transformations as regards the content or substance of human rights, (B) three shifts in their scope of application *ratione personae* and *ratione loci*, and (C) three dynamics at the institutional level. There exist, quite obviously, many overlaps and interdependencies, both among these nine perspectives and with respect to the topics covered in the other contributions to this volume.

Before delving into these fields, one should disclose, however, why reflections uttered and written down in 2021, do not devote a special part to the COVID-19 pandemic. This choice might seem odd, even imprudent to some. Yet, even when acknowledging, and deploring, the serious challenges arising from the pandemic for civil and political rights,[49] and the momentous consequences it entails for the economic, social and cultural rights of millions of people,[50] I do not expect major structural changes from it as regards the functioning of the international human rights system.[51] This is not meant to deny that the pandemic and its repercussions

[48] M Mutua, 'Is the Age of Human Rights Over?', in S McClennen and A Schulthesis Moore (eds), *The Routledge Companion to Literature and Human Rights* (London, Taylor & Francis, 2015); I Wuerth, 'International Law in the Post-Human Rights Era' (2017) *Texas Law Review* 279; S Moyn, 'How the Human Rights Movement Failed', www.nytimes.com/2018/04/23/opinion/human-rights-movement-failed.html.

[49] To provide just one example, lockdowns which many states had recourse to during the pandemic, not seldom several times, interfere with eg, the freedom of movement (Art 12 ICCPR; Art 2 of the Fourth Additional Protocol to the ECHR), the freedom of assembly and association (Arts 21 and 22 ICCPR; Art 11 ECHR), the right to private and family life (Arts 23 and 24 ICCPR; Arts 8 and 12 ECHR). In particular, bans on religious gatherings raise issues regarding the right to freedom of conscience and religion (Art 18 ICCPR; Art 9 ECHR) and court closures and trial delays encroach upon the right to a fair trial (Art 14 ICCPR; Art 6 ECHR); see, for instance, S Joseph, 'International Human Rights Law and the Response to the COVID-19 Pandemic' (2020) 11 *Journal of International Human Legal Studies* 249, 255.

[50] See in particular UN Committee on Economic, Social and Cultural Rights, *Statement on the coronavirus disease (COVID-19) pandemic and economic, social and cultural Rights* (17 April 2020), E/C.12/2020/1.

[51] There has been some debate on whether there was a need to adapt the derogation clauses regime in international human rights treaties (Art 4 ICCPR; Art 15 ECHR) to pandemic scenarios, but this can be dealt with on the basis of the existing law; see AT Müller and J Prantl, 'The COVID-19 pandemic as 'public emergency' – Health emergencies as triggers for derogation clauses in international human

may contribute, in manifold ways, to reinforce, and accelerate, ongoing processes of human rights erosion and deconstruction, but this does not make the pandemic a decisive factor in its own right, at least when compared with the impact of the dynamics described below.

A. Substance of Human Rights

First, the focus shall be on the content or substance of human rights: the history of international human rights could be told as a process of continuous accretion of human rights, starting with civil and political rights, on the one hand, and economic, social and cultural rights on the other. In this narrative, the first and second generations of human rights have been completed by a third layer of rights, namely collective rights in the decolonisation context such as the right to self-determination of peoples, the right to freely dispose of natural wealth and resources as well as the right to development.[52] Yet, this dynamic has not stopped there, but over the last decades various 'new' human rights have claimed acceptance. Some among them have successfully done so, others have not yet achieved the legal recognition that more 'established' human rights benefit from, at least not in a universal perspective.[53] The following three reflections relate to relevant trends that can be witnessed at the global level and that must be expected to significantly shape the development in the coming decade(s), namely digitisation, climate change and principled challenges to the universal aspirations of the international human rights project.

(1) There can be no doubt that digitisation and the many dynamics triggered by it pose a major human rights challenge. Reflections on 'human rights in the digital age'[54] abound, and rightly so. The problem already begins with adequately capturing and labelling the phenomenon. Some find it useful to distinguish between digitisation, digitalisation and digital transformation.[55] The complexity is augmented by the fact that this field is demanding in terms of scientific and technological insight – not a self-evident quality of lawyers in general and international human rights lawyers in particular. Furthermore, the challenges arising in such different fields

rights treaties' (2021) 3 *juridikum* 386, 394, with further references. For farther-reaching consequences of the pandemic for human rights see, eg, N Jain, 'Pandemics as Rights-Generators' (2020) 114 *American Journal of International Law* 677, 686.

[52] See in particular the common Art 1 of the ICESCR and the ICCPR as well as Arts 19 et seq of the African (Banjul) Charter on Human and Peoples' Rights (27 June 1981).

[53] See A Arnauld, K von der Decken and M Susi (eds), *The Cambridge Handbook of New Human Rights* (Cambridge, Cambridge University Press, 2020).

[54] See, eg, Keynote speech by M Bachelet, UN High Commissioner for Human Rights, 'Human rights in the digital age', www.ohchr.org/en/NewsEvents/Pages/DisplayNews.aspx?NewsID=25158&LangID=E.

[55] See J Bloomberg, 'Digitization, Digitalization And Digital Transformation: Confuse Them At Your Peril', www.forbes.com/sites/jasonbloomberg/2018/04/29/digitization-digitalization-and-digital-transformation-confuse-them-at-your-peril/?sh=673a8d3f2f2c; MM Gobble, 'Digitaliziation, Digitization, and Innovation' (2018) 4 *Research Technology Management* 56–59.

as social media, cybercrime, artificial intelligence, human enhancement, autonomous driving, but also autonomous weapon systems, etc affect a wide range of human rights (for instance, privacy, free speech, health, mobility, life, dignity), arguably leaving no sector untouched. There can be no doubt that a great many aspects of human life and existence will be subject to massive changes under the auspices of digitisation, and the human rights project cannot be insulated from it.[56] It is important to note, however, that this is not only an area of pitfalls and risks, but also of opportunities for strengthening and enhancing human rights.

(2) The second issue that deserves to be mentioned in its own right in the present context, is climate change. It is used here as a convenient catch-all term encompassing a broad range of phenomena such as sea-level rise, the deterioration of the habitat of fauna and flora and the consequent loss of biodiversity, overpopulation, rural depopulation and the ensuing megalopolis growth, the rise of natural disasters and migration[57] – and, yes, the increased likelihood of the emergence and proliferation of pandemics. As mentioned before with respect to digitisation, also climate change confronts us with a complex and truly global phenomenon that affects most diverse features of our existences and thus our human rights.

It is fascinating to see the great many efforts across the globe to tackle climate change via human rights-driven climate litigation. There are already numerous examples at the domestic level[58] as well as before international courts such as the European Court of Human Rights (ECtHR),[59] the Court of Justice of the European Union (CJEU),[60] in the Inter-American human rights system,[61] but also at the universal level[62] – and we will certainly see more of that to come in the coming decade. At the moment, the applicants are chiefly struggling with obtaining access

[56] See the growing body of case-law on the matter, notably of the European Court of Human Rights (ECtHR), eg *Delfi AS v Estonia*, No 64569/09 (ECtHR 2015); *Big Brother Watch and Others v The United Kingdom* No 58170/13, No 62322/14, No 24960/15 (ECtHR 2015), but also of the CJEU (see n 107 below).

[57] As regards the emerging challenges relating to 'climate refugees' see in particular UNHRC, Communication No 2728/2016 *Ioane Teitiota v New Zealand* UN DocCCPR/C/127/D/278/2016.

[58] See, for instance, Federal Constitutional Court Germany 1 BvR 2656/18, 1 BvR 288/20, 1 BvR 96/20, 1 BvR 78/20 (24 March 2021); *Verein KlimaSeniorinnen Schweiz and Others v Switzerland*, Tribunal federal, 5 May 2020, 1C_37_19; *Milieudefensie et al* v *Royal Dutch Shell*, Rechtbank Den Haag, 26 May 2021, ECLI:NL:RBDHA:2021:5339.

[59] A series of climate cases is pending before the ECtHR, notably *Duarte Agostinho and Others* v *Portugal and 32 Other states* No 39371/20, a complaint of six Portuguese teenagers against 33 state parties, as well its alter ego, a complaint by the Swiss 'KlimaSeniorinnen' ('Senior Women for Climate Protection') *Verein KlimaSeniorinnen Schweiz v Bundesrat* No 53600/20. See also the complaint by an Austrian suffering from Uhthoff's syndrome, a temperature-dependent version of multiple sclerosis, in which the state of health deteriorates significantly, especially in warm temperatures *Mex M* v *Austria* No 18859/21.

[60] CJEU Case T-330/18 *Carvalho and Others* v *Parliament and Council* [2018]; CJEU Case C-565/19 P *Carvalho and Others* v *Parliament and Council* [2021] (the so-called 'People's Climate Case').

[61] Petition to the Inter-American Commission on Human Rights Seeking to Redress Violations of the Rights of Children in Cité Soleil – Haiti [2021].

[62] As regards the UN Human Rights Committee see n 57 above; see also with respect to a petition filed by 16 children from 12 countries against Argentina, Brazil, France, Germany and Turkey in 2019 *Chiara Sacchi et al v Argentina* Committee on the Rights of the Child CRC/C/88/D/104-XX/2019 (8 October 2021).

to the respective fora due to *locus standi* issues.[63] To be sure, climate change is a momentous threat to humanity, but its negative effects are diluted in a twofold sense: on the one hand, they tend to affect not only a few, but many or all; on the other hand, climate change figures remotely in the chain of causality, with many other factors and actors intervening. This is a challenge indeed for a human rights protection system designed to deal with the responsibility of state parties of human rights conventions triggered by 'individualisable' violations of human rights. It is a serious hurdle to establish that, in the context of climate change, a given individual is the (at least indirect/potential) victim[64] of a violation of rights that is attributable to a specific state or a group of states which will, however, normally not include those states which account for the lion's share of greenhouse gas emission.

(3) Third, we can observe principled challenges to the universal aspirations of the international human rights project. Lofty promises such as 'All human beings are born free and equal in dignity and rights',[65] 'All human rights are universal'[66] or 'The universal nature of these rights and freedoms is beyond question',[67] while only a generation old, appear to be far away at a time where the human rights project is criticised – both from the inside[68] and the outside – as a Euro-centric or Occidentalist[69] endeavour or a (post-)colonial enterprise. The attacks come from too many sides to name them all: Human rights are said to be relative with regard to religious precepts (eg Islam[70] and the Christian right in the US) or, in a more secular perspective, to historical and cultural traditions (eg African States,

[63] See also in the context the limits to common interest litigation; for instance, with respect to the ECtHR *Gorraiz Lizarraga and Others v Spain* No 52543/00 (ECtHR 2004); with respect to the CJEU in the light of the so-called *Plaumann* criteria see n 59 above.

[64] See, eg, Art 1 Optional Protocol ICCPR or Art 34 ECHR; see AT Müller, 'Admissibility (of Individual Communications and Complaints)', in C Binder, M Novak, J Hofbauer and P Janig (eds), *Elgar Encyclopedia of Human Rights* (Cheltenham, Edward Elgar Publishing, 2022) II., with further references.

[65] Art 1 UDHR.

[66] Vienna Declaration, Nr 5.

[67] ibid, Nr 1; but see already the at least indirect recognition of cultural variations in ibid, Nr 5: 'While the significance of national and regional particularities and various historical, cultural and religious backgrounds must be borne in mind, it is the duty of States, regardless of their political, economic and cultural systems, to promote and protect all human rights and fundamental freedoms.'

[68] See in particular the efforts of Third World Approaches to International Law (TWAIL) to 'decolonise' international law, ie to expose that, at closer inspection, seemingly universal principles often reflect the interests of the Global North more than the Global South; see, eg, S Pahuja, *Decolonising International Law, Development, Economic Growth and the Politics of Universality* (Melbourne, Cambridge University Press, 2011). In this context, also the comparative international law movement merits mention, claiming that international law is not a monolith, but is open to variations in application and interpretation depending on the respective background; see notably M Koskenniemi, 'The Case for Comparative International Law' (2011) *Finnish Yearbook of International Law* 1, 8; A Roberts, P Stephan, P Verdier and M Versteeg, *Comparative International Law* (Oxford, Oxford University Press, 2018).

[69] See E Said, *Orientalism* (New York, Pantheon Books, 1978) and A Margalit, and I Buruma, *Occidentialism: The West in the Eyes of Its Enemies* (New York, The Penguin Press, 2004).

[70] See in particular the original version of the Cairo Declaration of the Organization of Islamic Cooperation on Human Rights (adopted on 5 August 1990, Conference of Foreign Ministers of the OIC), Art 24 ('All the rights and freedoms stipulated in this Declaration are subject to the Islamic Shari'ah.') and Art 25 ('The Islamic Shari'ah is the only source of reference for the explanation

China, but also indigenous peoples in Latin America), which appear to be able to form a coalition against 'the West' on the basis of the concept of 'traditional values of humankind',[71] or all at the same time (eg the 'Unholy Alliance' of the Russian Government and Russian Orthodox Church[72]). Calls for pluralism and exercises in identity politics, commendable and reprehensible motives lie close to each other in this debate. In a similar vein, techniques developed in international human rights law to accommodate such claims for diversity – for instance, reservations[73] to human rights treaties or the doctrines of proportionality,[74] margin of appreciation[75] or subsidiarity[76] – are ambiguous. They can be used either to strengthen or to weaken human rights. The battle for the integrity of the human rights project is far from over, and there can be no doubt that it will be one of the chief tasks on this decade's human rights agenda.

or clarification of any of the articles of this Declaration.'). This take on human rights that subjects them to religious rules and limitations was also at the basis of many reservations of Islamic countries to international human rights conventions, notably the Convention on the Elimination of All Forms of Discrimination against Women (adopted 19 December 1979, entered into force 3 September 1981) 1249 UNTS 13 (CEDAW) and the CRC; see www.treaties.un.org/pages/ViewDetails.aspx?src=TREATY&mtdsg_no=IV-8&chapter=4&clang=_en and www.treaties.un.org/pages/ViewDetails.aspx?src=IND&mtdsg_no=IV-11&chapter=4&clang=_en. One should also consider, however, the different approach taken by the updated version of the Arab Charter on Human Rights (Tunis, 22 May 2004) that only selectively refers to the precepts of Islam; see for instance ibid, Art 3(3) on the relation of men and women: 'Men and women are equal in respect of human dignity, rights and obligations within the framework of the positive discrimination established in favour of women by the Islamic Shariah, other divine laws and by applicable laws and legal instruments.'

[71] See notably the adoption on 9 October 2012 of HRC Resolution 21/3 on Promoting human rights and fundamental freedoms through a better understanding of traditional values of humankind: best practices, A/HRC/RES/21/3, notably its Nr 1 ('*Reaffirms* that a better understanding and appreciation of traditional values shared by all humanity and embodied in universal human rights instruments contribute to promoting and protecting human rights and fundamental freedoms worldwide') and Nr 2 ('*Recalls* the important role of family, community, society and educational institutions in upholding and transmitting these values').

[72] See further K Stoeckl, *The Russian Orthodox Church and Human Rights* (London, Routledge, 2014); eadem, *Russian Orthodoxy and Secularism* (Leiden, Brill, 2020).

[73] According to Art 2(1)(d) of the 1969 Vienna Convention on the Law of Treaties (adopted 22 May 1969, entered into force 27 January 1980) 1155 UNTS 331 (VCLT), a reservation allows a state 'to exclude or modify the legal effect of certain provisions of the treaty in their application to that State', thus to fine-tune its consent to an international (human rights) treaty. However, when making a reservation, a state has to respect the limits set by Art 19(c) of the VCLT, ie that reservation must not be 'incompatible with the object and purpose of the treaty'.

[74] See, eg, J Sieckmann, 'Proportionality as a Universal Human Rights Principle' in D Duarte and J Sampalo (ed), *Proportionality in Law: An Analytical Perspective* (Heidelberg, Springer Verlag, 2018) 3, 24.

[75] As regards the use of the margin of appreciation doctrine by the ECtHR see notably E Bjorge, *Domestic Application of the ECHR. Courts as Faithful Trustees* (Oxford, Oxford University Press, 2015) 178 et seq. At the same time, this doctrine is, at least *eo nomine*, not applied by the HRC and the IACtHR.

[76] See the 6th preambular paragraph of the ECHR, as introduced with the entry into force of Protocol Nr 15 on 1 August 2021: 'Affirming that the High Contracting Parties, in accordance with the principle of subsidiarity, have the primary responsibility to secure the rights and freedoms defined in this Convention and the Protocols thereto, and that in doing so they enjoy a margin of appreciation, subject to the supervisory jurisdiction of the European Court of Human Rights established by this Convention.'

B. Personal and Territorial Scope of Application of Human Rights

In the next steps, we shall analyse challenges arising from shifts in the scope of application *ratione personae* and *ratione loci* of human rights.

(4) As concerns the beneficiaries' or right-bearers' side, being human rights, they are evidently focused on the human person, more precisely on the individual human person. While the debate on collective or group human rights, peoples' rights, third generation rights, and so forth[77] is anything but new, today there are calls with a view to extend the personal scope of application of human rights even further. It is telling that the respective proposals are often linked to challenges that we have already identified at the substantive level: digitisation and climate change. One may point in this regard to the multifaceted debate on the (supposed or real) anthropocentrism or speciesism[78] of human rights law. A growing number of persons, activists, and scholars alike, seek to advance human rights – in an eco- or biocentric perspective – towards animal rights,[79] plant rights,[80] rights of rivers,[81] or even rights of 'nature as a whole' (*Pacha Mama*);[82] as regards the latter, these ideas of 'nuevo constitucionalismo latinoamericano' have also found their way into the case-law of the IACtHR, although so far somewhat timidly.[83] In a similar vein,

[77] See n 52 above.

[78] As regards the seminal work for the speciesism debate see P Singer, *Animal Liberation* (New York, HarperCollins,1975).

[79] See further A Peters, 'Rights of Human and Nonhuman Animals: Complementing the Universal Declaration of Human Rights' (2018) 112 *American Journal of International Law Unbound* 355, 360; eadem, *Animals in International Law* (Leiden, Brill, 2021).

[80] See S Butler, *Erewhon* (Trübner and Ballantyne, 1872), notably chapter XXVII: The Views of an Erewhonian Philosopher concerning the Rights of Vegetables; see further C Stone, 'Should Trees Have Standing–Toward Legal Rights for Natural Objects' [1972] *Southern California Law Review* 450, 487.

[81] For instance, in 2017, the Uttarakhand High Court ruled that the Indian rivers Ganga and Yamuna, the Gangotri and Yamunotri glaciers, as well as other related natural elements are 'legal persons'; see *Mohd. Salim v State of Uttarakhand and Others* The High Court of Uttarakhand at Nainital written petition no 126 (20 March 2014).

[82] The 2008 Constitution of Ecuador provides a particularly strong example in this regard. Already its preamble states: 'We women and men, the sovereign people of Ecuador […] *Celebrating* nature, the Pacha Mama (Mother Earth), of which we are a part and which is vital to our existence […]'. See in particular Art 10(2) ('Nature shall be the subject of those rights that the Constitution recognizes for it.') as well as Art 71: 'Nature, or Pacha Mama, where life is reproduced and occurs, has the right to integral respect for its existence and for the maintenance and regeneration of its life cycles, structure, functions and evolutionary processes. All persons, communities, peoples and nations can call upon public authorities to enforce the rights of nature. […]'. Also the preamble of the 2009 Constitution of Bolivia refers to the concept of 'Pachamama'. In addition, it adopts traditional principles that call for a life in harmony with nature that should make it possible to live a good life (*buen vivir*); see notably Art 8(1): 'The State adopts and promotes the following as ethical, moral principles of the plural society: ama qhilla, ama llulla, ama suwa (do not be lazy, do not be a liar or a thief), suma qamaña (live well), ñandereko (live harmoniously), teko kavi (good life), ivi maraei (land without evil) and qhapaj ñan (noble path or life).'

[83] IACtHR, *The Environment and Human Rights (State obligations in relation to the environment in the context of the protection and guarantee of the rights to life and to personal integrity), interpretation and scope of Articles 4(1) and 5(1) of the American Convention on Human Rights)* Advisory Opinion OC-23/17, 15 November 2017, para 62 (references omitted): 'The Court considers it important to stress

in view of the digital revolution, others already call for extending human rights also to artificial intelligence or robots.[84] The challenge in all this is to find the right balance between, on the one hand, keeping the human rights project inclusive (faithful to its emancipation narrative, as this has always been one of its characteristic traits, ie the emancipation of women, colonial peoples and persons with disabilities) and, on the other hand, avoiding dangers of erosion due to the inflation of human (or then better: fundamental or basic) right-bearers.

(5) Similar considerations apply to the converse side, namely the addressees of human rights. While international human rights law has always focused on the state, non-state actors are more than ever before identified as systemic risks to human rights:[85] armed groups,[86] terrorist organisations, the mafia, and in particular transnational corporations and, more recently, social media companies.[87] The horizontal effect of certain human rights is increasingly accepted, both in domestic and EU law.[88] At the level of international human rights law, duties

that, as an autonomous right, the right to a healthy environment, unlike other rights, protects the components of the environment, such as forests, rivers and seas, as legal interests in themselves, even in the absence of the certainty or evidence of a risk to individuals. This means that it protects nature and the environment, not only because of the benefits they provide to humanity or the effects that their degradation may have on other human rights, such as health, life or personal integrity, but because of their importance to the other living organisms with which we share the planet that also merit protection in their own right. In this regard, the Court notes a tendency, not only in court judgments, but also in Constitutions, to recognize legal personality and, consequently, rights to nature.' The IACtHR confirmed this statement also in its contentious jurisprudence; see *Indigenous Communities of the Lhaka Honhat (Our Land) Association v Argentina* [6 February 2020] IACtHR ser C No 400, para 203.

[84] See S Butler, *Erewhon* (London, Trübner and Ballantyne, 1872), notably chapters XXIII-XXV: The Book of Machines; see further M Coeckelbergh, 'Robot rights? Towards a social-relational justification of moral consideration' (2010) 12 *Ethics and Information Technology* 209, 221; D Gunkel, *Robot Rights* (Cambridge, The MIT Press, 2018).

[85] For a general overview, also addressing the various types of non-state actors, see notably P Alston (ed), *Non-State Actors and Human Rights* (Oxford, Oxford University Press, 2005); A Clapham, *Human Rights Obligations of Non-State Actors* (Oxford, Oxford University Press, 2006); R McCorquodale, 'Non-State Actors and International Human Rights Law', in S Joseph and A McBeth (eds), *Research Handbook on International Human Rights Law* (Cheltenham, Edward Elgar Publishing, 2010); M Nowak and K Januszewski, 'Non-State Actors and Human Rights in M Noortmann', in A Reinisch and C Ryngaert (eds), *Non-State Actors in International Law* (Oxford, Hart Publishing, 2015), with further references.

[86] See, eg, AT Müller, 'Human Rights Obligations of Armed Group' in R Geiß and H Krieger (eds), *The 'Legal Pluriverse' Surrounding Multinational Military Operations* (Oxford, Oxford University Press, 2019) 444 et seq., with further references.

[87] See, for instance, the developing case-law of the Facebook Oversight Board www.oversightboard.com/decision/. See in particular Case decision 2021-001-FB-FBR [5 May 2021] on the decision to restrict then-US President Donald Trump's access to posting content on his Facebook page and Instagram account; www.oversightboard.com/sr/decision/2021/001/pdf-english.

[88] See notably the case-law of the CJEU with respect to data protection (Art 8 of the Charter of Fundamental Rights of the EU [2012] OJ C326/02 (FRC)); see Case C-131/12 *Google Spain SL and Google Inc. v Agencia Española de Protección de Datos (AEPD) and Mario Costeja González* [2014]. See further the jurisprudence on anti-discrimination law, in particular with respect to age discrimination (Art 21 FRC) and the right to paid leave (Art 31(2) FRC); see Case C-144/04 *Werner Mangold v Rüdiger Helm* [2005] ECR I-09981; Case C-555/07 *Seda Kücükdeveci v Swedex GmbHCo. KG.* [2010] ECR I-00365; Case C-684/16 *Max-Planck-Gesellschaft zur Förderung der Wissenschaften eV v Tetsuji Shimizu* [2008]; Case C-619/16 *Sebastian W Kreuziger v Land Berlin* [2018].

of business actors have so far been limited[89] to *soft law* instruments such as the Ruggie Principles.[90] And yet, initiatives to institutionally capture at least the most powerful private actors are on the rise.[91] Also here, a differentiated assessment is necessary regarding what is to be gained from the formal extension of addressees of human rights obligations and to what extent such moves carry risks of dilution of responsibility and accountability. No doubt, also in 2030, the state will continue to stand in the arena as both the greatest protector of, and greatest threat to, human rights.

(6) The focus is also on the state in terms of human rights' scope *ratione loci*. A state is primarily bound to respect human rights within the confines of its territory. Yet, there exists a longstanding doctrine and practice of extraterritorial application of human rights, that is, however, fraught with many ramifications and also certain inconsistencies. We should expect the pertinent challenges to further rise in the decade to come. This is due to the growing importance of relevant activities of states beyond their international borders, be it on the high sea (eg in the context of migration,[92] labour rights, exploitation of natural resources, and environmental pollution), be it by creating 'twilight zones' between states under the guise of 'migration management',[93] be it by engaging in military operations on the

[89] However, individual responsibility of natural, not legal persons in the business context could arise in the context of international criminal responsibility; see Art 25(1) of the ICC Statute. See further, eg, D Stoitchkova, *Towards Corporate Liability in International Criminal Law* (Cambridge, Intersentia Publishers, 2010).

[90] UNHCR, *Guiding Principles on Business and Human Rights* (2011) HR/PUB/11/04. The 'Ruggie Principles' insist on the paramount role of the state in protecting human rights (see ibid, Part I), but address in their Part II the 'corporate responsibility to protect human rights'. While falling short of accepting a full-fledged duty of business enterprises to respect human rights (apart from the fact that the Ruggie Principles constitute merely a *soft law* instrument, they use in the relevant part language that is meant to make clear that no real duties are at stake; arg ibid, Nr 11: 'should' instead of 'shall'), the principles create a whole regime that should lead (notably transnational) corporations to integrate human rights compliance mechanisms in their business processes (in particular through human rights due diligence, including a human rights impact assessment). See in this context also the efforts to adopt a legally binding instrument to regulate, in international human rights law, the activities of transnational corporations and other business enterprises, 3rd revised draft, 17 August 2021, www.ohchr.org/Documents/HRBodies/HRCouncil/WGTransCorp/Session6/LBI3rdDRAFT.pdf, which does, however, not give rise to any individual duties on the part of the transnational corporations.

[91] See, for instance, the Draft Statute of the World Court of Human Rights, compiled by Manfred Nowak and Julia Kozma, which would also have jurisdiction with respect to human rights violations of non-state actors (see Art 7(4) of the Draft Statute); J Kozma, M Nowak, and M Scheinin, *A World Court of Human Rights: Consolidatet statute and commentary* (Wien, NWV Verlag, 2010). See further the 2019 Hague Rules on Business and Human Rights Arbitration; www.cilc.nl/project/the-hague-rules-on-business-and-human-rights-arbitration/.

[92] See, eg, *Hirsi Jamaa and Others v Italy* No 27765/09 (ECtHR 2012).

[93] See, for instance, as regards the practice of *devoluciones en caliente* or 'hot returns' by the Spanish border police at the Moroccan-Spanish border fence surrounding the city of Melilla, *N.D. and N.T. v Spain* No 8675/15 and 8697 (ECtHR 2020). See further *Ilias and Ahmed v Hungary* No 4727/15 (ECtHR 2019) and Case C-924/19 PPU and C-925/19 PPU *FMS and Others v Országos Idegenrendészeti Főigazgatóság Dél-alföldi Regionális Igazgatóság und Országos Idegenrendészeti Főigazgatóság* [2020] on the Röszke transit zone situated on the land border between Hungary and Serbia.

territories of other states,[94] more and more often amounting to outright situations of occupation.[95] In sum, we witness an increasing number and variety of zones that cannot be linked, for the purposes of human rights protection, to the state under whose sovereignty they fall. While there is no compelling need for human rights lawyers to go down the road of Foucault's *biopolitics*[96] or, more recently, Mbembe's *necropolitics*,[97] the increasing pressures arising from the proliferation of extraterritoriality have implications for the architecture of the human rights system as we know it. As already shown, one of the main areas in which those developments will take place is the migration/asylum field which will take centre stage again in the coming decade.

C. Institutional Level of Human Rights Protection

Finally, three brief remarks concerning the institutional side of human rights protection are in order, one in a horizontal and two in a vertical perspective.

(7) Finding and maintaining the right balance in the separation and interaction of the legislative, executive, and judicial powers is a never-ending mission. The relative gain in power of courts, notably constitutional courts, with respect to the protection of human rights has become and remains a characteristic feature of the separation of powers doctrine in this field. Partly, parliaments have even become used to abstain from exercising their powers – and discharging their responsibilities – in view of controversial social and ethical issues and thus to leave the decision to the judiciary: abortion, same-sex marriage, medically assisted reproduction, assisted suicide, etc. However, courts willing to receive the pass can face major difficulties in terms of (democratic) legitimacy; the challenge of the 'counter-majoritarian difficulty'[98] and its elitist connotations exists even if it is not clear, or articulated, what the democratic majority wants. These difficulties are even exacerbated to the extent courts are ready to enter the business of protecting economic and social rights by substituting themselves for the political discretion of the legislator.[99]

[94] See the decision of the German Federal Administrative Court BVerwG 6 C7.19 (25 November 2020) on the question whether German fundamental rights apply to US drone strikes in Yemen due to the fact that the US used the infrastructure of the Ramstein Air Base in Germany for that purpose.

[95] Even if only looking at Europe, several cases come to mind: Abkhazia, Crimea, Nagorno-Karabakh, Northern Cyprus, South Ossetia, Transnistria.

[96] M Foucault, *The Birth of Biopolitics: Lectures at the Collège de France, 1978–1979* (London, Palgrave Macmillan, 2008); see also G Agamben, *Homo Sacer: Sovereign Power and Bare Life* (Stanford, Stanford University Press, 1995).

[97] A Mbembe, *Necropolitics. Theory in Forms* (Durham, Duke University Press, 2019).

[98] A Bickel, *The Least Dangerous Branch* (New Haven, Yale University Press, 1986) 16.

[99] As to this aspect see in general C Binder, J Hofbauer, F Piovesan and A Úbeda de Torres (eds), *Research Handbook on International Law and Social Rights* (Cheltenham, Edward Elgar Publishing, 2020) and in particular AT Müller, 'The role of domestic actors in the implementation and enforcement of social rights' 280, 284, with further references.

Another noteworthy feature in the horizontal relationship of powers is the proliferation of, and increasing reliance on, *soft law* instruments emerging from the machinery of international organisations,[100] which is also due to the increasing difficulty or reluctance for states to agree on new formal instruments of human rights protection. While this can offer welcome opportunities to specify, adapt and progressively develop human rights guarantees, the lack of public debate in the domestic fora and of formal parliamentary approval may add to the (perceived or real) lack of democratic legitimacy of judicial decision-making, notably at the international level.[101]

(8) This takes us to the vertical perspective, and first to the interaction between the national and the international levels. Historically, we can observe with respect to the performance of international human rights law a certain asymmetry between relatively well-established substantive standards, on the one hand, and the structural weakness of the institutional system of human rights protection on the other. This state of affairs will not significantly change within the coming decade. In the European context, one can refer to the ECtHR as a noteworthy exception in this regard, but even the Strasbourg Court is not free from, and immune to, pressures and hostilities from outside.[102] The huge case-load prompted, and legitimised, state parties to devise (partly problematic) strategies for resource and docket management,[103] that have massively reduced the Court's accessibility, ie its ability to offer individuals a fair chance to have their complaint against the domestic authorities heard in an international forum.[104] At the same time, on the whole,

[100] In the international human rights context, see the widespread practice of the adoption of General Comments by human rights bodies, seeking to state in authoritative manner how the treaty provisions in question should be interpreted. In a similar vein, it has become common to adopt Guidelines, Codes of Conduct and the like. While they often emerge from a structured dialogue with relevant stakeholders, they remain *soft law* instruments. The International Court of Justice (ICJ) has meanwhile expressly acknowledged the 'in-between status' of the interpretation of binding human rights instruments by treaty bodies with a formalised mandate, but no competence to engage in law-making in the strict sense; ICJ, *Ahmadou Sadio Diallo (Republic of Guinea v Democratic Republic of the Congo)* (Merits) [2010] ICJ Rep 639, para 66.

[101] See further A Bodgandy and I Venzke (eds), *International Judicial Lawmaking* (Heidelberg, Springer, 2012); idem, *In Whose Name? A Public Law Theory of International Adjudication* (Oxford, Oxford University Press, 2014).

[102] In several Member States of the Council of Europe (eg Russia, Turkey, but also Switzerland and the UK, and Poland more recently) there have been political initiatives to limit the reach and impact of the ECHR (especially as interpreted by the ECtHR) on the domestic legal system. The claim whether there are tendencies of retrogression in the ECtHR case-law in view of such pressures is subject to academic debate; see the recent controversy of LR Helfer and E Voeten, 'Walking Back Human Rights in Europe?' (2020) 31 *European Journal of International Law* 797, 827; A Stone Sweet, W Sandholtz and M Andenas, 'Dissenting Opinions and Rights Protection in the European Court: A Reply to Laurence Helfer and Erik Voeten' (2021) 32 *European Journal of International Law* 897, 905; LR Helfer and E Voeten, 'Walking Back Dissents on the European Court of Human Rights: A Rejoinder to Alec Stone Sweet, Wayne Sandholtz and Mads Andenas' (2021) 32 *European Journal of International Law* 907, 913; A Stone Sweet, W Sandholtz and M Andenas, 'Walking Back Dissents: A Reply to Helfer and Voeten', www.ejiltalk.org/walking-back-dissents-a-reply-to-helfer-and-voeten/.

[103] This was done in the context of the so-called 'Interlaken process'; see www.rm.coe.int/processus-interlaken-eng/1680a059c7.

[104] Relevant measures include the reduction of the time period for filing a complaint from six to four months, but in particular the amendment of the inadmissibility criteria to the effect that an application

the ECtHR has managed to maintain its integrity and effectiveness and remains to stand as a powerful example for the feasibility and benefits of international human rights adjudication. In a somewhat ambiguous development, the Strasbourg Court has become even popular to its 'constituency' as inter-state complaints (Article 33 ECHR) seem to be on the rise in the last years, providing to the court very visible and high-profile, but also highly politicised cases where the human rights question is often only an instrumental one.[105]

(9) Finally, as regards the vertical relationship between universal and regional human rights protection, one should not realistically expect major institutional developments at the global level within the next ten years. Thus, regional human rights institutions will remain in the driver's seat. In addition to the already-mentioned ECtHR, this also brings the CJEU to the fore which seems eager to sharpen its profile as a human rights (or rather: fundamental rights[106]) court, at least in certain fields.[107] There are also promising signals from the Inter-American system.[108] It is much harder to assess how regional human rights protection in Africa and in other areas (ASEAN, the Arab world, etc) will fare, but next to many reasons of concern, there are also signs of hope, and in any event much potential waiting to be realised (eg the creation of Arab Court of Human Rights).[109]

will not be dealt with if it is clear from the beginning that the applicant has 'not suffered a significant disadvantage' (Art 35(3)(b) ECHR) and giving the authority to take this decision in the hands of a single judge (Art 27(1) ECHR). In addition, the preamble of the ECHR was amended to now expressly include the subsidiarity principle (see n 76 above), thus making clear that the ECtHR should not act as a 'fourth instance' vis-à-vis the domestic courts. See in this regard also ECtHR, *Kemmache v France* (No 3) No 17621 (ECtHR 1994) para 44; *Perlala v Greece* No 17721/04 (ECHR 2007) para 25; *G.J. v Trinidad and Tobago* (5 November 1991) Communication No CCPR/C/43/D/331/1988 para 5.2; S Joseph and M Castan, *The International Covenant on Civil and Political Rights* 3rd edn (Monash, Oxford University Press, 2013) 20; IACHR, *Santiago Marzioni v Argentina*, Case 11.673, Report No 39/96 (Inter-American Court of Human Rights 1997) para 51; IACHR, *Wilma Rosa Posadas v Argentina*, Petition 0015/00, Report No 122/01 para 10.

[105] Of the 30 inter-state complaints in the history of the ECtHR, more than half have been filed since 2007. 10 of them even date from the last three years; see *Ukraine v Russian Federation* (VII) No 38334/18 (ECtHR 2018), *Georgia v Russian Federation* (IV) No 39611/18 (ECtHR 2018), *Ukraine v Russian Federation* ((VIII) No 55855/18 (ECHR 2018), *Latvia v Denmark* No 9717/20 (ECtHR 2020), *Liechtenstein v the Czech Republic* No 35738/20 (ECtHR 2020), *Armenia v Azerbaijan* No 42521/20 (ECtHR 2020), *Armenia v Turkey* No 43517/20 (ECtHR 2020), *Armenia v Turkey* No 43517/20 (ECtHR 2020), *Azerbaijan v Armenia* No 47319/20 (ECtHR 2020), *Ukraine v Russian Federation* (IX) No 10691/21 (ECtHR 2021), *Russia v Ukraine* No 36958/21 (ECtHR 2021). See further I Risini, *The Inter-State Application under the European Convention on Human Rights. Between Enforcement of Human Rights and International Disputes* (Boston, Brill, 2018).

[106] It is telling that, while the ECHR refers – following the common usage – to 'human rights', the EU deliberately chose the term 'fundamental rights' for its FRC, thus arguably emphasising the constitutional aspirations of the Union law.

[107] See, for instance, with respect to data protection and privacy in the digital age n 88 above; see also Case C-311/18 *Data Protection Commissioner v Facebook Ireland Limited and Maximilian Schrems* [2020]; Case C-18/18 *Eva Glawischnig-Piesczek v Facebook Ireland Limited* [2020].

[108] See notably the engagement of the San José Court with respect to the rights of indigenous peoples and the rights of nature; see n 83 above.

[109] Statute of the Arab Court of Human Rights (adopted 7 September 2014), Council of the League of Arab States Res 7790. This gave rise to a lot of criticism, however; see, eg, K Magliveras and G Naldi 'The Arab Court of Human Rights: A Study in Impotence' (2016) 2 *Quebec Journal of International*

In various areas of international law-making, multilateral cooperation seems to work better now at the regional than the universal level (eg trade agreements). In this regard, one should not underestimate the positive effects that may spill over from other sectors (such as investment law).[110]

IV. Outlook

In the previous analysis, a sufficient amount of overlapping, but also counteracting and even contradicting dynamics has been identified to make the narrative of crisis appear as a highly appealing one. Yet, as crisis discourses can produce or at least reinforce perceptions of impotence and paralysis, the preferential option of the present contribution is, as stated in the beginning, the narrative of ambition.

This is not so much a call for human rights activism, but a plea, an exhortation of sorts, for academic ambition in the sense of a proactive, engaged reflection on human rights.[111] In this vision, this does also, but not primarily mean to devise ever 'new' human rights[112] or novel institutional arrangements,[113] but to explore even more thoroughly and with stronger commitment the premises and implications of the political, economic, social, demographic, ecological parameters within which the human rights project operates and evolves. This analysis and the conclusions to be drawn from it are markedly different from those of the 1990ies, but nothing forces the conclusion that it needs another generation for the human rights project to thrive.

Law 147, 172; for a contrasting account see A Almutawa, 'The Arab Court of Human Rights and the Enforcement of the Arab Charter on Human Rights' (2021) 3 *Human Rights Law Review* 506, 532.

[110] One example is the project of the 2019 Hague Rules on Business and Human Rights Arbitration (*supra* fn 91) that emerged from an investment law background.

[111] In the meaning of Aristotle's *Protrepticus*, but encouraging, in the present case, not so much to study philosophy, but human rights; see W Rabinowitz, *Aristotle's Protrepticus and the sources of its Reconstruction* (Berkeley, University of California Press, 1957).

[112] See n 53 above. This arguably also includes modesty with respect to efforts to create new legal instruments for particular groups of persons; see in this regard the campaign of the Global Alliance for the Rights of Older People for a special international human rights convention for elderly people on the model of the CRC and the CRPD; www.rightsofolderpeople.org/; see also for existing *soft law* on the matter UN Principles for Older Persons, UNGA, Principles for Older Persons (16 December 1991) A/Res/46/91.

[113] See n 91 above regarding the project of a World Court of Human Rights.

5

International Criminal Law in 2030

STEFANIE BOCK

Criminal law is traditionally perceived as a national matter. It is – at least at the outset – designed to protect national interests[1] and to defend and enforce the domestic legal order.[2] And although it is meanwhile commonly accepted that national criminal laws are in various ways influenced by international and/or European law, the German Constitutional Court, for example, stressed in its Lisbon judgment that decisions on substantive and formal criminal law are particularly sensitive for the ability of a constitutional state to democratically shape itself. As the Constitutional Court rightly pointed out, the preconditions for criminal liability and the concepts of a fair trial depend 'on cultural processes of previous understanding that are historically grown and also determined by language, and on the alternatives which emerge in the process of deliberation which moves the respective public opinion'.[3] External influences from the international sphere – in particular those aiming at an expansion of criminal liability – thus entail the risk of breaking with fundamental domestic values and disturbing the inherent coherence of the national criminal justice systems. This is all the more concerning given that the infliction of criminal punishment is the severest intrusion into citizens' rights available to a state bound by the rule of law.[4] Therefore, overcriminalisation, that is, the unjustified and/or disproportional use of criminal law, is a constant but often underestimated threat to liberty and human rights. In addition, if criminal

[1] M Böse, F Meyer and A Schneider, 'Comparative Analysis', in M Böse, F Meyer and A Schneider (eds), *Conflicts of Jurisdiction in Criminal Matters in the European Union. Volume I: National Reports and Comparative Analysis* (Baden-Baden, Nomos, 2013) 411, 436–437.

[2] K Ambos, *Treatise on International Criminal Law – Volume I: Foundations and General Part* 2nd edn (Oxford, Oxford University Press, 2021) 106–107.

[3] German Constitutional Court, Judgment of 30 June 2009, *BVerfGE* [Entscheidungen des Bundesverfassungsgerichts – Official Journal of Reportable Constitutional Court Decisions] 123, 267, 359–360, English translation available at www.bundesverfassungsgericht.de/SharedDocs/Entscheidungen/EN/2009/06/es20090630_2bve000208en.html;jsessionid=51C0CE93D6CFC6E05152B23F7C625 71D.2_cid377.

[4] *cf* only S Bock and F Stark, 'Preparatory Offences', in K Ambos et al. (eds), *Core Concepts in Criminal Law and Criminal Justice*. Vol I (Cambridge, Cambridge University Press, 2020) 54, 57.

law and criminal punishment is to have any positive effect[5] (like condemnation of certain behaviour, appeal to the citizen to respect the legal order or acknowledgement of the victim's suffering),[6] this presupposes that criminal law is applied and enforced in an efficient, meaningful and predictable way. In international criminal law, we have both: a risk of overcriminalisation and a risk of non-enforcement. To illustrate this, I will try to sketch out the recent and (possible) future developments in three areas: the exterritorial application of criminal law, European criminal law and the international criminal justice system stricto sensu.

I. Criminal Jurisdiction of National States

Broadly speaking, jurisdiction refers to the regulatory power of a state,[7] its right and power to administer justice and to carry out the rule of law.[8] According to the commonly used approach of the American Law Institute, three categories of jurisdiction may be distinguished, which, however, are often intertwined:[9]

(1) jurisdiction to prescribe, that is, the power of a state to make its national law applicable to the activities, relations, or status of persons, or the interests of persons in things (in particular by criminal legislation);
(2) jurisdiction to adjudicate, that is, the power of a state to subject persons or things to the process of its national courts; and
(3) jurisdiction to enforce, that is, the power of a state to induce or compel compliance or to punish noncompliance with its laws or regulations.[10]

[5] For a critical assessment of the (alleged) effectiveness of criminal law and its problematic side-effects see R Kölbel, 'Die dunkle Seite des Strafrechts. Eine kriminologische Erwiderung auf die Pönalisierungsbereitschaft in der strafrechtswissenschaftlichen Kriminalpolitik' (2019) 31 *Neue Kriminalpolitik* 249.

[6] For a recent overview on theories of punishment see T Hörnle, *A Framework Theory of Punishment*, MPI-CSL Working Paper 2021/01.

[7] K Ambos, *Treatise on International Criminal Law – Volume III: International Criminal Procedure* (Oxford, Oxford University Press, 2016) 207; A Mills, 'Rethinking Jurisdiction in International Law' (2014) 84 *British Yearbook of International Law* 187, 194.

[8] On the complexity and ambiguity of the term 'jurisdiction' D Helenius, 'The If, How, and When of Criminal Jurisdiction – What is Criminal Jurisdiction Anyway?' (2015) 3 *Bergen Journal of Criminal Law and Criminal Justice* 22.

[9] See, eg, H Satzger, *International and European Criminal Law* 2nd edn (München, Oxford, Baden-Baden, C. H. Beck, Hart Publishing, Nomos, 2018) § 3 mn 3 noting that 'whenever a state has criminal jurisdiction, the usual consequence is that the applicability only extends to own provisions of substantive criminal law'. The German law, for example, is based on the principle that German Courts apply only German Law. At the same time, whenever German substantive law is applicable, German Courts have international competence, see K Ambos, *Internationales Strafrecht. Strafanwendungsrecht – Völkerstrafrecht – Europäisches Strafrecht – Rechtshilfe* 5th edn (München, C. H. Beck, 2018) § 1 mn 3–5; P Mankowski and S Bock, 'Die internationale Zuständigkeit der deutschen Strafgerichte als eigene Kategorie des Internationalen Strafverfahrensrechts' (2008) 63 *Juristenzeitung* 555.

[10] American Law Institute, *Restatement of the Law, Third, The Foreign Relations Law of the United States, i: §§ 1 to 488* (Saint Paul, American Law Institute Publications, 1987) § 401.

In criminal matters, jurisdiction is closely linked with the power to punish,[11] which includes the right to define what conduct constitutes a criminal wrong and the right to sanction persons for noncompliance with criminal norms.[12] The establishment of criminal jurisdiction and the right to punish associated therewith must be legitimised, on the one hand, vis-à-vis the affected individuals because threats of punishment severely restrict their freedom of action. On the other hand, all other states are requested to tolerate that the prosecuting state exercises state power by penalising and punishing a certain act, which requires justification if a case is connected to more than one state.[13]

This international or inter-state dimension of criminal jurisdiction became apparent already in the famous *Lotus* ruling of the Permanent Court of International Justice in 1927.[14] Here, the Court held that international law does not prohibit states 'to extend the application of their laws and the jurisdiction of their courts to persons, property and acts outside their territory'. Rather, states were said to enjoy broad discretion in defining their jurisdiction, which 'is only limited in certain cases by prohibitive rules; as regards other cases, every State remains free to adopt principles which it regards as best and most suitable'. At the same time, however, the Court emphasised that a state 'should not overstep the limits which international law places upon its jurisdiction'.[15] The *Lotus* ruling seems 'somewhat ambiguous',[16] since the Court on the one hand leaves states a wide discretion to determine their jurisdiction, but on the other hand argues that the application of national laws to acts which have taken place abroad requires 'a permissive rule derived from international custom or from a convention'.[17] Meanwhile, the International Court of Justice has clarified that the exercise of jurisdiction generally presupposes a 'real link' or a 'genuine connection' between the case at hand

[11] Helenius (n 8) 24.

[12] *cf* S Bock, 'The Internationalisation of Criminal Law', in H-D Horn and S Bock (eds), *On the Correlation between National and International Law* (Marburg, Philipps-Universität Marburg – Publikationsserver, 2020) 29.

[13] Helenius (n 8) 24; see also M Böse, 'Vorbemerkungen zu § 3 StGB', in U Kindhäuser, U Neumann and H-U Paeffgen (eds), *Nomos Kommentar zum Strafgesetzbuch* 5th edn (Baden-Baden, Nomos, 2017) mn 12 ff, mn 40 ff.

[14] PCIJ, Judgment of 7 September 1927 – *France v Turkey* - *Case of the S S 'Lotus', PCIJ Series A* 10, 1. The facts of the underlying case were the following. In August 1926, the French steamship *Lotus* collided with the Turkish steamship *Boz-Kourt* on the high seas. The *Boz-Kourt* was cut in two and sank; eight Turkish nationals died. A few days later, the Turkish authorities arrested the first officer of the *Lotus*, D, a French citizen, put him on trial and sentenced him to 80 days' imprisonment for involuntary manslaughter. France argued that French courts have exclusive jurisdiction over French nationals and that Turkey had violated international law by prosecuting D.

[15] PCIJ, Judgment of 7 September 1927 – *France v Turkey* – *Case of the S S 'Lotus', PCIJ Series A* 10, 1 19. In the *Lotus* case, the Court found that limits imposed on states by international law were respected as 'the offence produced its effects on the Turkish vessel and consequently in a place assimilated to Turkish territory' and the prosecution of D was 'justified from the point of view of the so-called territorial principle', ibid 23.

[16] Ambos (n 7) 207; also, Bock (n 12) 31.

[17] PCIJ, Judgment of 7 September 1927 – *France v Turkey* – *Case of the S S 'Lotus', PCIJ Series A* 10, 1, 19.

and the state claiming jurisdiction.[18] Otherwise, the establishment or exercise of exterritorial criminal jurisdiction violates the principle of non-interference.[19] Classical and well-established factors, which – as a rule – legitimise the exercise of jurisdiction even if this affects the interests of other states, are the place of the offence, the nationality of the offender and the victim as well as the endangerment of essential state interests.[20] These links are also the basis for justifying the establishment of criminal jurisdiction vis-à-vis the defendant. They indicate that the adjudicating state has a legitimate interest in restricting the defendant's freedom of action and in enforcing its national norms by punishing him or her for non-compliance. Moreover, they contribute to the predictability of criminal law. In order to be able to foresee if and which criminal law consequences a certain conduct has, the individual must be able to estimate which national jurisdiction he or she may face.

Despite this need for dual legitimation, states tended in the last years to broaden the territorial scope of their national laws. This is, first, arguably a consequence of the increased use of criminal law as tool to promote and enforce national values. To illustrate this by example: Article 37 of the Convention of the Council of Europe on Preventing and Combating Violence Against Women and Domestic Violence,[21] the so-called Istanbul Convention, obliges the state parties to ensure that the intentional conduct of forcing an adult or a child to enter into a marriage is criminalised. According to Article 44(2) Istanbul Convention, states shall 'endeavour' to criminalise forced marriages committed abroad if the offence is directed against one of their nationals or a person who has her or his habitual residence in their territory. This extension of jurisdiction shall not be made dependent on whether the act is also criminalised by the territorial state (Article 44(3) Istanbul Convention). Germany has fully implemented these provisions and now allows[22] for the prosecution of forced marriages[23] even if committed abroad and regardless of the law in force at the location of the offence, provided (inter alia) that the act is directed against a person who has her or his domicile or usual residence

[18] See ICJ, Judgment of 6 June 1955 – *Liechtenstein v Guatemala – Nottebohm Case, ICJ-Reports* 1955, 4, 25 f (concerning the right to grant diplomatic protection); *cf* also ICJ, Judgment of 5 February 1970 – *Belgium v Spain – Case Concerning Barcelona Traction, Light and Power Company, Limited, ICJ-Reports* 1970, 3, 42.

[19] Ambos (n 7) 206–210; Bock (n 12) 31.

[20] Mills (n 7) 196 ff; Satzger (n 9) § 4 mn 3; Ambos (n 7) 209; Bock (n 12) 31.

[21] CETS No. 210. The Istanbul Convention was adopted on 11 May 2011 and entered into force on 1 August 2014.

[22] The German Procedural Code (*Strafprozessordnung*) – although essentially based on the principle of mandatory prosecution – grants the prosecution broad discretion to discontinue the prosecution of crimes committed abroad, *cf* s 153c of the German Procedural Code.

[23] Forced marriage is a punishable offence in terms of s 237 of the German Criminal Code (*Strafgesetzbuch* – StGB), which reads as follows: 'Whosoever unlawfully with force or threat of serious harm causes a person to enter into a marriage shall be liable to imprisonment from six months to five years. The act shall be unlawful if the use of force or the threat of harm is deemed inappropriate for the purpose of achieving the desired outcome.' Official translation of the StGB available at www.gesetze-im-internet.de/englisch_stgb/.

in Germany.[24] Imagine now that M – an Afghan national who has been living in Germany for ten years – takes her 16-year-old daughter D (who is also an Afghan national with permanent residence in Germany) for a holiday trip to Afghanistan. There she introduces D to the 20-year-old P and demands from D to marry P right on the spot. Otherwise, she would disown D and return to Germany without her. D is scared and agrees to marry P.[25] Supposing that M's behaviour is not criminal under Afghan national law, it seems questionable if Germany has the right to bring in other – foreign – norms as a kind of external evaluation standard. The German legislator deemed it necessary to expand the German law to such cases in order to avoid that the criminal prohibition of forced marriages is undermined by such 'holiday marriages'.[26] This approach seems understandable as it aims at the transnational protection of women residing in Germany. Nevertheless, it is questionable if Germany's claim of jurisdiction can be justified vis-à-vis Afghanistan (international/state level) and M (individual level). Germany is linked to the case only by the residence of the victim D. Its jurisdiction can be based merely on the so-called domicile principle.[27] This, however, is a relatively new concept, which can be found in some international instruments,[28] but arguably does not yet enjoy full recognition. In addition, the exterritorial application of the German criminal prohibition of forced marriages is not limited by a double criminality requirement; that is, it is not made dependent on that the territorial state also qualifies the respective conduct as a criminal wrong. Germany thus ignores and, in a way, undermines Afghanistan's sovereign decision not to criminalise forced marriages and forces Afghanistan to tolerate an exercise of foreign state power to a (predominantly) domestic incident.[29] This interference cannot be justified by reference to the Istanbul Convention. This is a mere regional instrument of the Council of

[24] The relevant § 5 No. 6 lit. c) StGB on 'Offences committed abroad with specific domestic connection' provides: 'Regardless of which law is applicable at the place where the offence was committed, German criminal law applies to the following offences committed abroad: [...] offences against personal liberty [...] in the cases under section 237 if the offender is a German national at the time of the offence or if the offence is directed against a person whose domicile or habitual residence is in Germany at the time of the offence.' For a comparative overview on the increased use of the domicile principle as an alternative to the classical principle of active or passive personality see N Beyer, *Personelle Strafgewalt – Ein Plädoyer für das Domizilprinzip im Lichte grenzüberschreitender Migration* (Tübingen, Mohr Siebeck, 2020) 191 et seq.

[25] Example taken from Bock (n 12) 32.

[26] Bundestag, *Beschlussempfehlung und Bericht des Ausschusses für Recht und Verbraucherschutz (6. Ausschuss) a) zu dem Gesetzentwurf der Fraktionen der CDU/CSU und SPD – Drucksache 18/2601 – Entwurf eines ... Gesetzes zur Änderung des Strafgesetzbuches – Umsetzung europäischer Vorgaben zum Sexualstrafrecht b) zu dem Gesetzentwurf der Bundesregierung – Drucksache 18/2954 – Entwurf eines ... Gesetzes zur Änderung des Strafgesetzbuches – Umsetzung europäischer Vorgaben zum Sexualstrafrecht* 12.11.2014, BT-Drs. 18/3202, 26.

[27] The domicile principle is the modern variant or – to be more precise – expansion of the classical principle of personality, which allows states to prosecute crimes committed abroad by or against their nationals. The domicile principle replaces the traditional nationality requirement by introducing residence as a sufficient link; Ambos (n 7) 219; Bock (n 12) 32.

[28] Ambos (n 7) 219.

[29] Bock (n 12) 33.

Europe, which is not binding on Afghanistan (and has so far been ratified only by 34 states).[30] Moreover, the Convention does not strictly oblige, but merely encourages the state parties to prosecute forced marriages on the basis of the passive domicile principle.[31]

The absence of the double criminality requirement makes it also hard to justify the German claim of punishment vis-à-vis M. Her behaviour is in line with the laws of the territorial state (which at the same time is the state of her nationality). To demand from her to respect also the laws of her daughter's state of residence even when both are in another country considerably restricts her freedom of action and may (in particular in cases in which the defendant is not aware of the victim's home of residence) conflict with the principle of culpability and the right to a fair trial if and because the defendant might (unexpectedly for him or her) be subjected to a foreign jurisdiction which is alien to him or her.[32]

Second, the territorial extension of national criminal laws is probably a reaction to increasing globalisation. The new freedoms of movement may be used for criminal purposes; actions in one state might impair the interests of another state or indirectly affect its national legal order. The prime example is the debate on criminal law regulation of cybercrime. Offences committed on the internet and their effects can hardly be located in a physical sense, but are nevertheless in a way ubiquitous. This is an enormous challenge for the application of the traditional jurisdictional principles. Should, for example, the fact that a hate post (however defined) on Facebook can be read anywhere throughout the world, be a sufficient link to all states and empower them to assess the post on the basis of their respective national criminal laws?[33] Another important question is the regulation of transnational business activities and the protection of human rights in this

[30] Other treaties recognise a right to marry (or not to marry) a person of one's choice (see, eg, Art 23 of the International Covenant on Civil and Political Rights), but there is no international consensus that an infringement of this right constitutes a criminal wrong, M Böse, '§ 5 StGB', in U Kindhäuser, U Neumann and H-U Paeffgen (eds), *Nomos Kommentar zum Strafgesetzbuch* 5th edn (Baden-Baden, Nomos, 2017) mn 6.

[31] See the differences between Art 44(1) of the Istanbul Convention ('Parties *shall take* the necessary measures' to establish jurisdiction on the basis of the territorial principle etc) and para 2 ('Parties *shall endeavour to take* the necessary measures' to establish jurisdiction on the basis of the passive personality/domicile principle) emphasis added.

[32] With a view to the absolute passive domicile principle, Ambos (n 7) 222; also Satzger (n 9) § 4 mn 26.

[33] For an overview on the discussion, see Satzger (n 9) § 4 mn 6 ff; in more detail, L Wörner, 'Einseitiges Strafanwendungsrecht und entgrenztes Internet?' (2012) 7 *Zeitschrift für Internationale Strafrechtsdogmatik* 458; J Hörnle, *Internet Jurisdiction – Law and Practice* (Oxford, Oxford University Press, 2021). In a decision from 2000, the German Federal Court of Justice favoured a broad application of German Criminal Law on (at least) certain communicative acts on the internet and upheld the conviction of an Australian citizen for incitement of masses (s 130 StGB) because he was found to have denied crimes committed under the rule of National Socialism on an Australian website hosted on an Australian server, German Federal Court of Justice, Decision of 12 December 2000, BGHSt [Entscheidungen des Bundesgerichtshofes in Strafsachen – Official Journal of Reportable Federal Supreme Court Decisions] 46, 212; more reluctant German Federal Court of Justice, Decision of 3 May 2016 (2017) 37 *Neue Zeitschrift für Strafrecht* 146.

context. With respect to claims brought by victims, Article 9 of the recent draft of the UN's Business and Human Rights Treaty[34] foresees concurrent jurisdiction of the courts of the State where:

(a) the human rights abuse occurred and/or produced effects; or
(b) an act or omission contributing to the human rights abuse occurred;
(c) the legal or natural persons alleged to have committed an act or omission causing or contributing to such human rights abuse in the context of business activities, including those of a transnational character, are domiciled; or
(d) the victim is a national of or is domiciled.

This very broad provision which establishes various links for jurisdiction will surely influence the debate on the exterritorial use of criminal law in the fight against transnational human rights violations.

Already these few examples suggest that in the next years to come, states will continue to broaden the territorial scope of their criminal laws. This will increase the number of conflicts of jurisdiction, which may result in sovereignty conflicts on the international and undue restrictions of liberty rights on the individual level. In particular, it remains to be seen if and how states – alone or acting in international cooperation – will be able to avoid overcriminalisation, unjust dual punishments, prosecutorial forum shopping, and legal insecurities resulting from complex and overlapping jurisdictional regimes.

II. European Criminal Law

In the European context, the national criminal justice systems of EU Member States are in many ways influenced by Union law.[35] In addition to more indirect techniques of 'Europeanisation' like the 'neutralisation' of criminal norms that are incompatible with Union law[36] or the interpretation in conformity with Union law,[37]

[34] Legally Binding Instrument to Regulate in International Human Rights Law, the Activities of Transnational Corporations and Other Business Enterprises, third revised draft from 17 August 2021, prepared by the Intergovernmental Working Group on Transnational Corporations and Other Business Enterprises with Respect to Human Rights of the United Nations Human Rights Council.

[35] For an overview, see K Ambos and S Bock, 'Brexit and the European Criminal Justice System – An Introduction' (2017) 28 *Criminal Law Forum* 191, 193 ff with further references.

[36] *cf* Satzger (n 9) § 7 mn 78 ff; Ambos and Bock (n 35) 193–194. In its famous *Taricco* case, the Court of Justice of the European Union (CJEU) held that national rules on prescription which have the effect that in a considerable number of cases, the commission of serious fraud will escape criminal punishment, are incompatible with the duty of the Member States to counter EU-fraud with deterrent and effective measures as required by Art 325 TFEU and must therefore be disapplied. According to the CJEU, this is because the offences will usually be time-barred before the criminal penalty laid down by law can be imposed by a final judicial decision CJEU, Judgment of 8 September 2015, C-105/14 – *Criminal Proceedings against Ivo Taricco and Others*.

[37] Member States are required to interpret their (criminal) law in such a way that it conforms to Union law, as otherwise it would be displaced by Union law in case of collision, ECJ, Judgment of 10 April 1984, Case 14/83 – *Sabine von Colson and Elisabeth Kamann v Land Nordrhein-Westfalen*; Ambos and Bock (n 35) 194.

the Lisbon Treaty grants the Union broad competencies to approximate the substantive and procedural laws of the Member States. According to Article 83(1) TFEU, the European Parliament and the Council,

> by means of directives adopted in accordance with the ordinary legislative procedure, [can] establish minimum rules[38] concerning the definition of criminal offences and sanctions in the areas of particularly serious crime with a cross-border dimension resulting from the nature or impact of such offences or from a special need to combat them on a common basis.

In addition, the ancillary competence enshrined in Article 83(2) TFEU empowers the Union to 'establish minimum rules with regard to the definition of criminal offences and sanctions' to implement Union policies if this is 'essential to ensure the effective implementation' of the policy in question. In principle, approximation of criminal laws thus may follow or accompany any extra-penal harmonisation measure. Over the last years, the EU made broad use of these competencies and introduced harmonisation measures inter alia in the areas of sexual exploitation of children and child pornography,[39] market abuse,[40] cybercrime[41] and fraud to the Union's financial interests.[42]

These directives, however, are not based upon an overall, coherent criminal policy[43] that specifies what conduct deserves punishment and which interests or goods are worthy of criminal protection.[44] The Council's 'conclusion on model provisions, guiding the Council's criminal law deliberations'[45] are a step in the right direction and contain some useful guidelines on the use and boundaries of criminal law and the structure of criminal norms. However, they remain rather vague and were rejected by the Commission as too restrictive and non-binding.[46]

[38] Art 83 TFEU does not allow for a fully-fledged unification of laws, but only for the adoption of minimum requirements, that is, Union-wide minimum standards regarding the punishability of certain forms of conduct and the corresponding punishments – a kind of minimum penalty for 'minimum conduct' valid across the Union, Ambos and Bock (n 35) 196; Satzger (n 9) § 7 mn 42.

[39] Directive 2011/93/EU of the European Parliament and of the Council of 13 December 2011 on combating the sexual abuse and sexual exploitation of children and child pornography, and replacing Council Framework Decision 2004/68/JHA [2000] OJ L334/1.

[40] Directive 2014/57/EU of the European Parliament and of the Council of 16 April 2014 on criminal sanctions for market abuse (market abuse directive) [2014] OJ L173/179.

[41] Directive 2013/40/EU of the European Parliament and of the Council of 12 August 2013 on attacks against information systems and replacing Council Framework Decision 2005/222/JHA [2013] EU L218/8.

[42] Directive 2017/1371/EU of the European Parliament and of the Council of 5 July 2017 on the fight against fraud to the Union's financial interests by means of criminal law [2018] OJ L198/29 (PIF-Directive).

[43] For a comprehensive proposal for a European criminal policy, see European Criminal Policy Initiative, 'The Manifesto on European Criminal Policy 2011' (2011) 1 *European Criminal Law Review* 86.

[44] In more detail, C Prittwitz, 'Lissabon als Chance zur kriminalpolitischen Neubesinnung. Das Manifest zur Europäischen Kriminalpolitik', in K Ambos (ed), *Europäisches Strafrecht post-Lissabon* (Göttingen, Universitätsverlag Göttingen, 2011) 29; European Criminal Policy Initiative (n 43) 92–103.

[45] Doc. 16542/09 of 27 November 2009.

[46] *cf* J Vogel, 'Die Strafgesetzgebungskompetenzen der Europäischen Union nach Art. 83, 86 und 325 AEUV', in K Ambos (ed), *Europäisches Strafrecht post-Lissabon* (Göttingen, Universitätsverlag Göttingen, 2011) 41, 53–54.

In its own paper on criminal policy, the Commission basically refers to the limits on the Union's criminal law competencies as set out in primary law (in particular: the principles of conferral, subsidiarity and proportionality, respect for fundamental rights as enshrined in the EU Charter of Fundamental Rights),[47] but does not offer additional thoughts on the theoretical foundation and limitation of criminal norms. Rather, the Union tends to use criminal law as an 'ordinary' regulatory tool to combat socially unwanted behaviour[48] and to enhance the mutual trust between Member States and the national judiciaries.[49] This ignores that – due to its invasive character and its significant impact on fundamental rights – criminal law is and must be the last resort of social control; its use requires careful justification. Article 6 of Directive 2011/93/EU, for example, requires the Member States to penalise the solicitation of children for sexual purposes, that is, the proposal by means of information and communication technology, by an adult to meet a child who has not reached the age of sexual consent, for the purpose of committing an offence concerning sexual abuse or sexual exploitation.[50] This provision aims at the criminalisation of a preparatory act that is committed long before the actual commission of a sexual crime; it refers to a neutral conduct which is quite remote from the threatened harm (proposal to meet), but is performed with a guilty mind (intention to commit a sexual crime). Such a 'pre-dating' of criminal liability is not unproblematic as it might overstretch the legitimate boundaries of criminal law and lead to an undue criminalisation of purely 'internal' matters.[51] In addition, the legitimacy and acceptability of criminal law also depends on its coherence. If, for example, active corruption is defined more broadly in the PIF-Directive than in the EU-Anti-Corruption-Convention,[52] this endangers the understandability of and trust in the (European) criminal justice system.[53]

[47] European Commission, *Towards an EU Criminal Policy: Ensuring the Effective Implementation of EU Policies Through Criminal Law*, 20 September 2011, COM(2011) 573 final, 6 ff.

[48] See European Commission, *EU Criminal Policy*, 2: criminal law as tool to 'strengthening the enforcement of EU policies'.

[49] ibid 3.

[50] A similar provision can be found in 18 USC § 2422. Other states have also criminalised forms of cyber grooming but have adopted a more restrictive approach. Art 167 of the Código Penal of Costa Rica, for example, requires that the defendant establishes an erotic or sexual communication with the Child. According to Art 131B of the New Zealand Crimes Act, a person is liable for sexual grooming if, having met or communicated with a person under the age of 16 years (the young person) on an earlier occasion, he or she takes one of the following actions: (i) intentionally meets the young person; (ii) travels with the intention of meeting the young person; (iii) arranges for or persuades the young person to travel with the intention of meeting him or her (provided that the person intends to commit a sexual offence with respect to the young person). Art 131B thus does not merely penalise the communicative act as such, but requires (at least) that the person has made some efforts to actually meet the child.

[51] For further examples, see European Criminal Policy Initiative (n 43) 94–95. In general on the legitimation of preparatory offences and pre-dated criminal liability, Bock and Stark (n 4) 65–84. On the worldwide tendency to pre-date criminal liability in the fight against terrorism see the country reports in K Roach (ed), *Comparative Counter-Terrorism Law* (Cambridge, Cambridge University Press, 2015).

[52] Convention drawn up on the basis of Art K.3(2)(c) of the Treaty on European Union on the fight against corruption involving officials of the European Communities or officials of Member States of the European Union [1997] OJ C195/2.

[53] According to Art 4(2)(a) PIF-Directive, '"passive corruption" means the action of a public official who, directly or through an intermediary, requests or receives advantages of any kind, for himself or

More worrisome than the lack of a theoretical foundation of European criminal law, however, is the Union's focus on the efficiency of law enforcement. At a time when crimes are often committed across borders, states increasingly depend on mutual support in the gathering of evidence or the arrest of suspects. Therefore, the EU has created a unique system of international cooperation based on the principle of mutual recognition (Article 82(1) TFEU). This principle basically requires that judgments and judicial decisions made in one Member State have to be recognised and enforced in all other Member States even when the outcome would be different if their own national laws were applied.[54] Mutual recognition is – if fully implemented – very effective as it allows for a kind of 'free movement of judicial decisions' and an unhampered cross-border enforcement of criminal law.[55] It can be seen as a counterpart to, or a safeguard against the right to free movement, which is prone to misuse for criminal purposes.[56] Nevertheless, fast-track international cooperation as enabled by the principle of mutual recognition has the inherent risk of undermining procedural safeguards and the fairness of the proceedings.[57]

Meanwhile, the European Union has made some efforts to harmonise the rights of the defendant: the Directive on the right to interpretation and translation,[58] for example, requires Member States to ensure that suspected or accused persons who do not speak or understand the language of the criminal proceedings concerned are provided with interpretation during criminal proceedings and receive written translations of essential documents. The Directive on the right to information[59] foresees that suspects or accused receive information about certain procedural rights (including a Letter of Rights in case of arrest). Directive 2013/48/EU[60]

for a third party, or accepts a promise of such an advantage, to act or to refrain from acting in accordance with his duty or in the exercise of his functions in a way which damages or is likely to damage the Union's financial interests'. Art 2(1) of the Anti-Corruption-Convention additionally requires that the official acts 'in breach of his official duties'.

[54] ECJ, Judgment of 11 February 2003, Joined Cases C-187/01 and C-385/01 – *Criminal Proceedings against Hüseyin Gözütok (C-187/01) and Klaus Brügge (C-385/01)* para 33; Satzger (n 9) § 8 mn 26; K Ambos, *European Criminal Law* (Cambridge, Cambridge University Press, 2018) 20–21.

[55] Ambos (n 54) 21; Bock (n 12) 39.

[56] *cf* also Satzger (n 9) § 8 mn 26.

[57] See A Erbežnik, 'The Principle of Mutual Recognition as a Utilitarian Solution, and the Way Forward' (2012) 2 *European Criminal Law Review* 4; M Thunberg Schunke, 'The Manifesto on European Criminal Procedure Law; a commentary on the perspective of mutual recognition and violations of defence rights' (2015) 5 *European Criminal Law Review* 46; Satzger (n 9) § 8 mn 27; Ambos (n 54) 21–22; with a particular view to the European Arrest Warrant, D Mansell, 'The European Arrest Warrant and Defence Rights' (2012) 2 *European Criminal Law Review* 37.

[58] Directive 2010/10/EU of the European Parliament and of the Council of 20 October 2010 on the right to interpretation and translation in criminal proceedings [2010] OJ L280/1.

[59] Directive 2012/13/EU of the European Parliament and of the Council of 22 May 2012 on the right to information in criminal proceedings [2012] OJ EU L142/1.

[60] Directive 2013/48/EU of the European Parliament and of the Council of 22 October 2013 on the right of access to a lawyer in criminal proceedings and in European arrest warrant proceedings, and on the right to have a third party informed upon deprivation of liberty and to communicate with third persons and with consular authorities while deprived of liberty [2013] OJ EU L294/1.

enshrines the right of access to a lawyer, which is complemented by a right to legal aid.[61] Further directives aim at strengthening the presumption of innocence, the right to be present at the trial,[62] or the procedural position of children suspected or accused of a crime.[63] These are important measures for ensuring a fair treatment of defendants. However, the directives are fragmentary in nature, that is, they merely deal with selected aspects and are not integrated in an overall human rights approach towards transnational criminal proceedings. Moreover, some directives merely confirm certain minimum standards (which, in their essence, are already included in the European Convention of Human Rights) and are phrased so vaguely that they can easily be undermined in practice.[64] It is, thus, questionable if these directives are a sufficient compensation or countermeasure for the increase in police and prosecutorial powers.

This is, all the more, true if one was to look at the institutionalisation of European Criminal Law. Europol maintains a comprehensive information system which includes a wealth of personal data, assists the national authorities in the gathering and analysis of intelligence and provides advice on (transnational) investigation;[65] Eurojust supports and improves judicial co-operation in cross-border prosecutions as a kind of documentation and service centre[66] and the newly created European Public Prosecutor even has the power to indict and prosecute crimes against the Union's financial interests before national criminal courts.[67] For the defence, there is no comparable 'institutional back-up'. The legitimacy of future European Criminal Law will, to a great extent, depend on whether or not the EU can find a balance between the fight against transnational crime and the effective protection of defence rights.

III. International Criminal Law stricto sensu

Another highly dynamic area of internationalisation is the International Criminal Justice System created for the global prosecution of the international core

[61] Directive 2016/1919/EU of the European Parliament and of the Council of 26 October 2016 on legal aid for suspects and accused persons in criminal proceedings and for requested persons in European arrest warrant proceedings [2016] OJ EU L297/1.

[62] Directive 2016/343/EU of the European Parliament and of the Council of 9 March 2016 on the strengthening of certain aspects of the presumption of innocence and of the right to be present at the trial in criminal proceedings [2016] OJ EU L65/1.

[63] Directive 2016/800/EU of the European Parliament and of the Council of 11 May 2016 on procedural safeguards for children who are suspects or accused persons in criminal proceedings [2016] OJ L132/1.

[64] In more detail, European Criminal Policy Initiative, 'A Manifesto on European Criminal Procedure Law' (2013) 8 *Zeitschrift für Internationale Strafrechtsdogmatik* 430; also Thunberg Schunke (n 57) 46.

[65] In more detail, J Ruthig and M Böse, '§ 20. Europol', in M Böse (ed), *Europäisches Strafrecht* 2nd edn (Baden-Baden, Nomos, 2021) 1039.

[66] In more detail, MA Zöller and S Bock, '§ 21. Eurojust und EJN', in M Böse (ed), *Europäisches Strafrecht* 2nd edn (Baden-Baden, Nomos, 2021) 1073.

[67] In more detail, MA Zöller and S Bock, '§ 22. Europäische Staatsanwaltschaft', in M Böse (ed), *Europäisches Strafrecht* 2nd edn (Baden-Baden, Nomos, 2021) 1073.

crimes – genocide, crimes against humanity, war crimes and the crime of aggression. When the Statute of the International Criminal Court (ICC) was adopted in 1998 and entered into force in 2002, this new institution was met with great enthusiasm and hailed as the mark of a new era.[68] International Criminal Tribunals were believed (and expected) to bring justice to those responsible for serious violations of human rights and humanitarian law, put an end to such violations and prevent their recurrence, secure justice and dignity for victims, establish a record of past events, promote national reconciliation, re-establish the rule of law, and contribute to the restoration of peace.[69]

Given these high hopes and expectations, the ICC was kind of doomed to disappoint. In its almost 20 years of operation, the ICC has only produced seven final judgments on individual responsibility for core crimes[70] – four persons were convicted for crimes against humanity and/or war crimes (these cases are still in the reparation stage);[71] four persons were acquitted;[72] one of these acquittals led the Court to vacate an arrest warrant in a related case.[73] In three cases, the Pre-Trial Chambers declined to confirm the charges against the defendant,[74] respectively

[68] On the background of the establishment of the ICC, see CM Bassiouni, 'Chronology of Efforts to Establish an International Criminal Court' (2015) 86 *Revue Internationale de Droit Pénal* 1163, who concludes at 1179: 'In the post-confrontational era, the people of the world have high expectations for a new world order in which peace is more than the absence of war, and justice more than hollow slogans. The establishment of an international court, which can effectively and fairly prosecute international and transnational crimes, irrespective of how high or mighty the perpetrator may be, is part of these high expectations. Indeed, any system of justice must be fair, impartial, and even-handed'.

[69] *cf*, UNSC, *The Rule of Law and Transitional Justice in Conflict and Post-Conflict Societies – Report of the Secretary-General*, 13 August 2002, S/2004/616, mn 38.

[70] Another final judgment of the ICC deals with offences against the administration of justice in connection with the case *Prosecutor v Bemba Gombo*, ICC (AC), Judgment of 8 March 2018, ICC-01/05-01/13-2275 – *Prosecutor v Bemba Gombo et al – Judgment on the appeals of Mr Jean-Pierre Bemba Gombo et al against the decision of Trial Chamber VII entitled 'Judgment pursuant to Article 74 of the Statute'*.

[71] ICC (AC), Judgment of 1 December 2014, ICC-01/04-01/06-3121-Red – *Prosecutor v Lubanga – Public redacted Judgment on the appeal of Mr Thomas Lubanga Dyilo against his conviction*; ICC (TC II), Judgment of 7 March 2014, ICC-01/04-01/07-3436 – *Prosecutor v Katanga – Judgment pursuant to article 74 of the Statute*; ICC (TC VIII), Judgment of 27 September 2016, ICC-01/12-01/15-171 – *Prosecutor v Al Mahdi – Judgment and Sentence*; ICC (AC), Judgment of 30 March 2021, ICC-01/04-02/06-2666 – *Prosecutor v Ntaganda – Public redacted Version of Judgment on the appeals of Mr Bosco Ntaganda and the Prosecutor against the decision of Trial Chamber VI of 8 July 2019 entitled 'Judgment'*.

[72] ICC (AC), Judgment of 7 April 2015, ICC-01/04-02/12-271 – *Prosecutor v Ngudjolo Chui*; ICC (AC), Judgment of 8 June 2018, ICC-01/05-01/08-3636 – *Prosecutor v Bemba Gombo – Judgment on the appeal of Mr Jean-Pierre Bemba Gombo against Trial Chamber III's 'Judgment pursuant to article 74 of the Statute'*; ICC (AC), Judgment of 31 March 2021, ICC-02/11-01/15-1400 – *Prosecutor v Gbagbo and Blé Goudé – Judgment in the appeal of the Prosecutor against Trial Chamber I's decision on the no case to answer motions*.

[73] ICC (PTC II), Decision of 19 July 2021, ICC-02/11-01/12-90 – *Prosecutor v S Gbagbo – Decision on the Prosecutor's request to vacate the effect of the Warrant of Arrest issued against Ms Simone Gbagbo*.

[74] ICC (PTC I), Decision of 8 February 2010, ICC-02/05-02/09-243 – *Prosecutor v Abu Garda – Decision on the Confirmation of Charges*; ICC (PTC II), Decision of 23 January 2012, ICC-01/09-02/11-382 – *Prosecutor v Kenyatta – Decision on the Confirmation of Charges Pursuant to Article 61(7)(a) and (b) of the Rome Statute*; ICC (PTC I), Decision of 16 November 2011, ICC-01/04-01/10-465 – *Prosecutor v Mbarushimana – Decision on the Confirmation of Charges*.

the Prosecution had to withdraw charges due to insufficient evidence.[75] Another case was terminated at trial stage, because the Trial Chamber found that there was 'no case to answer' for the defence, that is, the Prosecution had not presented sufficient evidence on which a reasonable Trial Chamber could convict the accused.[76]

Naturally, the effectiveness and efficiency of a criminal justice system cannot and must not be measured (only) by a Court's output, and even less by its conviction rate.[77] Acquittals and terminations of proceedings are an integral part of a fair trial system which respects the fundamental rights of the defendants. At least some of the mentioned decisions, however, reveal general problems and deficits of the international criminal justice system.

The ICC and its procedural law are a mixture (mainly) of elements from the common and the civil law tradition. The practical application of this system sui generis poses a challenge to the actors trained in and influenced by their respective national systems and thereby carrying with them the burden of their limited national perspectives.[78] In their separate opinion on the Appeals Chamber judgment on the acquittal of Jean Pierre Bemba, Judges Van den Wyngaert and Morrison quite frankly described this 'clash of culture' and its effect on the daily work of the Court as follows:

> [i]t is important to recognise that the strong divergence in how we [the judges of the Appeals Chamber] evaluate the Conviction Decision is not just a matter of difference of opinion, but appears to be a fundamental difference in the way we look at our mandates as international judges. We seem to start from different premises, both in terms of how the law should be interpreted and applied and in terms of how we conceive of our role as judges.[79]

It gives cause for concern if leading judges indicate that even after (at the time of the decision) 15 years, the ICC has neither developed a common understanding of the basic premises of its work and the general principles it is based upon nor a common self-concept. This, on the one hand, may lead to divergent decisions,[80]

[75] ICC (OTP), Notice of 5 December 2014, ICC-01/09-02/11-983 – *Prosecutor v Kenyatta – Notice of withdrawal of the charges against Uhuru Muigai Kenyatta*; ICC (OTP), Notification of 11 March 2013, ICC-01/09-02/11-687 – *Prosecutor v Muthaura – Prosecution notification of withdrawal of the charges against Francis Kirimi Muthaura.*

[76] ICC (TC Va), Decision of 5 April 2016, ICC-01/09-01/11-2027 – *Prosecutor v Ruto and Sang – Public redacted version of Decision on Defence Applications for Judgments of Acquittal.*

[77] This is also stressed in European Parliament Research Service, *Achievements and Challenges 20 Years after the Adoption of the Rome Statute*, 13 July 2018, 10.

[78] In more detail, K Ambos and S Bock, 'Procedural Regimes', in L Reydams, J Wouters and C Ryngaert (eds), *International Prosecutors* (Oxford, Oxford University Press, 2012) 488, 530 ff, 541.

[79] ICC (AC), Judgment of 8 June 2018, ICC-01/05-01/08-3636-Anx2 – *Prosecutor v Bemba Gombo – Judgment on the appeal of Mr Jean-Pierre Bemba Gombo against Trial Chamber III's 'Judgment pursuant to Article 74 of the Statute' – Separate Opinion of Judge Van den Wyngaert and Judge Morrison*, para 4.

[80] See, eg, the controversy on the admissibility of witness proofing (that is, the substantive preparation of a witness and his or her testimony): While some Chambers of the ICC reject this practice because it might hamper the ascertaining of the truth, others endorse proofing sessions as they are believed to ensure the efficient use of court time and a fair determination of the cases; see, on the one hand, for example, ICC (PTC I), Decision of 9 November 2006, ICC-01/04-01/06-679 – *Prosecutor v Lubanga – Decision on the Practices of Witness Familiarisation and Witness Proofing*; ICC (TC I),

which in turn can violate the principle of equality before the law and undermine the credibility and legitimacy of the court. On the other hand, internal discrepancies and self-insecurities may make the ICC particularly vulnerable for political pressure. This became obvious in the Afghanistan situation. In a meanwhile notorious decision, the Pre-Trial Chamber denied the Prosecutor's Request for opening a *proprio motu* investigation (*cf* Articles 13(c), 15 ICC Statute). Although the Chamber agreed that there were reasonable grounds to believe that crimes falling within the jurisdiction of the ICC had been committed not only by the Taliban and other armed groups, but also by Afghan and US military forces and the CIA,[81] it concluded that international proceedings would not serve the interests of justice in terms of Article 53(1)(c) ICC Statute. As the preliminary investigations in Afghanistan had been particularly long and difficult, the Chamber assumed that prosecutions were unlikely to succeed and thus ran the risk to frustrate the hopes of victims raised by the investigations.[82] The Prosecutor should, according to the PTC, invest her resources in situations which have 'more realistic prospects to lead to trials'.[83]

This decision was obviously influenced by power politics:[84] when assessing the prospects of further action by the Court, the Chamber referred to the 'scarce cooperation obtained by the Prosecutor'[85] and noted that

> subsequent changes within the relevant political landscape both in Afghanistan and key States (both parties and non-parties to the Statute), coupled with the complexity and volatility of the political climate still surrounding the Afghan scenario, make it extremely difficult to gauge the prospects of securing meaningful cooperation from relevant authorities for the future, whether in respect of investigations or of surrender of suspects.[86]

Decision of 1 December 2007, ICC-01/04-01/06-1049 – *Prosecutor v Lubanga – Decision Regarding the Practices Used to Prepare and Familiarise Witnesses for Giving Testimony at Trial*; ICC (TC III), Decision of 18 October 2010, ICC-01/05-01/08-1016 – *Prosecutor v Bemba Gombo – Decision on the Unified Protocol on the Practices Used to Prepare and Familiarise Witnesses for Giving Testimony at Trial*; ICC (TC I), Decision of 2 December 2015, ICC-02/11-01/15-355 – *Prosecutor v L. Gbagbo and Blé Goudé – Decision on Witness Preparation and Familiarisation*, and, on the other hand, ICC (TC V), Decision of 2 January 2013, ICC-01/09-01/11-524 – *Prosecutor v Ruto and Sang – Decision on Witness Preparation*; ICC (TC VI), Decision of 16 June 2015, ICC-01/04-02/06-652 – *Prosecutor v Ntaganda – Decision on Witness Preparation*; ICC (TC X), Decision of 17 March 2020, ICC-01/12-01/18-666 – *Prosecutor v Al Hassan – Decision on Witness Preparation and Familiarisation*.

[81] ICC (PTC II), Decision of 12 April 2019, ICC-02/17-33 – *Situation in Afghanistan – Decision Pursuant to Article 15 of the Rome Statute on the Authorisation of an Investigation into the Situation in the Islamic Republic of Afghanistan*, paras 47–48.

[82] ibid, para 96.

[83] ibid, para 95.

[84] In more detail, S Bock and N Bülte, 'The Politics of International Justice', in S Sayapin, N Quenivet, G Kemp, and N Zambrana-Tevar (eds) *International Conflict and Security Law*, Vol II (The Hague, TMC Asser Press, forthcoming).

[85] ICC (PTC II), Decision of 12 April 2019, ICC-02/17-33 – *Situation in Afghanistan – Decision Pursuant to Article 15 of the Rome Statute on the Authorisation of an Investigation into the Situation in the Islamic Republic of Afghanistan*, para 91.

[86] ibid, para 94.

This accepts that opposition to the Court yields (positive) results and, thus, sends the political message to states: if they resist the Court strongly enough, no investigations will take place, or proceedings will collapse. Meanwhile, the decision of the PTC was squashed on appeal.[87] The Appeals Chamber dealt predominantly with the difficult relationship between prosecutorial independence and judicial supervision,[88] but also stated obiter dicta that the PTC's reasoning 'was cursory, speculative and did not refer to information capable of supporting it'.[89]

This clear commitment to the mandate of the ICC and the idea that justice must be put beyond politics, however, cannot hide the fact that the enforcement of international criminal law is hampered by political interferences and the lack of will of some states to cooperate with the ICC and to assist the Court in investigating and prosecuting the 'worst crimes known to humanity'. In the 'no case to answer' decision in the *Ruto and Sang* case, Judge Robert Fremr stated that the investigations and the ability of the prosecution to produce reliable and compelling evidence was seriously affected by 'a disturbing level of interference with witnesses, as well as inappropriate attempts at the political level to meddle with the trial and to affect its outcome'.[90] Another example of the dependency of the international criminal justice system on the goodwill of the respective political players is the backlash caused by the issuance of arrest warrants against the then head of Sudan, Omar al-Bashir.[91] It was argued that they might interfere with a peace process for which the participation of the Sudanese Government appeared necessary. Especially the African Union, and for a time France and Great Britain too, tried to convince the UNSC to suspend investigations and prosecutions for 12 months (*cf* Article 16 ICC Statute), but failed to do so.[92] Nevertheless, several state parties of the ICC refused to arrest and surrender al-Bashir, which constituted – at least in the view of the ICC –[93] a breach of their cooperation obligations.[94]

[87] ICC (AC), Decision of 5 March 2020, ICC-02/17-138 – *Situation in Afghanistan – Judgment on the appeal against the decision on the authorisation of an investigation into the situation in the Islamic Republic of Afghanistan.*

[88] In more detail, L Poltronieri Rossetti, 'The Pre-Trial Chamber's Afghanistan Decision: A Step Too Far in the Judicial Review of Prosecutorial Discretion?' (2019) 17 *Journal of International Criminal Justice* 585; T Mariniello, 'Judicial Control over Prosecutorial Discretion at the International Criminal Court' (2019) 19 *International Criminal Law Review* 979.

[89] ICC (AC), Decision of 5 March 2020, ICC-02/17-138 – *Situation in Afghanistan – Judgment on the appeal against the decision on the authorisation of an investigation into the situation in the Islamic Republic of Afghanistan*, para 49.

[90] ICC (TC Va), Decision of 5 April 2016, ICC-01/09-01/11-2027 – *Prosecutor v Ruto and Sang – Public redacted version of Decision on Defence Applications for Judgments of Acquittal*, para 147.

[91] ICC (PTC I), Decision of 4 March 2009, ICC-02/05-01/09-1 – *Prosecutor v Al Bashir – Warrant of Arrest for Omar Hassan Ahmad Al Bashir*; ICC (PTC I), Decision of 12 July 2010, ICC-02/05-01/09-95 – *Prosecutor v Al Bashir – Second Warrant of Arrest for Omar Hassan Ahmad Al Bashir.*

[92] See D Bosco, *Rough Justice – The International Criminal Court in a World of Power Politics* (Oxford, Oxford University Press, 2014) 142–148; Bock and Bülte (n 84) (forthcoming).

[93] The states have justified their non-cooperation in the *al-Bashir* case with reference to Art 98(1) Rome Statute according to which the Court may not proceed with a request for surrender or assistance which would require the requested state to act inconsistently with respect to the state immunity of a third state. In more detail on the complex relationship between Arts 27 and 98 of the Rome Statute, see Ambos (n 7) 617–625 with further references.

The decision of the Office of the Prosecutor (OTP) of December 2020 to close the preliminary examination into alleged war crimes by British troops[95] gives the impression that powerful (western) states with a generally efficient and functional criminal justice system can quite easily prevent or undermine international prosecutions. In its report, the OTP concluded that there is a reasonable basis to believe that members of UK armed forces in Iraq committed the war crimes of wilful killing, torture and inhuman treatment, rape and other forms of sexual violence.[96] The efforts of the UK to investigate these crimes were criticised as very lengthy (they span over more than ten years)[97] and ineffective.[98] According to the OTP, 'the examination of thousands of allegations has resulted in not one single case being submitted for prosecution: a result that has deprived victims of justice'.[99] The UK justified the resulting impunity gap basically with the complexity of the situation and a lack of concrete and reliable evidence. In light of this, the OTP felt unable to demonstrate that there have been unjustified delays in the British proceedings or that they were in any other way conducted in a manner which is inconsistent with an intent to bring the perpetrators to justice.[100] Despite remaining concerns about the decision-making processes of the competent British authorities and their evidentiary assessment of the facts of the case, it could not be proven that the UK is unwilling to genuinely carry out the investigations and prosecutions. Thus, it remained doubtful whether the evidentiary threshold of Article 17 ICC Statute[101] on the admissibility of cases was met and the OTP felt impelled to close its preliminary examination – an alarming decision which was described as the implicit admission that 'an appearance of justice is all that is required to neutralise an ICC criminal investigation and get away with war crimes and torture at the highest levels'.[102]

To cut a long story short, the ICC is under political pressure, suffers from a lack of international support and struggles with itself, its mandate and its role in the international criminal justice system. Against this background, one may be

[94] ICC (PTC I), Decision of 13 December 2011, ICC-02/05-01/09-140 – *Prosecutor v Al Bashir – Decision pursuant to article 87(7) of the Rome Statute on the refusal of the Republic of Chad to comply with the cooperation requests issued by the Court with respect to the arrest and surrender of Omar Hassan Ahmad Al Bashir*; ICC (PTC II), Decision of 6 July 2017, ICC-02/05-01/09-302 – *Prosecutor v Al Bashir – Decision under article 87(7) of the Rome Statute on the non-compliance by South Africa with the request by the Court for the arrest and surrender of Omar Al-Bashir*.

[95] ICC (OTP), *Situation in Iraq/UK – Final Report*, 9 December 2020.

[96] ibid, paras 113, 493.

[97] ibid, paras 425 ff.

[98] ibid, paras 443 ff, 481 ff.

[99] ibid, para 496.

[100] ibid, para 502.

[101] According to the principle of complementarity as enshrined in Art 17 ICC Statute, the ICC is designed as a court of last resort which merely steps in when the national authorities fail to address the matter themselves. National investigations and prosecutions thus take precedence; proceedings before the ICC are admissible only if the competent state is unwilling or unable genuinely to carry out the investigation or prosecution, in more detail, Ambos (n 7) 271 ff.

[102] A Schueller, *The ICC, British War Crimes in Iraq and a Very British Tradition*, OpinioJuris, 11 December 2020, opiniojuris.org/2020/12/11/the-icc-british-war-crimes-in-iraq-and-a-very-british-tradition/.

tempted to predict that in the next years to come, the ICC will remain or become a paper tiger; that it will conduct a few, more or less symbolic trials without really making a meaningful contribution to the overall goal of ending impunity for the international core crimes.

But – and here I am more optimistic – one must not underestimate the symbolic value of the ICC and its catalytic effect on the national criminal justice systems. First of all, the ICC Statute contains the clear message that the commission of the international core crimes – including the highly political crime of aggression – constitutes criminal wrong and is subject to judicial evaluation. This influences – even if no prosecution takes place – the interrelation of the political and legal sphere; the ICC Statute and its underlying values have become part of the international (political) discourse and are used as a kind of evaluation standard. By its very existence, the ICC contributes to the juridification (and the corresponding de-politicisation) of international law. This can already be seen in the OTP's decision in the Iraq situation. As disappointing as the closure of investigations may be, one must not overlook that a strong western government had to explain and justify its prosecutorial efforts before an international body and that its failures and omissions were made public in an official report. This – in combination with the announcement of the Prosecution to reopen investigations if it receives further information concerning improper interference with UK proceedings[103] and (hopefully) political pressure from the international community – may stimulate genuine domestic prosecutions.

The idea that the ICC can serve as a catalyst for national proceedings is also the basis for the Prosecutor's approach of positive complementarity, which aims at encouraging the national judiciary to conduct their own proceedings.[104] The recent closure of the preliminary examination of the situation in Colombia, for example, was linked with an agreement between the OTP and the Colombian Government in which the latter committed itself to support the national judiciary and other accountability mechanisms and to cooperate further closely with the OTP.[105] In addition, many states have implemented the ICC's core crimes into national law; some even allow for the universal prosecution of genocide, crimes against humanity and war crimes. This is, for example, the case in Germany with its Code of Crimes Against International Law (*Völkerstrafgesetzbuch*). Having overcome some initial reluctance to prosecute international crimes committed abroad,[106] the German Federal Prosecutor meanwhile plays an active role

[103] ICC (OTP), *Situation in Iraq/UK – Final Report*, para 505.

[104] In more detail, Ambos (n 7) 327 ff.

[105] ICC (OTP), *Cooperation Agreement between the Office of the Prosecutor of the International Criminal Court and the Government of Colombia*, 28 October 2021; for a first assessment, see K Ambos 'The Return of "Positive Complementarity"', EJIL:Talk!, 3 November 2021, www.ejiltalk.org/the-return-of-positive-complementarity/.

[106] S Bock, 'Western Sahara and Universal Jurisdiction in Germany' (2010) 43 *Revue Belge de Droit International* 43, 54 ff.

in the global fight against impunity. Apart from monitoring the activities of the German *Bundeswehr*, one focus of the Federal Prosecutor lies on the prosecution of so-called foreign fighters who travel to conflict areas like Syria to participate in armed conflicts and later return to Germany. He has also initiated trials concerning the Yazidien genocide[107] and indicted former members of the Assad regime for torture as a crime against humanity –[108] a trial followed closely by the world press.[109] Similar proceedings take place in other countries.[110]

The national prosecution of international crimes is not without challenges and risks: the reconstruction of events that happened thousands of kilometres away from the Court is difficult, the gathering and assessment of evidence is hampered by cultural and linguistic barriers and the Court is faced with the information needs of a foreign society. Arguably, the national procedural laws need some updates in order to guarantee fair and efficient prosecutions of international crimes.[111] But this is the future. In the next decade to come, we will witness an increase in the decentral, national enforcement of international law and these proceedings will make a significant contribution to the fight against impunity for international crimes and the global protection of human rights.

[107] On 25 October 2021, the Higher Regional Court of Munich convicted Jennifer W inter alia for membership in a terrorist organisation and crimes against humanity, www.justiz.bayern.de/gerichte-und-behoerden/oberlandesgerichte/muenchen/presse/2021/30.php. The proceedings against her husband before the Higher Regional Court of Frankfurt are still ongoing. About a month later, the Higher Regional Court of Frankfurt convicted her husband inter alia for genocide to life imprisonment, https://ordentliche-gerichtsbarkeit.hessen.de/sites/ordentliche-gerichtsbarkeit.hessen.de/files/PI%2053ste1204120%20%28Urteil%20Taha%20Al%20J.%29_0.pdf.

[108] See, in more detail, the trial monitoring reports by the Syria Justice and Accountability Centre and the Marburg International Research and Documentation Centre for War Crimes Trials, available at syriaaccountability.org/.

[109] For an overview on universal jurisdiction proceedings in Germany, see C Safferling and G Petrossian, 'Universal Jurisdiction and International Crimes in German Courts – Recent Steps Towards Exercising the Principle of Complementarity after the Entry into Force of the Rome Statute' (2021) 11 *European Criminal Law Review* 242.

[110] *cf*, the briefing papers on universal jurisdiction by the Open Society Justice Initiative, available at www.justiceinitiative.org/publications/universal-jurisdiction-law-and-practice-in-the-netherlands.

[111] On the respective German discussion, D Bentele, 'Völkerstrafprozesse in Deutschland voranbringen – Eine rechtspolitische Betrachtung' (2016) 11 *Zeitschrift für Internationale Strafrechtsdogmatik* 803–806; S Bock and M Wagner, 'Nationale Strafverfolgung von Völkerrechtsverbrechen – in kleinen Schritten weitergedacht' (2020) 73 *Neue Juristische Wochenschrift* 3146.

6

Global Trade in 2030

ANTONIOS KOUROUTAKIS

I. Introduction

Trade of goods and services is a vital activity going hand in hand with the development of humankind. In fact, trade has followed the pace of human development; from the initial activity of the exchange of goods, nowadays we have moved to a global trade model. When the structure of the international economy was built after World War II, with the World Bank (WB) and International Monetary Fund (IMF), global trade was not officially institutionalised in the Bretton Woods agreement. While the initiative to establish the International Trade Organization (ITO) failed, the vacuum was filled by the General Agreements on Tariffs and Trade (GATT). Eventually, in April 1994 an agreement was reached and the World Trade Organization (WTO) was established.[1]

Whilst WTO is the largest (and arguably the most important) international economic organisation, with 164 Member States as of today, the puzzle of global trade is complemented by a plethora of regional integration arraignments: namely Free Trade Areas (FTA), such as the US, Mexico and Canada Agreement replacing the North American Free Trade Agreement (NAFTA),[2] Customs Unions (CU), such as MERCOSUR in South America comprising Argentina, Brazil, Paraguay, Uruguay, and Venezuela[3] and Single Markets such as the European Union (EU).[4]

Unlike standard international economic organisations, such as the World Bank and the International Monetary Fund, the architecture of the WTO was embedded with constitutional aspirations.[5] In particular, it had a deliberative assembly,

[1] Marrakesh Agreement Establishing the World Trade Organization, 15 April 1994.

[2] See Pub.L. 116–113 Agreement between the United States of America, the United Mexican States, and Canada, 29 January 2020.

[3] For more details see M Toscano, F Filho, L Lixinski, M Belén and O Giupponi, *The Law of MERCOSUR* (Oxford, Hart Publishing, 2010) and GL Gardini, 'MERCOSUR: What You See Is Not (Always) What You Get' (2011) 17 *European Law Journal* 683.

[4] See Treaty of the European Union and Treaty Functioning of the European Union, Official Journal of the European Union 2012/C 326/01.

[5] On the constitutionalisation of the WTO see DZ Cass, *The Constitutionalization of the World Trade Organization: Legitimacy, Democracy, and Community in the International Trading System* (Oxford, OUP, 2005).

a permanent administration and a dispute resolution system complemented by efficient enforcement mechanisms.[6] This remark led to the observation that the WTO system incorporates elements that resemble the idea of constitutionalism.

From the literature review, it seems that there is no consensus on what we mean by the term 'constitutionalism', as different authors examine this concept from different perspectives.[7] For the purpose of this chapter, constitutionalism is to mean three different things. First, governance is arranged among different institutions, second, the polity shares common values and agenda, and third, powers exercised are limited.[8] All these three combined legitimise the exercise of power. Constitutionalism is about who exercises power and the limits that are imposed on governments. Such limits, in essence, are legal constraints on politics, and codified in most of the cases in constitutional texts and documents.

Global constitutionalism is about international norms playing a role similar to the role that constitutional principles play in constitutional legal orders.[9] In terms of form, global governance has emerged exercising powers and functions similar to national governments, for instance with institutions exercising lawmaking, executive and judicial functions. In terms of substance, norms are bidding for actors in the international arena, states and private entities alike.

Global constitutionalism, compared to state constitutionalism has a different perspective. State constitutionalism faces power from the perspective of the nation state, while global constitutionalism has a more downwards perspective facing state power from an international and supranational perspective.

A more holistic approach is proposed and termed as societal constitutionalism,[10] which covers both national, and transnational phenomena. As Joerges clarifies

> 'societal constitutionalism' is a metaphor that seeks to capture three interdependent phenomena: the 'politicisation' of markets; the emergence of governance arrangements which need to acknowledge the problem-solving capacities and managerial qualities of the private sphere; and the transformation of nation-state governance in transnational constellations.[11]

[6] Several authors highlight the tripartite division of function in the WTO, however the author argues that what makes the WTO a unique international organisation is its efficient mechanism to enforce the decisions of its dispute resolution system.

[7] See AS Sweet, 'Constitutionalism, Legal Pluralism, and International Regimes' (2009) 16 *Indiana Journal of Global Legal Studies* 621. For more details on the development of constitutionalism, see D Grimm, *Constitutionalism: Past, Present, and Future* (Oxford, OUP, 2016).

[8] A Godden and J Morison, 'Constitutionalims', in R Grote, F Lachenmann and R Wolfrum (eds), *Max Planck Encyclopedia of Comparative Constitutional Law* (Oxford, OUP, 2017).

[9] See DS Law, 'The Evolution and Ideology of Global Constitutionalism' (2011) 99 *California Law Review* 1163; E Young, 'The Trouble with Global Constitutionalism' (2003) 38 *Texas International Law Journal* 527–545.

[10] See D Sciulli, *Theory of Societal Constitutionalism* (Cambridge, CUP, 1992); G Teubner, 'Societal Constitutionalism: Alternatives to State-centered Constitutional theory?' in C Joerges et al. (eds), *Transnational Governance and Constitutionalism* (Oxford, Hart Publishing, 2004) 3–28.

[11] C Joerges, 'Constitutionalism in Postnational Constellations: Contrasting Social Regulation in the EU and in the WTO', in C Joerges and EU Petersmann (eds), *Constitutionalism, Multilevel Trade Governance and Social Regulation* (Oxford, Hart Publishing, 2006) 526.

While a plethora of articles and books are devoted to Global Constitutionalism in relation to trade,[12] this chapter focuses on the status quo, and the (alleged) crisis of global trade with the aim to discuss its prospects for the next ten years to come. In doing so, it will first map the status quo of global constitutionalism, and in particular, the role and the function of the WTO. In addition, it will elaborate on other more advanced integration arrangements that complement the governance of trade, the supranational constitutionalism.[13]

The second part will be more forward looking. It will examine global constitutionalism and in particular the tension between global constitutionalism and state sovereignty. Such tension is recorded in two instances: first, the analysis will begin with the crisis in the WTO dispute resolution system, and in particular the blockage of the appointments in the Appellate Body and the interim solution. Second, the analysis will elaborate in the tension recorded within global and supranational constitutionalism due to the lack of harmonisation and the conflict between public laws.

II. From the Institutionalisation of the World Trade to its Constitutionalisation

The following part will examine the path of world trade regulation from its institutionalisation to its constitutionalisation. It will first examine the establishment of the WTO and its main features. Then it will proceed with the elements that led to the constitutionalisation of world trade. It will argue that the sophisticated enforcement mechanisms of the WTO judicial branch, the WTO panels in combination with the global reach of the organisation were the key elements.

Before the establishment of the United Nations (UN) in 1954, the Westphalian Model provided that nation states may autonomously dictate its own norms and rules. In the international sphere, though, as no legal system is complete, and self-contained, co-existing states interacted in different ways and they influenced each other.[14]

However, with the establishment of the UN, a global constitutional system replaced the Westphalian world order. While with the Westphalian world order, the nation enjoyed regulatory autonomy without restrictions, with the creation

[12] C Joerges and EU Petersmann, (eds) *Constitutionalism, Multilevel Trade Governance and Social Regulation* (Oxford, Hart Publishing, 2006); M Neves, *Transconstitutionalism* (Oxford, Hart Publishing, 2013); A O'Donoghue, *Constitutionalism in Global Constitutionalisation* (Cambridge, CUP, 2014).

[13] Supranational constitutionalism, which is a feature of advanced trade models between states, lies between WTO constitutionalism and state constitutionalism and combines features from both. For more details about supranational constitutionalism see See C Joerges, 'Constitutionalism in Postnational Constellations: Contrasting Social Regulation in the EU and in the WTO', in C Joerges and E U Petersmann (eds), *Constitutionalism, Multilevel Trade Governance and Social Regulation* (Oxford, Hart Publishing, 2006) 527.

[14] G Mousourakis, *Comparative Law and Legal Traditions; Historical and Contemporary Perspectives* (Cham, Springer, 2019) 3.

of the UN, the nation state's sovereignty became subject to the influence of the world community. At the same time, as Archibugi stresses 'the presence of intergovernmental organizations (IGOs) is an indicator of the willingness to expand at the interstate level a number of democratic principles (formal equality between member states, public accountability, rule of law'.[15]

On top of that, states have become interconnected in a plethora of ways. Through bilateral and multilateral treaties, states coordinate their legal framework, harmonise their laws and mutually recognise states' courts' judgments.[16]

The political constitution of the world order found within the UN was complemented with an economic constitution. The economic global constitution was designed in the Bretton Woods agreements. Financial institutions such as the International Monetary Fund and the World Bank were founded, however, the economic global constitution was not completed as the effort to establish an International Trade Organisation was unsuccessful. Temporarily, states dedicated to international cooperation signed an international agreement, the General Agreement on Tariffs and Trade (GATT) and committed to international trade and the elimination of trade barriers.[17]

The world economic constitution was complemented, eventually, in 1995 with the successful foundation of the WTO, which was built upon the GATT system. The WTO, in reality, codified and integrated the key principles of the GATT agreements enforcing the laissez faire approach in trade. As Godden and Morison put it, these financial institutions, together with the UN, 'have engendered a new form of constitutionalism that transcends traditional regional boundaries'.[18]

As a result, the nation state and government's power at the national level changed.[19] Governments' policy making in relation to trade was restricted so as to leave more space to the market players. Most importantly, trade disputes were adjudicated before the WTO dispute settlement system, which proved to be a reasonably effective mechanism to resolve disputes.[20]

A. WTO Constitutionalism

The regulation of trade has been and is a key issue for domestic politics. For instance, states might put forward key policies for the support of a local sector,

[15] D Archibugi, 'Cosmopolitan Democracy and Its Critics: A Review' (2004) 10 *European Journal of International Relations* 437, 448.

[16] Mousourakis (n 14).

[17] CP Bown and DA Irwin, 'The GATT's Starting Point', in M Elsig, B Hoekman and J Pauwelyn, *Assessing the World Trade Organization; Fit for Purpose?* (Cambridge, CUP, 2017) 45.

[18] A Godden and J Morison, 'Constitutionalims', in R Grote, F Lachenmann and R Wolfrum (eds), *Max Planck Encyclopedia of Comparative Constitutional Law* (Oxford, OUP, 2017).

[19] About the erosion of the state's power, especially in relation to trade, see D Chalmers 'Administrative Globalisation and Curbing the Excesses of the State', in C Joerges and EU Petersmann (eds), *Transnational Governance and Constitutionalism* (Oxford, Hart Publishing, 2004) 351.

[20] WJ Davey, 'The WTO Dispute Settlement System: The First Ten Years' (2005) 8 *Journal of International Economic Law* 17.

such as the textile industry or agriculture. Moreover, in regulations about trade, core values are enshrined. For instance, some states may rule out Genetically Modified Organisms (GMOs) for food and safety reasons or because they cause controversy or remain a divisive issue in society. In addition, it is possible that states would want to enhance their cooperation with certain states and exclude others.

However, such trade policies might violate core provisions of the WTO. To begin with, the WTO unlike ordinary international organisations does not simply regulate interstate trade relations. It also sets up quasi-legislative processes and adjudicatory institutions for the interpretation and enforcement of these rules with a sophisticated dispute resolution system.[21]

According to WTO rules (Article 11), while Member States are allowed to impose tariffs on imports, they are not allowed to impose quantitative restrictions,[22] such as absolute bans, embargoes, etc unless an exception is applied.

Furthermore, the WTO requires Member States not to discriminate among their trading partners and in case they grant a trading partner a special customs duty rate for one of their products, then they are required to extend the same special customs duty rate for all other WTO members in relation to the like products (the so called most-favoured-nation (MFN) treatment).[23]

As a general exception to the MFN principle, states though are allowed to create agreements of closer integration such as custom unions and free trade areas with exclusive trade rules to facilitate trade between the party states.[24]

Moreover, the WTO requires Member States to treat imported and locally produced products the same way,[25] as well as foreign and domestic services[26] and foreign and local trademarks, copyrights and patents[27] according to the national treatment principle.

As a result, the WTO is fundamentally based on the principle of equality, and in particular on the dimension of non-discrimination either among trading partners or the dimension of non-discrimination between local and international products or services. Such principle resembles the right based approach, which is a core element of national constitutionalism.[28]

On the top of that, the WTO system is complemented by a sophisticated dispute resolution mechanism. In particular, the WTO dispute settlement system, which

[21] See JH Jackson, *The World Trading System: Law and Policy of International Economic Relations* 2nd edn (Cambridge, MA, MIT Press, 1997) 58.

[22] Art 11 GATT.

[23] Art 1 GATT. MFN is also a priority in the General Agreement on Trade in Services (GATS) (Art 2) and the Agreement on Trade-Related Aspects of Intellectual Property Rights (TRIPS) (Art 4).

[24] Art 24 GATT.

[25] Art 3 GATT.

[26] Art 17 GATS.

[27] Art 3 TRIPS.

[28] In general, at a national level, human rights create limits on what government can do especially in their relationship with ordinary citizens. In relation to human rights in the WTO system see EU Petersmann, 'The WTO Constitution and Human Rights' (2000) 3 *Journal of International Economic Law* 19.

was based on the rules, procedures and practices developed under the GATT,[29] is activated in case a Member State enacts a trade policy, which compatibility with WTO agreements is disputed.

The whole framework of the WTO dispute resolution system is regulated by the 'Understanding on Rules and Procedures Governing the Settlement of Disputes', also known as Dispute Settlement Understanding (DSU).[30] In particular, the WTO body responsible for the adjudication of disputes is the Dispute Settlement Body (DSB).[31]

The first stage of the dispute settlement is consultation attempts, and if they fail, then the DSB selects a panel to deliver a ruling (report) based on the facts of the case. However, such ruling is not final; it must be circulated to all WTO members, and unless appealed or rejected by consensus becomes the DSB's final decision.[32] In case the parties decide to appeal, the dispute is presented before three members of the WTO Appellate Body. The stage before the WTO Appellate Body is critical as it was put, as the

> Appellate Body reports provide the only avenue for obtaining a binding resolution in many WTO disputes since, once a panel report has been appealed, the DSB cannot act on the matter until the completion of the appeal.[33]

The WTO dispute settlement system is exclusive and compulsory for any legal dispute related to trade,[34] as reflected in Article 23 of the DSU. A declination of jurisdiction made by a panel would violate the rights of the Member States, as well as the panel obligations under the DSU.[35] Therefore, the DSU precludes the use of other *fora* for the resolution of WTO related disputes.[36]

While most complaints concern the violation of the principle of non-discrimination established with GATT, quite often complains are submitted in relation to other WTO agreements.[37] In fact, under the auspices of the WTO a

[29] For more details see World Trade Organization, *A Handbook on the WTO Dispute Settlement System* 2nd edn (Cambridge, CUP, 2017) 4.

[30] The DSU was annexed to the 'Final Act' signed in Marrakesh in 1994, see WTO Agreement, Annex 2.

[31] See WTO Agreement, Annex 2, Art 2.

[32] Dispute Settlement Rules: Understanding on Rules and Procedures Governing the Settlement of Disputes, Marrakesh Agreement Establishing the World Trade Organization, Annex 2, Arts 4, 6, 7, 11, 12, 15 Apr. 1994, 1869 UNTS 401, 33 ILM 1226.

[33] 'United States Continues to Block New Appellate Body Members for the World Trade Organization, Risking the Collapse of the Appellate Process' (2019) 113 *American Journal of International Law* 822.

[34] K Kwak and G Marceau 'Overlaps and Conflicts of Jurisdiction between the World Trade Organization and Regional Trade Agreements' (2003) 41 *The Canadian Yearbook of International Law* 83, 85.

[35] Appellate Body Report, *Mexico-Tax Measures on Soft Drinks and Other Beverages*, WT/DS308/AB/R, (2006) [7.4–7.9].

[36] I Van Damme, 'Treaty Interpretation by the WTO Appellate Body' (2010) 21 *European Journal of International Law* 605.

[37] From data collected between 1995 to 2014, 387 complaints were submitted in relation to GATT: 104 complaints in relation to subsidies and countervailing measures, 73 complaints in relation to Agriculture, 48 complaints in relation to technical barriers to trade, 42 complaints in relation to Sanitary and Phytosanitary Measures, 44 complaints in relation to Impost Licensing, 40 complaints in relation to trade related investment measures, and 34 complaints about trade related aspects of intellectual

plethora of agreements are reached resembling the function of the legislator within constitutional systems with separation of powers. Suffice to mention here the Agreement on Agriculture and the Agreement on the Application of Sanitary and Phytosanitary Measures (also known as SPS), which were negotiated during the Uruguay Round and entered into force on 1 January 1995, the Agreement on Import Licensing Procedures, the Agreement on Subsidies and Countervailing Measures, and the recently reached Trade Facilitation Agreement in Bali, in December 2013 at the Ninth Ministerial Conference and came into force in 2017.

Such agreements, in principle, are difficult to reach as they require consensus. Nonetheless, once they are reached, their interpretation is left to a two-thirds supermajority.[38] As a result, such agreements bind the Member States and restrict national policy making on trade, and in case a Member State fails to comply, it might be subject to sanctions and repercussions from the DSB Body based on the WTO dispute resolution mechanism.

We may, thus, conclude that the WTO system is composed by a plethora of agreements, which bind the Member States and restrict their power. On top of that, in case of a breach of these agreements, sanctions are imposed and most importantly such agreements effectively override the domestic political will. All this establishes the system of WTO Constitutionalism with features similar to the concept of domestic constitutionalism.

B. Regional Integration Arrangements: The Enhanced Supranational Constitutionalism

Between WTO constitutionalism and state constitutionalism, WTO's framework is the matrix for another form of constitutionalism, the supranational. Supranational constitutionalism lies between WTO constitutionalism and state constitutionalism and combines features from both. As mentioned above, according to Article 24 of the GATT agreement, WTO Member States are allowed to create agreements of closer integration with exclusive trade rules to facilitate trade between the party states.[39]

There are three main models of closer trade integration: the first model, which we may understand as offering 'light integration' contains the free trade areas, such as the United States–Mexico–Canada Agreement (USMCA). Member States in free trade areas have a common internal trade policy (for instance free movement of goods) but pursue a different external policy. The second model, offering more integration, is the Custom Union with common internal and external policy, for

property rights. For the full list of data see 'WTO Dispute Settlement, 20 years Resolving trade disputes between WTO members', available at www.wto.org/english/thewto_e/20y_e/dispute_brochure20y_e.pdf (last accessed 10 October 2021).

[38] See Marrakesh Agreement Establishing the World Trade Organization, Art 9.

[39] Art 24 GATT.

instance common customs and tariff barriers with third countries. A prime example is MERCOSUR in South America comprising Argentina, Brazil, Paraguay, Uruguay, and Venezuela with its own dispute resolution system.[40]

One of the most successful paradigms of custom unions, is BENELUX, between Belgium, the Netherlands and Luxembourg, which foreshadowed and provided the model for future European integration and the EU as a whole. The EU is the most advanced model of integration having at its heart a single market.[41] This single market is comprised of common internal and external trade policy in combination with more sophisticated tools of integration such as the removal of physical barriers (for instance, paperwork, customs controls), the removal of technical barriers (namely production standards) and the removal of fiscal barriers (namely custom fees) and even with a common currency.

Nowadays the model of the EU underpins a new paradigm of a union of independent sovereign states constrained though by the text of the treaties and core values such as the rule of law, democracy and human rights protection; what I call supra-constitutionalism.

However, this model is not unique as similar models exist elsewhere such as the Caribbean Community (CARICOM)[42] CARICOM is located throughout the Caribbean and has 15 full members, 5 associate members and 8 observers founded by the Revised Treaty of Chaguaramas. The predecessor to CARICOM was the Caribbean Free Trade Agreement, established in 1965. The Caribbean Free Trade Agreement was replaced by the Treaty of Chaguaramas which established the CARICOM on 4 July 1973. The treaty also established the Caribbean Single Market and Economy) (revised in 2001) and the Caribbean Court of Justice.[43]

Interestingly, the common trade policy and the ideals of the WTO for free trade have a spill over effect and in the most advanced models of integration, the unions of Member States form supranational institutions.[44] As a result, in such a model of integration, a delegation of powers takes place from national institutions to common intergovernmental institutions, with shared values, a uniform legal framework, and, most importantly, with the power to enact interstate rules with hierarchical status over national laws. Interestingly, such a normative framework is

[40] For more details see RE Vinuesa, 'The MERCOSUR Settlement of Disputes System' (2006) 5 *The Law & Practice of International Courts and Tribunals* 77.

[41] Stone actually describes the relation of the EU constitutionalism and WTO constitutionalism in the following way: 'the European Union (EU) occupied the opposite extreme, and other regime forms, including the General Agreement on Tariffs and Trade (GATT) and the then-new World Trade Organization (WTO), occupied the middle ground.' See A Stone Sweet, 'Constitutionalism, Legal Pluralism, and International Regimes' (2009) 16 *Indiana Journal of Global Legal Studies* 621, 622.

[42] On CARICOM see D O'Brien, 'CARICOM: Regional Integration in a Post-Colonial World' (2011) 17 *European Law Journal* 630. Similar organisations are the Eurasian Economic Union which was signed on 29 May 2014 by Belarus, Kazakhstan and Russia, and came into force on 1 January 2015 and the Cooperation Council for the Arab States of the Gulf which was signed on 25 May 1981 and includes Bahrain, Kuwait, Oman, Qatar, Saudi Arabia, and the United Arab Emirates.

[43] J Kocken and G van Roozendaal, 'Constructing the Caribbean Court of Justice: How Ideas Inform Institutional Choices' (2012) 93 *European Review of Latin American and Caribbean Studies/Revista Europea de Estudios Latinoamericanos y del Caribe* 95.

[44] N MacCormick, 'Beyond the Sovereign State' (1993) 56 *Modern Law Review* 1.

typically coupled with supranational courts guaranteeing the uniform application of such framework.

As it was accurately put,

> Global Constitutionalism is not about abolishing sovereign states, but about integrating them globally and building the appropriate legal and institutional infrastructure to empower them to better fulfil their function to respect, protect and fulfil the rights of those under their jurisdiction.[45]

The application of such global or supranational constitutionalism after years and decades of trials has raised questions about the legitimacy of such transnational governance. This led to an inevitable tension between global constitutionalism and state sovereignty. The following section will examine the tension as it is recorded in both global constitutionalism and supranational constitutionalism.

III. Global Constitutionalism: Challenges and Perspectives

A. Concerns in Relation to Global Constitutionalism

The development of global constitutionalism implies that more and more power moves upwards from national and local governments to a supranational level. As Zurn explained,[46] the three elements of the current status quo seems to be:

1. the autonomy of the nation-state is restricted as the nation state has to harmonise its policies within international institutions;
2. national political actors still depend on their national constituencies, but they also need recognition at international level; and
3. the nation state remains a key player in the global system.

However, the enhancement of global constitutionalism affects directly or indirectly the life of citizens around the world.[47] This leads to tension between global constitutionalism and national constitutionalism and counter forces are created. As Godden and Morison state, while the centre of political power continues to move upward, recent years have been marked by the emergence of nationalism and a peculiar form of 'neo-Westphalianism'.[48]

[45] M Kumm, J Havercroft, J Dunoff and A Wiener, 'Editorial: The end of 'the West' and the future of global constitutionalism' (2017) 6 *Global Constitutionalism* 1, 9.

[46] M Zurn, 'The State in the Post-National Constellation – Societal Denationalization and Multi-Level Governance', ARENA Working Paper, 35/1999 available at www.sv.uio.no/arena/english/research/publications/arena-working-papers/1994-2000/1999/wp99_35.htm.

[47] E C. Ip, 'Globalization and the future of the law of the sovereign state' (2010) 8 *International Journal of Constitutional Law* 636.

[48] A Godden and J Morison, 'Constitutionalims' in R Grote, F Lachenmann and R Wolfrum (eds), *Max Planck Encyclopedia of Comparative Constitutional Law* (Oxford, OUP, 2017).

A serious concern that is reasonably raised is that global constitutionalism differs from constitutionalism in terms of essence. While constitutionalism is a limit on national governments emanating from national sovereignty, global constitutionalism is seen as the imposition of limits and constrains on national governments by external sources. However the supranational institutions with control lack legitimacy, accountability and are not subject to checks and balances. This is actually a paradox as at the global scale there is governance without governments, and power without accountability.

Such tension is not new, as it is a new dimension in an old and ongoing pathology of national constitutionalism.[49] National constitutionalism equally suffers from the question of delegation of powers, especially from the legislature to the executive, weakening the nexus of accountability and representation in the decision making process.[50] In a similar manner, global constitutionalism suffers from the delegation of powers from national institutions to supranational with limited accountability and representation at the decision making process.

Such lack of legitimacy inevitably led to the creation of counter political forces as articulated by Brexit and the election of President Trump in the US.[51] On the one hand Brexit meant that the UK departed from the close trading union with the EU, and trade relations between the UK and EU Member States will no longer be subject to a free trade agreement.[52] On the other hand, the election of President Trump did not only signal a more protectionist environment in trade with higher tariffs, but also impacted the trade relations of the US with third countries. Suffice to mention here that the US has withdrawn from the Trans-Pacific Partnership, which is a 12-country trade agreement.[53]

While global constitutionalism was meant to complement state constitutionalism, these tendencies demonstrate that the forces within the state are still central and enduring.

At the global level, WTO constitutionalism has for several years been facing serious challenges, due to counter forces at national level. In particular, the dispute settlement of the WTO was under a state of uncertainty, as the US was blocking the appointment of new Appellate Body Members at WTO Appeal Panels.[54] As the Appellate Body plays a key role in the WTO dispute resolution system, the vacant

[49] For more analysis see PL Lindseth, 'Democratic Legitimacy and the Administrative Character of Supranationalism: The Example of the European Community' (1999) 99 *Columbia Law Review* 628, 630ff.

[50] About the history of delegation of powers see P Craig, *Administrative Law* 7th edn (London, Sweet and Maxwell, 2008) [15–002]. Furthermore, about the UK Parliament's efforts to control delegated powers see A Kouroutakis, *The Constitutional Value of Sunset Clauses; An Historical and Normative Analysis* (Abingdon, Routledge, 2017) 66.

[51] M Kumm, J Havercroft, J Dunoff and A Wiener, 'Editorial: The end of 'the West' and the future of global constitutionalism' (2017) 6 *Global Constitutionalism* 1.

[52] EU–UK Trade and Cooperation Agreement (TCA) signed on 30 December 2020.

[53] See Trans-Pacific Partnership Agreement, signed on 4 February 2016.

[54] About the stance of the US to block new Appellate Body Members see 'United States Continues to Block New Appellate Body Members for the World Trade Organization, Risking the Collapse of the Appellate Process' (2019) 113 *American Journal of International Law* 822, 824.

seats in the Appellate Body inevitably leads to the paralysis of the WTO dispute resolution system.

Obviously, the systemic failure in the adjudication of cases threatens a key feature of WTO constitutionalism, and such development highlights, the dependency of the global constitutionalism and in particular of the multilateral rules-based trading system from the Member States and national sovereignty. Interestingly, it suffices for one Member State to challenge the whole edifice of the WTO constitutionalism.

Such a development indicates the key role of the nation state in global constitutionalism. As it was accurately put: 'while constitutionalism is now a global phenomenon, it has yet to supersede the boundaries of sovereignty, still so central to regional constitutional thought'.[55]

However, while the crisis in the WTO dispute resolution system is still present, and while WTO parties seek a solution to stop the paralysis of the Appellate Body, an interim proposal was adopted among several parties, including the EU and China. In particular, the Multi-party Interim Appeal Arbitration Arrangement (MPIA) recently was agreed in compliance with Article 25 of the Dispute Settlement Understanding.[56] According to this solution, a parallel appellate system is created which will be binding only for the Member States that join the interim appeal arbitration arrangement.

However, such solutions come with pros and cons. On the positive side, this interim arrangement offers a solution to the crisis on the WTO adjudication system. A plethora of countries have accepted such a solution, which at least ensures that the WTO dispute resolution system will keep on functioning for a number of countries. Such a solution offers an appellate review which is of paramount importance to preserve the coherence and effectiveness of the WTO dispute resolution system. Such an interim agreement shows that WTO members were committed to the WTO multilateral rules-based trading system and were not willing to give up the WTO dispute settlement system. With this temporary solution, they have kept the system functioning until a permanent solution is reached. Furthermore, this interim solution signals that one member of the WTO cannot block and undermine the values of the WTO dispute settlement system, and in general the values of such a system. The endurance of the WTO dispute settlement system might force the US to cooperate and have the WTO Appellate Body reactivated and fully functional.

However, the downside of this solution is that the MPIA subverts the original system, which might not have a real chance of being reactivated. It is indicative

[55] A Godden and J Morison, 'Constitutionalism', in R Grote, F Lachenmann and R Wolfrum (eds), *Max Planck Encyclopedia of Comparative Constitutional Law* (Oxford, OUP 2017).

[56] Statement on a mechanism for developing, documenting and sharing practices and procedures in the conduct of WTO disputes JOB/DSB/1/Add.12, 30 April 2020. For criticism on this new mechanism see H Gao, 'Finding a Rule-Based Solution to the Appellate Body Crisis: Looking Beyond the Multiparty Interim Appeal Arbitration Arrangement' [2022] *Journal of International Economic Law* forthcoming.

that such an agreement, while it is termed interim and temporary, is not subject to any sunset clause. In particular, it states that 'the MPIA will remain in effect only until the Appellate Body is again fully functional'.[57]

Additionally, such interim solutions might not be short-lived as it is possible that ten years from today, the appointments at the WTO Appellate Body will be still blocked. Accordingly, such an interim solution might prove to be more permanent; as it is often said, nothing is more permanent than a temporary solution. Hence, it is probable that the WTO Constitutionalism will continue to function with such interim configuration for the following decade.

All in all, the paralysis of the Appellate Body caused by one Member State shows that power and national sovereignty trumps trade and disturbs global constitutionalism in relation to international trade rules and procedures. At the same time, the interim solution is an unorthodox way[58] to circumvent the problem and indicates that global constitutionalism, regardless of the reluctance from some states, endures and finds ways to retain and restore order at a global level.

B. Legal Pluralism and Conflict of Public Laws

Trade has always been the force of legal interaction between different legal orders and between different norms. From the antiquity and the period of *pax romana*, the establishment of Roman *ius civile* was seen as a barrier to trade as foreign merchants and trades had little 'inclination to conform to the tedious formalities of the Roman ius civile'.[59] This limited conformity led to the birth of *ius gentium* regulating the relationships between Roman citizens and foreigners and between foreigners from different regions. As Mousourakis puts it

> in contrast to the *ius civile*, the *ius gentium* was thus characterised by its simplicity, adaptability and emphasis on substance rather than form. For that reason, not only foreigners but also Roman citizens often relied on it as a means for resolving legal disputes.[60]

Such was an early form of legal pluralism.

In the contemporary era, legal pluralism reappears especially with the foundation of regional integration arrangements of supranational nature, such as the EU

[57] See Statement On A Mechanism For Developing, Documenting And Sharing Practices And Procedures In The Conduct Of WTO Disputes, 30 April 2020 [15].

[58] However, such an unorthodox way was also used at EU level with the adoption of the Treaty on Stability, Cooperation and Governance (also known as Fiscal Compact) which was adopted as an independent and in reality complementary treaty to the EU Treaties once two Member States of the EU, in particular the UK and Czech Republic, did not sign it.

[59] Gai Institutiones or Institutes of Roman Law by Gaius, with a Translation and Commentary by the late E Poste, fourth edition, revised and enlarged by EA Whittuck, with an historical introduction by AHJ Greenidge, (Oxford, Clarendon Press, 1904) [12].

[60] G Mousourakis, *Comparative Law and Legal Traditions: Historical and Contemporary Perspectives* (Cham, Springer, 2019) 53.

and CARICOM.[61] Different legal orders co-exist, interact, influence each other, and even havr their supreme judicial authorities engaging in institutional dialogue

In principle, in supranational structures, multilateral agreements harmonise rules and recognise each other's judgments. In theory, the expectation was that such interaction will reshape even core values. Suffice to mention here that world trade was seen as an interdependence force, which connects countries and integrates different aspects of the economy. Such interconnection creates interdependency between states and regions, and the expectation was that such spill over effect will bring together and harmonise legal and political values alike.

In particular, before China's accession to the WTO, the expectation was that trade and the laissez faire values of the WTO would move China's regime closer to a more democratic system of governance. President William J Clinton argued that '[j]ust as democracy helps make the world safe for commerce, commerce helps make the world safe for democracy. It's a two-way street.'[62] Moreover, his successor, George W Bush, claimed that 'when we promote open trade, we are promoting political freedom. Societies that open to commerce across their borders will open to democracy within their borders, not always immediately, and not always smoothly, but in good time.'[63]

At the same time, pertaining to supranational constitutionalism, it was taken for granted that states entering supranational institutions like the EU, would uphold the principles of free trade and democracy alike.

However, such expectations were not met. On the one hand, the political system in China not only remained intact, but also tightened its control over several areas such as media, civil society, business etc.[64] On the other hand, the recent legal reforms in Hungary and Poland, two Member States in the EU, that have dismantled the authority of the courts, weakened checks and balances and created barriers to the opposition, led to an unprecedented democratic backsliding.[65]

Having said that, it seems that the debate on the nexus between the globalisation of trade and democracy is far from settled, and on top of that, the harmonisation of values did not materialise. In the near future and in the years to come, it is more probable that the tension will escalate. While Francis Fukuyama, after the dissolution of the Soviet Union predicted the universalisation of 'Western liberal

[61] ibid 169 ff. See also LM Friedman, *The Legal System: A Social Science Perspective* (Russell Sage Foundation, 1975) and MB Hooker, *Legal pluralism: an introduction to colonial and neo-colonial laws* (Oxford, Clarendon Press, 1976). In relation to legal pluralism and constitutionalism, see G Tusseau, *Debating Legal Pluralism and Constitutionalism: New Trajectories for Legal Theory in the Global Age* (Cham, Springer, 2020) and A Stone Sweet, 'Constitutionalism, Legal Pluralism, and International Regimes' (2009) 16 *Indiana Journal of Global Legal Studies* 621.

[62] See www.issues2000.org/Celeb/BillClintonFreeTrade.htm (last accessed 27 November 2004).

[63] See Office of the Press Secretary, The White House, Remarks, by the President to the Council of the Americas, 7 May 2001; www.whitehouse.gov/news (last accessed 8 May 2001).

[64] About the state of democracy in China see Freedom House Report on China available at freedomhouse.org/country/china/freedom-world/2020 (last accessed 10 October 2021).

[65] For more details see T Ginsburg and A Huq, *How to Save a Constitutional Democracy* (Chicago, University of Chicago Press, 2018) 68ff and 99ff.

democracy as the final form of human government',[66] recent developments around the world show that such expectations were not fully met. Interestingly, a new type of regime emerged, the so called illiberal democracy.[67] Illiberal democracy functions based on the ordinary election process, however, political actors with power bypass constitutional limits, distort checks and balances, and turn the rules of the political process in their favour by establishing an uneven playing field.[68] Such an autocratic approach to politics will definitely affect free trade as autocrats are expected to be keener to take protectionist measures and to be hostile vis a vis lower tariffs in international trade.[69] A fortiori, autocrats would be less keen to join trade agreements which by default limit the scope of their autocratic policy making and impose constraints based on free trade values.[70]

Interestingly, in supranational structures, harmonisation of laws in some cases fails, as norms often contradict each other. Indeed, the most critical facet of the plurality of sources is when different public laws are in conflict. In systems with imperfect constitutionalism such as the systems of supranational constitutionalism, the conflict between public rules lacks hierarchical structures.[71] On the other hand, in systems with perfect constitutionalism such as the nation state constitutionalism, the conflict is resolved via the hierarchical structure of the norms and the precedent force from supreme courts in the judicial pyramid. However, in relation to the supranational constitutionalism of the EU, Joerges clarifies:

> what is 'constitutional' about such an exercise? Any kind of 'supranational constitutionalism' has to 'juridify' a paradox. It has to create a type of unity which maintains diversity. Conflict of laws is committed to precisely this objective. 'Unitas in pluralitate', the motto of the European Union according to Article IV–1 of the Draft Constitutional Treaty, can be read as a constitutional conflict-of-laws paradigm.[72]

In practice, though, supranational constitutionalism suffers from setbacks due to conflicting norms and decisions. Suffice to mention here the recent case from the Federal Constitutional Court rendered on 5 May 2020 which challenged the Public

[66] F Fukuyama, 'The End of History?' (1989) 16 *The National Interest* 3.

[67] F Zakaria, 'The Rise of Illiberal Democracy' (1997) 76 *Foreign Affairs* 22.

[68] For more details on political self-entrenchment in illiberal democracies see A Kouroutakis, 'Legitimate and Illegitimate Political Self-entrenchment and Its Impact on Political Equality' (2021) 15 *ICL Journal* 4.

[69] In line with the above, Mansfield et al have modeled that trade agreement between democracies have fewer trade barriers compared to trade agreements between democracies and autocracies. For more details see E Mansfield, H Milner and P Rosendorff, 'Free to Trade: Democracies, Autocracies and International Trade' (2000) 94 *American Political Science* 305.

[70] Mansfield and Milner argued that democracies are keener to enter into free trade agreements compared to autocracies. See ED Mansfield and HV Milner, *Vetoes, and the Political Economy of International Trade Agreements* (Princeton, Princeton University Press 2012).

[71] As Joerges states, in systems of supranational constitutionalism, 'there is simply no political authority available which could ensure the type of normative coherence that we can expect within constitutional democracies'. See C Joerges, 'Constitutionalism in Postnational Constellations: Contrasting Social Regulation in the EU and in the WTO', in C Joerges and EU Petersmann (eds), *Constitutionalism, Multilevel Trade Governance and Social Regulation* (Oxford, Hart Publishing, 2006) 527.

[72] See Joerges and Petersmann (n 71) 494.

Sector Purchase Programme (PSPP) of the European Central Bank (ECB), while it questioned the authority of the European Court itself, as the supreme interpreter of Union law.[73]

A more direct challenge to the authority of the European Court came recently from the Constitutional Tribunal of Poland which rejected the principle of the primacy of EU law over national legislation and constitutional provisions in certain judicial matters.[74]

Apart from the aforementioned conflicts, the harmonisation and uniformity of laws is a dynamic and never-ending process. Nowadays, divergent norms and conflicting rules are enacted due to the development of new problems and the birth of new products and forms of services. For instance, the regulation of crypto-currencies and regulatory sandboxes create centrifugal forces with the enactment of divergent laws emanating from different legal systems within the same supra-national legal order.

As a result, on the one hand, the lack of clear hierarchical structures render the rules and the procedures of global constitutionalism vulnerable, as different centres enact divergent laws exacerbating the lack of uniformity. On the other hand, the need to regulate new problems inevitably leads to the enactment of divergent rules.

In existing enhanced and advanced trade co-operations like the EU, the conflict between public norms and the competition between adjudicative authorities in supranational constitutionalism will remain a threat on the unity and coherence of such systems. Such tension is possible to remain, at least in the years to come. After all, the past has taught us that deeper integration coupled with the manifestation of centrifugal forces is an inherent feature of supranational organisations.

[73] Federal Constitutional Court, Judgment of 5 May 2020, 2 BvR 859/15, 2 BvR 980/16, 2 BvR 2006/15, 2 BvR 1651/15. The decision handed down by the German Court initiated a dialogue among institutions and provoked a number of responses from EU Institutions. The European Court, in a press release, stated that 'the Court of Justice alone – which was created for that purpose by the Member States – has jurisdiction to rule that an act of an EU institution is contrary to EU law', and, in doing so, found an unorthodox way to respond to the decision of the Federal Constitutional Court. See Press Release No 58/20, 'Press Release Following The Judgment of The German Constitutional Court of 5 May 2020' (8 May 2020). Moreover, the ECB responded that it takes note of the German Federal Constitutional Court's judgment and at the same time it recalled the judgment of the Court of Justice of the European Union which ruled in December 2018 that 'the ECB is acting within its price stability mandate'. See Press Release, 'ECB Takes Note of German Federal Constitutional Court Ruling And Remains Fully Committed To Its Mandate' (5 May 2020). Finally, a statement was made by the President of the European Commission according to which it was reaffirmed that 'the Union's monetary policy is a matter of exclusive competence; that EU law has primacy over national law and that rulings of the European Court of Justice are binding on all national courts'. See Statement by President Von Der Leyen, 10 May 2020.

[74] See Reuters, 'Polish Court Rules Some EU Law Is Unconstitutional, Deepening Dispute' (7 October 2021) available at www.reuters.com/world/europe/polish-constitutional-tribunal-some-articles-eu-treaties-unconstitutional-2021-10-07/ (last accessed 10 October 2021). In response to this ruling the Commission issued a statement and expressed its concern about the state of the rule of law in Poland and reminded the primacy of EU Law in relation to national law and the binding nature of the decisions of the European Court. See Statement by the European Commission on the decision of the Polish Constitutional Tribunal of 14 July (15 July 2021).

While the tension between public norms is expected to intensify due to the centrifugal forces, which have surged at national level, paradoxically, it is possible that closer union among different states to enhance free trade will multiply. To begin with, it is widely recognised that trade cooperation, at least at a peripheral level, is beneficial for the economy. More and more states facing fierce global competition are finding it more acceptable to see the erosion of their national sovereignty and their subjection to supranational constitutionalism in return of the benefits of free trade.

Free trade areas pose the minimum threat to national sovereignty and rationally speaking, the benefits from such trade agreements, such as welfare creation, job creation and the strengthening of regional supply chains, to a greater extent outweigh the isolation forces at the national level. Consequently, it is possible to see more and more free trade areas.[75] Suffice to mention here the move from China, which on 16 September 2021 submitted a request to accede to the Comprehensive and Progressive Trans-Pacific Partnership (CPTPP) trade agreement.[76] Interestingly, a year before, in 2020 the Regional Comprehensive Economic Partnership (RCEP), a free trade agreement, was signed among 15 nations of the Asia-Pacific region and is projected to come into effect in 2022,[77] which covers a market of almost 30 per cent of the world's population (2.2 billion people).[78]

That said, the global competition in trade, and the benefits from free trade, which outweigh the concerns over the preservation of national sovereignty, might force states to join forces in trade policies, rather than to stay isolated and left behind. In line with this, it is possible to see further integration in customs unions around the world towards the model of common markets. The close cooperation between states in customs unions might be the driving force to multiply the benefits by enhancing trade cooperation. In addition, the wealth created and the enhanced cooperation between states in common markets may also be a model that some states might want to follow. However, the tensions within common markets due to the conflict of public laws might create counter forces against further integration.

IV. Conclusion

World trade has always been an important economic activity with significant implications on the transformation of the world order and national sovereignty

[75] According to the Asia Regional Integration Center there is a continuous proliferation of free trade agreements. For instance by comparing the number of free trade agreements in relation to the Asia and Pacific region, in 2000, 5 Free Trade Agreements were signed, while in 2017, 70 Free Trade Agreements. For more information see Plurilateral FTAs by WTO Notification and Status, 2000 and 2017 available at aric.adb.org/fta.

[76] 'China Applies To Join Pacific Trade Pact To Boost Economic Clout', *Reuters* (17 September 2021) available at www.reuters.com/world/china/china-officially-applies-join-cptpp-trade-pact-2021-09-16/.

[77] Regional Comprehensive Economic Partnership (RCEP), signed on 15 November 2020.

[78] See 'Joint Leaders' Statement on The Regional Comprehensive Economic Partnership (RCEP)' available at rcepsec.org/wp-content/uploads/2020/11/RCEP-Summit-4-Joint-Leaders-Statement-Min-Dec-on-India-2.pdf.

alike. Wars that have broken out due to conflicts in world trade and international relations have diminished. Nowadays, in the regulation of world trade, the WTO system plays a key role in its constitutionalisation. The WTO system is composed of a plethora of agreements. Such agreements bind and restrict Member States, while sanctions are imposed by the sophisticated WTO dispute resolution system, in case such agreements are violated. All this establishes the system of WTO Constitutionalism with features similar to the concept of domestic constitutionalism.

In addition, WTO constitutionalism is complemented by integration agreements, by closer trade unions between states, such as free trade areas, but also with more enhanced systems, such as single markets. Constitutionalism in such single markets is more advanced as decisions at supranational level have a binding force overriding norms emanating from national level.

However, the emergence of global constitutionalism and supranational constitutionalism has led to the creation of counter forces at the national level. Such national forces, as has been seen, led to the blockade of the WTO dispute resolution system, and to the potential paralysis of WTO constitutionalism. An interim solution was adopted with the Multi-party Interim Appeal Arbitration Arrangement which was recently agreed and became operational. Such a solution demonstrates the limits of global constitutionalism, as single states are in a position to block the whole system. At the same time, such an interim solution is indicative on the wide-spread commitment on the mechanism of global constitutionalism, as states cooperate to bypass barriers. However, it is probable that such a temporary solution might become more permanent.

In addition, the tension between the nation state and global constitutionalism is exacerbated due to the conflict between public norms, and the absence of a central authority with a hierarchical structure. This conflict of public norms reflects the reaction of the sovereign state.

While sovereign states show resistance to closer trade integration, a paradox might appear in the years to come. On the one hand, free trade agreements will possibly multiply despite the resistance from counter forces in favour of national sovereignty, as the benefits from global trade outweigh any concern. On the other hand, such centrifugal forces will remain intact and thus conflicts of public norms will remain and possibly intensify in the most advanced models of trade co-operations. What remains to be seen is whether the integration in existing customs unions and common markets will become deeper as a way to resolve the tensions in the conflict of public norms.

PART THREE

Actors

7

Institutions in 2030

STEFANIE EGIDY

I. Introduction

Public institutions are called upon to live up to the challenges ahead. Their path of creating and recreating policy answers will be paved with change, whether it emerges organically or is adopted consciously. The ensuing institutional adjustments will correspond closely to the pending real-world problems and shape the face of constitutionalism in 2030. Therefore, the nature of these challenges will determine which institutional responses prove most instrumental. For instance, the climate crisis does not merely constitute a policy problem, but demands answers to the intergenerational divide of legislative decision making, the present bias of institutions, and the time inconsistency of lawmaking.[1] Similarly, the ongoing COVID-19 pandemic calls for institutional approaches that ensure the decision-makers' capacity to react rapidly to new developments in a separation of powers framework and to incorporate the necessary expertise in accordance with their democratic mandate.

Despite their many differences, constitutions around the world imply a demand for institutional design features that promote and strengthen the resilience of constitutional actors. I suggest that 'institutional resilience' provides a viable framework for assessing the power of these actors to withstand unwanted influence and their ability to cope with transformation and crises. Taking a closer look at likely future challenges allows me to uncover, which specific features of institutional design could prove beneficial for the institutions in charge of resolving these issues within a framework of constitutionalism. This question has normative

[1] See RJ Lazarust, 'Super Wicked Problems and Climate Change: Restraining the Present to Liberate the Future' (2009) 94 *Cornell Law Review* 1153, 1159–79; see JB Ruhl, 'General Design Principles for Resilience and Adaptive Capacity in Legal Systems – With Applications to Climate Change Adaptations' (2011) 89 *North Carolina Law Review* 1373 (applying resilience theory to climate change law); see also RH Weaver and DA Kysar, 'Courting Disaster: Climate Change and the Adjudication of Catastrophe' (2017) 93 *Notre Dame Law Review* 295, 296 (positing that 'Climate change challenges the capacity of law').

overtones. The approach chosen is not merely predictive, but also prescriptive. I will focus on policymaking institutions on a national level, namely the legislative and the executive branch, and reserve an inspection of the fate of political parties and social movements to my two esteemed co-contributors.[2] I will identify three institutional strategies that could help both branches to accommodate the challenges ahead. While the chapter takes into account a variety of jurisdictions, its main references stem from the European Union (EU) and the United States (US), a choice that will shape the conclusions drawn.

The chapter proceeds in three steps. First, I will ground my analysis on the insights created through foresight studies, which explore probable future scenarios and outline the relevant variables for potential policy responses. The concept of foresight provides a useful starting point because it identifies the upcoming challenges that policymaking institutions will face, allowing one to ponder about the matching strategies of constitutional institutional design. Second, I will analyse the societal and political impact of three key challenges over the next eight years that call for an institutional accommodation. Third, I will suggest three mechanisms of institutional design that could help increase the resilience of institutions vis-à-vis the impending challenges.

II. The Future in Foresight

A prediction of what constitutionalism may look like in 2030 has to rest on certain assumptions about the development of the state of the world. This also applies more generally to building any policy agenda that takes a prospective approach and seeks to set up the social and legal system for the future. This, again, closely relates to the study of foresight.[3] Foresight is an academic discipline that aims to understand and forecast long-term future developments and their impact in a methodologically systematic way.[4] Foresight studies can inform public policymakers as well as private actors and enable them to prepare for the transformations ahead (so-called strategic foresight).[5] Thus, international institutions, governmental actors, and

[2] P Starski, 'Political Parties', ch 8 in this volume; T Dumbrovsky, 'Popular Movements', ch 9 in this volume.

[3] See generally KA Piirainen and RA Gonzalez, 'Theory of and within Foresight – "What Does a Theory of Foresight Even Mean?"' (2015) 96 *Technological Forecasting and Social Change* 191 (outlining the theoretical dimension of foresight).

[4] D Canyon, 'Simplifying Complexity with Strategic Foresight and Scenario Planning' (2018) *Daniel K. Inouye Asia Pacific Center for Security Studies, Occasional Paper October 2018* 1, 1 (emphasising that 'Strategic foresight is a recent discipline, originating in the 1960s').

[5] A Oliveira et al, 'A Systemic and Contextual Framework to Define a Country's 2030 Agenda from a Foresight Perspective' (2019) 11 *Sustainability* 6360 (discussing the role of foresight in the national implementation of the Agenda 2030); see also M Sinclair, E Sadler-Smith and GP Hodgkinson, 'The Role of Intuition in Strategic Decision Making' in LA Costanzo and RB MacKay (eds), *Handbook of Research on Strategy and Foresight* (Cheltenham, Edward Elgar, 2009) (analysing the role of intuition and rationality in strategic foresight).

global companies all study the future in foresight in order to employ 'anticipatory governance'.[6] The EU in particular is heavily engaged in using strategic foresight to 'future-proof EU policymaking'.[7] The underlying idea is not to predict the future – as this would be a laborious and unsatisfactory task given the many contingencies – but to identify the most important dimensions of future development, outline different potential states of the world, and think through possible responses and strategies to prepare.[8] In that, concrete foresight studies both shape and make visible what institutions assume about the future.

The state of constitutionalism in 2030 will depend on the global experiences over the course of the next decade. The different nations as well as international actors will meet these challenges with a continually evolving set of policies. Their respective institutions need to be prepared to step up to meet the tasks ahead, all the while remaining committed to the applicable constitutional rules. Due to this interdependence between real-world conditions and constitutionalism, I will base the following analysis on existing foresight studies, which identify impending challenges that could or that should prompt changes to the design of the institutions in charge. I will begin by introducing the concept of foresight studies and by explaining why an analytical view of constitutionalism in 2030 should be anchored in empirical insight (A.). Then, I will draw attention to a few important limitations of the methodology of foresight (B.).

A. Concept

Foresight can be defined as 'the discipline of exploring, anticipating and shaping the future to help building and using collective intelligence in a structured and systemic way to anticipate developments'.[9] It offers a methodological basis that enables different actors to improve and strengthen their policymaking efforts. Thus, foresight becomes an instrument to counter behavioural and cognitive limits

[6] MJ Burrows and O Gnad, 'Between "Muddling through" and "Grand Design": Regaining Political Initiative – The Role of Strategic Foresight' (2018) 97 *Futures* 6, 9; A Hines and J Gold, 'An Organizational Futurist Role for Integrating Foresight into Corporations' (2015) 101 *Technological Forecasting and Social Change* 99 (emphasising the increasing use of foresight by corporate actors).

[7] Commission, '2020 Strategic Foresight Report. Strategic Foresight – Charting the Course Towards a More Resilient Europe' (Communication) COM (2020) 493 final 2–5 (outlining the foresight efforts of the European Union); see also F Gaub, 'Global Trends to 2030. Challenges And Choices For Europe' (European Strategy and Policy Analysis System 2019); see also Burrows and Gnad (n 6) 6 (analysing 'the Dahrendorf Foresight Process[, which] was initiated as a pilot project to improve the EU's foresight capabilities' in the area of foreign security policy).

[8] T Fuller and K Loogma, 'Constructing Futures: A Social Constructionist Perspective on Foresight Methodology' (2009) 41 *Futures* 71 (developing insights on the epistemological value of foresight); Burrows and Gnad (n 6) 9, 11; E Störmer et al, 'Foresight – Using Science and Evidence to Anticipate and Shape the Future' in V Šucha and M Sienkiewicz (eds), *Science for Policy Handbook* (Amsterdam, Elsevier, 2020) 129–30.

[9] Website of the European Commission, Strategic foresight, www.ec.europa.eu/info/strategy/strategic-planning/strategic-foresight_en.

of planning and adapting to future events.[10] Therefore, many public actors, but also large corporate ones, have set up their own foresight units.[11] The goal of foresight is to create a framework within which to envision and deliberate about how to shape the future development.[12] Its careful implementation can also strengthen institutional resilience.[13] Foresight includes observing ongoing developments and outlining their possible direction as well as detecting events that foreshadow impending crises. 'Unknown unknowns' or 'black swan events' remain unpredictable by definition.[14] However, even though hardly anyone specifically anticipated the financial crisis of 2007–2009 or the current global coronavirus pandemic, it was common knowledge that financial crises and pandemics are recurring events.[15] Despite the fact that specific problems will only surface once an emergency strikes, institutions can well prepare themselves in a more general manner. This is why, for instance, the US Federal Emergency Management Agency (FEMA) utilises strategic foresight to enhance preparedness.[16]

Foresight studies rely on a variety of methods for generating the necessary insight.[17] Commonly, they employ qualitative methods, supplemented with semi-quantitative methods, which can be evaluated along four dimensions – creativity, expertise, interaction, evidence – and selected accordingly.[18] Thereby, they fill a gap left by those quantitative studies that rely on existing data to calculate the probability of future events and therefore have limited adaptive and

[10] Burrows and Gnad (n 6) 12, 14; Canyon (n 4) 2–3.

[11] R Popper, 'How Are Foresight Methods Selected?' (2008) 10 *Foresight* 62, 78 (mapping foresight methods used by governmental actors, firms, trade bodies, NGOs and the research community); JM Greenblott et al, 'Strategic Foresight in the Federal Government: A Survey of Methods, Resources, and Institutional Arrangements' (2019) 11 *World Futures Review* 245 (discussing foresight within the US federal Government); R Vecchiato and C Roveda, 'Strategic Foresight in Corporate Organizations: Handling the Effect and Response Uncertainty of Technology and Social Drivers of Change' (2010) 77 *Technological Forecasting and Social Change* 1527 (focusing on corporate foresight).

[12] Canyon (n 4) 2.

[13] Commission, '2021 Strategic Foresight Report. The EU's capacity and freedom to act' (Communication) COM (2021) 750 final 20 (outlining that 'Developing strategic foresight capabilities can help assess the impending risks and better prepare to deal with crises and emerging opportunities').

[14] See L Ilmola and E Rovenskaya, 'Three Experiments: The Exploration of Unknown Unknowns in Foresight' (2016) 106 *Technological Forecasting and Social Change* 85 (exploring methods for addressing 'ontological uncertainty' in foresight).

[15] CM Reinhart and KS Rogoff, *This Time Is Different. Eight Centuries of Financial Folly* (Princeton, Princeton University Press, 2009); J Piret and G Boivin, 'Pandemics Throughout History' (2021) 11 *Frontiers in Microbiology* 1.

[16] See FEMA, 'Crisis Response and Disaster Resilience 2030: Forging Strategic Action in an Age of Uncertainty' (2012) *Progress Report Highlighting the 2010-2011 Insights* (highlighting its own strategic foresight initiative); Greenblott et al, 'Strategic Foresight in the Federal Government' (outlining strategic foresight efforts within the US federal Government).

[17] See R Popper, 'Foresight Methodology', in L Georghiou et al (eds), *The Handbook of Technology Foresight. Concept and Practice* (Cheltenham, Edward Elgar, 2008) (presenting 33 different methods of conducting foresight analyses); see also Popper (n 11) (empirically analysing the use of and selection criteria for different foresight methods).

[18] See Popper (n 17) 54–55.

innovative potential.[19] Often, foresight studies use a combination of literature review, futures workshops, scenario-building exercises, expert panels, surveys, and brainstorming.[20] In order to build scenarios, the organisers of foresight studies usually gather a group of experts. Depending on the goal of the study, the invitees can include scientists from a diverse set of fields, policymakers, but also key stakeholders, in order to reflect the differences between the sectors of society.[21] Some foresight studies of public entities also incorporate citizen participation.[22] The invited group usually tackles one central question, which narrows down the direction of inquiry and the relevant time frame, and thus shapes the outcome.[23] On this basis, the group members proceed through several rounds of brainstorming in which they are prompted to collect their knowledge, jointly to challenge their assumptions, and to develop ideas about potential trends and future developments.[24] Subsequently, the participants synthesise their findings and generate a variety of explorative scenarios of the future, often carving out the different constitutive dimensions of these scenarios.[25] Ultimately, the groups outline possible policy responses, compare their trade-offs and synergies, and prioritise between the underlying strategies.[26]

[19] Burrows and Gnad (n 6) 9.

[20] Popper (n 11) 69–81.

[21] Popper (n 17) 60; B Rasmussen, PD Andersen and K Borch, 'Managing Transdisciplinarity in Strategic Foresight' (2010) 19 *Creativity and Innovation Management* 37 (addressing the transdisciplinary nature of foresight); O Saritas, LA Pace and SIP Stalpers, 'Stakeholder Participation and Dialogue in Foresight' in K Borch, S Dingli and MS Jørgensen (eds), *Participation and Interaction in Foresight* (Cheltenham, Edward Elgar, 2013) (discussing stakeholder participation).

[22] The EU Joint Research Center conducted citizen workshops to explore 'The Future of Government 2030+', see L Vesnic-Alujevic et al, *The Future of Government 2030+: A Citizen Centric Perspective on New Government Models* (Luxemburg, Publications Office of the European Union, 2019); E Amanatidou, 'Beyond the Veil – The Real Value of Foresight' (2014) 87 *Technological Forecasting and Social Change* 274, 274–76 (stressing the participatory dimension of foresight); see also E Amanatidou, '"Foresight Process Impacts: Beyond Any Official Targets, Foresight Is Bound to Serve Democracy"' (2017) 85 *Futures* 1 (examining the participatory value of foresight); see also L Vesnic-Alujevic, 'Imagining Democratic Societies of the Future: Insights from a Foresight Study' (2021) 3 *Futures & Foresight Science* e60 (studying foresight created through citizen engagement).

[23] See Vesnic-Alujevic et al (n 22) (exploring: 'How will citizens, together with other actors, shape governments, policies and democracy in 2030 and beyond?'); see 'A strategic foresight study of the European information space in 2035', Annex to S Lewandowsky et al, 'Technology and Democracy. Understanding the Influence of Online Technologies on Political Behaviour and Decision-Making' (Luxembourg, Publications Office of the European Union, 2020) 113–39 (asking workshop participants 'to identify all the drivers of change that would affect the European information space over the next 15 years that they could think of').

[24] Popper (n 17) 55–56.

[25] C Bezold, 'Lessons from Using Scenarios for Strategic Foresight' (2010) 77 *Technological Forecasting and Social Change* 1513 (laying out experiences with scenario development); see generally T Durand, 'Scenarios as Knowledge Transformed into Strategic "Representations": The Use of Foresight Studies to Help Shape and Implement Strategy' in LA Costanzo and RB MacKay (eds), *Handbook of Research on Strategy and Foresight* (Cheltenham, Edward Elgar 2009).

[26] Oliveira et al (n 5) 2 (referencing the important role of 'assessing interlinkages, trade-offs and synergies between global targets[,] policy evaluation and design[, and] prioritization of … targets').

B. Caveats

Foresight studies are not a panacea. Indeed, their theoretical limitations have been widely discussed.[27] In the present context, I would merely like to point out one limitation of relying on foresight analysis, as well as one necessary assumption.

First, the limitation originates in the path dependence of foresight analysis. The outcome of a foresight study will always depend on the composition of the group asked to generate ideas, and on the specific question guiding the process. Both aspects are contingent on the overall goal an actor pursues through a concrete foresight study. Foresight is a means to an end. The reason why a certain institution – be it public or private, national or international, large or small – engages in foresight will influence which participants it invites and how it frames the central question. A biased selection of group members will usually lead to output that is biased as well – with regard to the trends identified, the scenarios created, and the potential policy responses suggested.[28] In particular, the output can reflect the deficits of an underrepresentation of experts with knowledge about certain regions, a lack of diversity, but also an imbalance in the representation of different industries. The initiator's policy preferences and goals also determine the time horizon, the subject matter, and the geographical focus of the core question. Moreover, the aim of foresight studies is not always open-ended, especially for the growing number of corporate foresight studies. Some actors might have already set the future direction of their policies in advance and employ foresight as a strategy for justifying the policy choices made. Foresight then creates a pretext on which these actors can rely when faced with criticism of their choices by presenting a future vision and tying to it a call for action. Without insight into these processes, it will be hard to detect the policy influence on foresight studies, which is why they need to be received with caution.

Second, constructing a constitutional projection on the building blocks of foresight relies on the assumption that the state of the world matters for the design of institutions. Foresight thus has to be able to inform policymaking and in turn impact institutional design, which both must be responsive to that influence. This interdependence will often already appear within the foresight scenarios. At least the studies used as reference points in this chapter (originating in the EU) largely assume a set of generic democratic institutions, which means that a possible

[27] A Fergnani and TJ Chermack, 'The Resistance to Scientific Theory in Futures and Foresight, and What to Do about It' (2021) 3 *Futures & Foresight Science* 1 (initiating a debate about the role of theory in the field of foresight); see also A Fergnani and TJ Chermack, 'Toward a Science of Futures and Foresight: Response to 10 Experts' Commentaries' (2021) 3 *Futures & Foresight Science* 1 (responding to criticism).

[28] Burrows and Gnad (n 6) 12, 14 (emphasising the importance of a heterogeneous group composition); A Bonaccorsi, R Apreda and G Fantoni, 'Expert Biases in Technology Foresight. Why They Are a Problem and How to Mitigate Them' (2020) 151 *Technological Forecasting and Social Change* 119855 (analysing expert biases in foresight).

democratic decay would deserve special attention. Nevertheless, I will assume that the (already diverging) constitutional frameworks will remain in place without major overhaul in the majority of countries throughout the next eight years, a time frame that is short enough to span just about two legislative periods in most systems.[29]

III. Impending Institutional Challenges

Two foresight reports of the EU will serve as starting points for the following analysis.[30] Both of them project real-world challenges and suggest possible policy solutions, which in turn will influence the make-up and design of the responsible governing institutions. From the scenarios these foresight reports outline, I will select three challenges that contain a powerful institutional dimension: climate change (A.), the technological transformation (B.), and democratic decline (C.). They all create a demand for smart institutional design strategies and therefore have reformative power for institutions. Notably, I will not outline substantive solutions to these developments. Therefore, questions such as which green policies would be feasible for various public actors will remain unanswered. Instead, the focus lies on the underlying institutional challenge, eg, the time inconsistency and intergenerational divide of policymaking.[31] Naturally, this focus omits many grave and urgent challenges directly affecting human well-being, such as global hunger, economic inequality, or war and terrorism.[32] These global problems mainly call for substantive solutions instead of changes to institutional design. Other important challenges will be neglected because they are as yet unknown or deemed unlikely to arise. A forecast in 2010 would have almost certainly disregarded a global pandemic occupying the world in 2020. The impact of the current COVID-19 pandemic will likely still be relevant in 2030. COVID-19 has caused an unexpected shock to institutions all around the globe. Since the virus itself will – hopefully – be more or less contained eight years from now, this pandemic is not among the challenges selected for closer inspection, but will rather serve as a reference point throughout the chapter. While it is a public-health crisis at heart, the COVID-19 pandemic has put a magnifying lens to the current deficiencies of our constitutional systems, among others the still insufficient digital and

[29] See ED Bó and M Rossi, 'Term Length and Political Performance' (Cambridge, National Bureau of Economic Research, 2008) w14511 26 (finding that the legislative term in most countries has a duration of four or five years).

[30] Commission, '2020 Strategic Foresight Report', COM (2020) 493 final; Commission, '2021 Strategic Foresight Report', COM (2021) 750 final.

[31] See above (n 1).

[32] See United Nations General Assembly, 'Transforming our world: the 2030 Agenda for Sustainable Development' (Resolution) A/RES/70/1 14–16, 21, 25–26 (Goals 2, 10, and 16).

information infrastructure in most countries, the increase of nationalist and populist forces, as well as a rise in science scepticism, fuelling a democratic decline.[33]

A. Climate Change

The arguably most pressing crisis throughout the next decade (and beyond) will be climate change. Combatting it is one of the Sustainable Development Goals of the United Nations and the European Union identifies it as one of four key global trends to account for when moving towards the year 2050.[34] Scientists warn that rapid action is crucial to curtail the worst consequences of global warming.[35] There is ample evidence to forecast the imminent and long-term serious consequences of climate change.[36] The certainty and gravity of this prediction exceed other expected crises. The consequences of climate change will severely impact the living conditions on this planet and cause global problems on a massive scale, among them hunger, death, mass migration, natural disasters and increasing extreme weather events, pollution, a destruction of ecosystems, and a loss of biodiversity.[37] The scientific background is both common knowledge and subject to populist denial.[38] Global warming is human-induced, its root cause lies in the increasing amount of CO_2 and methane emitted into the atmosphere.[39] Scientists warn that if not limited, ideally to a warming rate of 1.5°C compared to pre-industrial levels, global warming will cause irreversible damage.[40] Accordingly, the international

[33] S Faraj, W Renno and A Bhardwaj, 'Unto the Breach: What the COVID-19 Pandemic Exposes about Digitalization' (2021) 31 *Information and Organization* 1; P Guasti, 'The Impact of the COVID-19 Pandemic in Central and Eastern Europe. The Rise of Autocracy and Democratic Resilience' (2020) 7 *Democratic Theory* 47; R Brubaker, 'Paradoxes of Populism during the Pandemic' (2021) 164 *Thesis Eleven* 73; DA Stecula and M Pickup, 'How Populism and Conservative Media Fuel Conspiracy Beliefs about COVID-19 and What It Means for COVID-19 Behaviors' (2021) 8 *Research & Politics* 1.

[34] United Nations General Assembly, 'Transforming our world', A/RES/70/1 23 (Goal 13); Commission, '2021 Strategic Foresight Report, COM (2021) 750 final 1; see also United Nations Economist Network, 'Shaping the Trends of Our Time' (Report), 16 September 2020, 2, 7.

[35] Intergovernmental Panel on Climate Change (IPCC), 'Summary for Policymakers' in V Masson-Delmotte et al (eds), *Climate Change 2021: The Physical Science Basis. Contribution of Working Group I to the Sixth Assessment Report of the Intergovernmental Panel on Climate Change* (Switzerland, IPCC, 2021) 36–40.

[36] ibid 15–30.

[37] C Mbow et al, 'Food Security' in P Shukla et al (eds), *Climate Change and Land: an IPCC special report on climate change, desertification, land degradation, sustainable land management, food security, and greenhouse gas fluxes in terrestrial ecosystems* (2019).

[38] AM McCright and RE Dunlap, 'The Politicization of Climate Change and Polarization in the American Public's Views of Global Warming, 2001–2010' (2011) 52 *The Sociological Quarterly* 155; see generally S Lewandowsky et al, 'Misinformation and Its Correction: Continued Influence and Successful Debiasing' (2012) 13 *Psychological Science in the Public Interest* 106, 109–10, 113, 119–22, 124 (discussing the role of climate change misinformation).

[39] C Mbow et al (n 37) 5–14, 36–38.

[40] Intergovernmental Panel on Climate Change (IPCC), 'Global Warming of 1.5°C. An IPCC Special Report on the impacts of global warming of 1.5°C above pre-industrial levels and related global greenhouse gas emission pathways, in the context of strengthening the global response to the threat of climate change, sustainable development, and efforts to eradicate poverty' (2018).

Paris Agreement contains a commitment of its 195 signatories to 'Holding the increase in the global average temperature to well below 2°C above pre-industrial levels and pursuing efforts to limit the temperature increase to 1.5°C above pre-industrial levels'.[41] The countries' goal is 'to strengthen the global response to the threat of climate change, in the context of sustainable development and efforts to eradicate poverty'.[42] Policy action is needed to realise this commitment, most importantly a reduction of greenhouse gas emissions, inter alia, through a transition from coal and fossil-based energy sources to low carbon energy, mainly to renewable energy sources.[43]

Despite its specific, policy-centred nature, conquering climate change requires an institutional transformation that tackles the time inconsistency problem.[44] Just recently, the German Constitutional Court emphasised that a present inaction or hesitancy to cut CO_2 emissions 'pose[s] an irreversible legal risk to future freedom' and creates future costs.[45] Due to the large time span between the necessary action and its consequences, the climate crisis is an intergenerational issue. The constituency today is not identical with that of 2050 and beyond, who will suffer the consequences of the present inertia.[46] In general, this set-up is inclined to produce behavioural biases in decision-makers.[47] Most importantly, behavioural economics of intertemporal choice suggests that present bias, myopia, and the prevention paradox influence the commitment of today's legislators to obviating the climate emergency of the future.[48] This specific quality of climate change creates a demand for institutional solutions.[49]

[41] Paris Agreement to the United Nations Framework Convention on Climate Change, 12 December 2015, T.I.A.S. No. 16-1104 Art 2(1)(a).

[42] ibid Art 2(1).

[43] Commission, '2020 Strategic Foresight Report', COM (2020) 493 final 22 (mentioning other policy strategies, such as 'preserving biodiversity, developing a clean and circular economy, achieving a toxic-free environment').

[44] See generally B Harstad, 'Technology and Time Inconsistency' (2020) 128 *Journal of Political Economy* 2653, 2654–62 (addressing the time inconsistency problem in climate change mitigation).

[45] Bundesverfassungsgericht [German Federal Constitutional Court] [BVerfG], Order of the First Senate of 24 March 2021, 1 BvR 2656/18, available at www.bundesverfassungsgericht.de/SharedDocs/Entscheidungen/EN/2021/03/rs20210324_1bvr265618en.html, especially para 171, 182ff; see also K Pittel, 'The Intertemporal Distribution of Climate Policy Burdens and the Decision of the German Constitutional Court' (2021) 22 *CESifo Forum* 5 (discussing the 'intertemporal dimension of climate policy burdens').

[46] See, eg, BVerfG (n 45) paras 183, 192–93.

[47] See especially Lazarust (n 1) 1173–79.

[48] ibid 1173–79 (discussing the cognitive effects of myopia, procrastination, the availability and the representativeness heuristic); see also S Grünewald, 'Climate Change as a Systemic Risk – Are Macroprudential Authorities up to the Task?' (2020) 62 *EBI Working Paper Series* 1, 5; J Zhao and Y Luo, 'A Framework to Address Cognitive Biases of Climate Change' [2021] *Neuron* 1.

[49] See Lazarust (n 1) (arguing for 'design features' such as 'asymmetric precommitment strategies'); see also R Cunningham, 'Climate Change and Open Data: An Information Environmentalism Perspective' in M Rimmer (ed), *Intellectual Property and Clean Energy* (Singapore, Springer, 2018) (emphasising the importance of information for resolving climate change).

B. Technological Transformation

Currently, we are in the midst of a technological transformation with a profound impact on many areas of life. The EU Foresight Report 2021 includes it as one of the four 'structural global trends towards 2050'.[50] Digitalisation and automatisation transform entire industries, the working environment, and social connectivity. Even though all of these facets pose institutional challenges, I will focus on how the emergence of new information and communication technology transforms democratic behaviour and shapes demands on public institutions.

The last two decades have shown the potential, but also the dangers, of a rapidly developing online information sphere. While the online environment has made protests and mobilisation possible in many cases, the internet has not fulfilled its early promises of democratising the world.[51] Rather, it has brought many challenges that we are only beginning to understand. Today, the analogous and the digital world are inseparably intertwined. Both citizens and governments use the digital sphere for core democratic purposes.[52] Citizens inform themselves online, deliberate on a variety of topics especially on social media, interact with government officials, consume news, and contribute to political and social causes.[53] Correspondingly, political parties advertise online, and state institutions open up online avenues for citizen participation.[54] At the same time, the nature of digital communication creates new opportunities to interfere with democratically relevant processes. Threats stem not only from cyber-attacks by foreign or domestic state and non-state enemies,[55] but also from manipulation from within a political system. In particular, the architecture of social media creates an opportunity structure for disinformation, misinformation, threats to privacy, and discrimination, thus providing a channel for an unprecedented abuse of power and creating a fertile ground for sowing public distrust.[56] Due to the demands

[50] Commission, '2021 Strategic Foresight Report', COM (2021) 750 final 1, 3–4; see also Commission, '2020 Strategic Foresight Report' COM (2020) 493 final 29–30.

[51] See, eg, N Persily, 'Can Democracy Survive the Internet?' (2017) 28 *Journal of Democracy* 63, 71–72 (connecting democratic protests, such as the Arab Spring demonstrations, with the US presidential campaign of Donald Trump); see also JT Jost et al, 'How Social Media Facilitates Political Protest: Information, Motivation, and Social Networks: Social Media and Political Protest' (2018) 39 *Political Psychology* 85 (portraying the potential of online fora to foster protest).

[52] See US Supreme Court, *Packingham v North Carolina*, 137 S. Ct. 1730, 1735 (2017), Justice AM Kennedy (writing: 'While in the past there may have been difficulty in identifying the most important places (in a spatial sense) for the exchange of views, today the answer is clear. It is cyberspace – the "vast democratic forums of the Internet" in general [...] and social media in particular.').

[53] JM Balkin, 'The First Amendment Is an Information Policy' (2012) 41 *Hofstra Law Review* 1, 9 (stating that democratic behaviour consists of 'interconnected activities: deliberating, debating, spreading information, organizing like-minded individuals, forming and maintaining political parties and civil society organizations, protesting, petitioning, picketing, voting in elections, and governing').

[54] Lewandowsky et al (n 23) 73, 84.

[55] See Commission, '2020 Strategic Foresight Report', COM (2020) 493 final 30; Commission, '2021 Strategic Foresight Report', COM (2021) 750 final 4.

[56] L Frischlich and E Humprecht, 'Trust, Democratic Resilience, and the Infodemic' (2021) *Policy Paper Series*, Israel Public Policy Institute.

of the attention economy, both information acquisition and content creation occur under a completely different framework than they did just 20 years ago.[57] Content is increasingly designed to attract attention and generate more clicks and engagement.[58] Highly polarising content is therefore valuable because it is capable of triggering intense reactions.[59] Information acquisition is driven by algorithms, which can microtarget individuals for commercial, but also political purposes.[60] This endangers data privacy, but also opens the floodgates for manipulative behaviour that is practically almost invisible to the individual user.[61] In response, digital literacy and resilience to disinformation and manipulation become increasingly important for citizens.[62] Public institutions at large are so far still struggling to tackle this set of problems. In particular, attempts to regulate the global private companies that govern the social communication space are still being tried and tested.[63]

Moreover, public institutions have mostly shied away from using digital technology to their advantage and creating an inclusive, informative, and trustworthy information space. Generally, they have already failed at establishing a digital information infrastructure that can accommodate the rapidly growing amount of available data. The recent COVID-19 pandemic has highlighted this deficit both with regard to data availability and accessibility.[64] Demands for increased access to data has, time and time again, met the pushback of public institutions. The constitutional importance of these challenges creates a stark demand for improved institutional design.

C. Democratic Decline

A third institutional challenge is the development towards democratic decline, sometimes even coined democratic decay.[65] A long line of literature already

[57] Lewandowsky et al (n 23) 15–16, 22–23, 27–38.

[58] ibid 5, 49–50, 62.

[59] ibid 5, 50.

[60] FJ Zuiderveen Borgesius et al, 'Online Political Microtargeting: Promises and Threats for Democracy' (2018) 14 *Utrecht Law Review* 82; D Susser, B Roessler and HF Nissenbaum, 'Online Manipulation: Hidden Influences in a Digital World' (2018) 4 *Georgetown Law Technology Review* 1; A Kozyreva, S Lewandowsky and R Hertwig, 'Citizens Versus the Internet: Confronting Digital Challenges With Cognitive Tools' (2020) 21 *Psychological Science in the Public Interest* 103, 117; see also Lewandowsky et al (n 23) 5, 29–34, 99.

[61] Lewandowsky et al (n 23) 29–34.

[62] Kozyreva, Lewandowsky and Hertwig (n 60) 104–05, 136–41; Frischlich and Humprecht (n 56) 5, 22.

[63] See, eg, Commission, 'Proposal for a Regulation of the European Parliament and of the Council on contestable and fair markets in the digital sector (Digital Markets Act)' (Communication) COM (2020) 842 final.

[64] Commission, '2020 Strategic Foresight Report', COM (2020) 493 final 30–31.

[65] See especially TG Daly, 'Democratic Decay: Conceptualising an Emerging Research Field' (2019) 11 *Hague Journal on the Rule of Law* 9; see also J Gerschewski, 'Erosion or Decay? Conceptualizing

diagnoses this global problem of constitutionalism that affects many different countries.[66] Aziz Z. Huq and Tom Ginsburg describe two types of threats that constitutional liberal democracies can face, 'authoritarian reversion' in the sense of a 'collapse into authoritarianism' and 'constitutional retrogression', which consists of 'incremental changes to legal regimes and institutions'.[67] Notably, it is only the latter development that the strategies suggested below could remedy.

The symptoms of such democratic decline are manifold. Most importantly, they include an erosion in the protection of human rights and a weakening of the rule of law, two of the most basic commitments of constitutionalism.[68] Institutions that are supposed to safeguard democracy are faced with populist political pressure and growing extremism.[69] The destructive forces can stem from inside and outside of the respective system. Institutions, of course, do not exist in a void, but in some ways exhibit signs of the underlying tensions within the constituency of a given system. Growing distrust of public actors and the media, populist movements, racism, and rising economic inequality all seem to contribute to some extent to democratic decline.[70] Certainly, part of the solution will lie in addressing these problematic circumstances directly.[71] Yet, I suggest that certain instruments of institutional design may prove to be helpful to push back against democratic decline. Some crises can put additional erosive pressure on constitutional systems, for instance the Great Recession and the COVID-19 pandemic, so that institutional solutions to these crises simultaneously aid the overall democratic health of institutions.[72]

Causes and Mechanisms of Democratic Regression' (2021) 28 *Democratization* 43; B Bugarič, 'Central Europe's Descent into Autocracy: A Constitutional Analysis of Authoritarian Populism' (2019) 17 *International Journal of Constitutional Law* 597 (studying, i.a., Hungary and Poland); T Drinóczi and A Bień-Kacała, 'Illiberal Constitutionalism: The Case of Hungary and Poland' (2019) 20 *German Law Journal* 1140 (studying Hungary and Poland); P Guasti, 'Populism in Power and Democracy: Democratic Decay and Resilience in the Czech Republic (2013–2020)' (2020) 8 *Politics and Governance* 473 (studying the Czech Republic); R Markowski, 'Plurality Support for Democratic Decay: The 2019 Polish Parliamentary Election' (2020) 43 *West European Politics* 1513 (studying Poland); GW Shin, 'South Korea's Democratic Decay' (2020) 31 *Journal of Democracy* 100 (studying South Korea).

[66] S Levitsky and D Ziblatt, *How Democracies Die* (London, Crown Publishing, 2019); T Ginsburg and AZ Huq, *How to Save a Constitutional Democracy* (Chicago, University of Chicago Press, 2018); MA Graber, S Levinson and M Tushnet (eds), *Constitutional Democracy in Crisis?* (New York, Oxford University Press, 2018).

[67] AZ Huq and T Ginsburg, 'How to Lose a Constitutional Democracy' (2018) 65 *UCLA Law Review* 78, 92–99.

[68] ibid 83, 87–89, 96 (focusing on three elements: 'elections, speech and association rights, and the rule of law').

[69] JL Cohen, 'Populism and the Politics of Resentment' (2019) 1 *Jus Cogens* 5.

[70] See generally D King and RM Smith, 'Populism, Racism, and the Rule of Law in Constitutional Democracies Today', in Graber, Levinson and Tushnet (eds) (n 66) (discussing populism in constitutional democracies); see also S Ganesh, 'Economic Inequality and Constitutional Democracy' in Graber, Levinson and Tushnet (eds) (n 66) (explaining why inequality matters).

[71] See, eg, Commission, 'On the European democracy action plan' (Communication) COM (2020) 790 final.

[72] See MA Graber, S Levinson and M Tushnet, 'Constitutional Democracy in Crisis?: Introduction' in Graber, Levinson and Tushnet (eds) (n 66) 3–4.

All of these developments test the resilience of current constitutional systems and their institutions, sometimes with sobering results. Democratic decline often festers below the surface. During the Trump presidency, many deficiencies of the US political system came to light that were previously hidden under a veil of compliance with informal constitutional practices guiding and restraining the behaviour of those in power. Against that general backdrop, it will be one of the major challenges for countries around the world to build or rebuild responsive democratic institutions that can withstand these pressures in the future and save constitutional democracies already in decline.[73]

IV. Resilient Institutional Design

These impending challenges call for resilient institutional design. This constitutes the key thesis of the following part. Developing ideas about how to strengthen institutions so they are prepared to meet the future challenges is a task for scholars of constitutionalism. As Mark Graber points out, '[t]he design of governing institutions is particularly important for securing constitutional purposes that require government choices among competing policies, none of which are prohibited by the constitutional text.'[74] Similarly, policymaking institutions are well aware of the importance of resilient institutions in preparing for the future.[75] The EU Foresight Report 2020 defines resilience as 'the ability not only to withstand and cope with challenges but also to undergo transitions in a sustainable, fair, and democratic manner'.[76] The report relates resilience to an analysis of an institution's capacity and vulnerability with regard to current challenges, such as 'the green and digital transition'.[77] The report, however, does not detail specific mechanisms and instruments that institutions have to be endowed with or establish in order to become more resilient. Law, and in particular constitutional law, plays a major role in generating, shaping, and safeguarding institutional resilience.[78]

[73] See generally Ginsburg and Huq (n 66).

[74] MA Graber, *A New Introduction to American Constitutionalism* (Oxford, Oxford University Press, 2013) 224. See also ibid 51 (demanding that 'Governing institutions must be carefully designed because many constitutional purposes cannot be directly secured by constitutional law, fiat, or exhortation').

[75] See only Commission, '2021 Strategic Foresight Report', COM (2021) 750 final 20 (listing 'strengthening the resilience of institutions' as one of ten future goals); see also Commission, '2021 Strategic Foresight Report', COM (2020) 493 final 2–3, 5–7 (declaring resilience as the 'central theme' and 'new compass').

[76] Commission, '2021 Strategic Foresight Report', COM (2020) 493 final 2, 6; see W Merkel and A Lührmann, 'Resilience of Democracies: Responses to Illiberal and Authoritarian Challenges' (2021) 28 *Democratization* 869, 871–74 (understanding resilience as a system's ability 'to withstand [challenges, stresses, and assault] without changes, to adapt through internal changes, and to recover without losing the democratic character of its regime and its constitutive core institutions, organizations, and processes'); see also TL Humby, 'Law and Resilience: Mapping the Literature' (2014) 4 *Seattle Journal of Environmental Law* 85, 99–104 (summarising the legal literature on resilience).

[77] Commission, '2021 Strategic Foresight Report', COM (2020) 493 final 2, 41.

[78] JB Ruhl, B Cosens and N Soininen, 'Resilience of Legal Systems. Toward Adaptive Governance' in M Ungar (ed), *Multisystemic Resilience* (Oxford, Oxford University Press, 2021) 512–14.

Resilient institutions are capable of providing stability reliably when facing volatile situations.[79] Against this backdrop, I will discuss three different institutional strategies that could increase the resilience of the legislature and the executive as the main policymaking governing branches. Incorporating these features could strengthen democracies and help them overcome the hurdles ahead, even though the individual contributions will be modest and their success will depend on the specific context of their implementation.[80]

All of the strategies centre around the fundamental role of information for policymaking institutions. Legislative as well as executive bodies around the world have a growing need for data that can form the basis for solving the complex challenges and crises they face. Moreover, both branches constantly generate new insights with each law they enact, as long as they pay attention to the experiences made with the application of the legal rules. These feedback loops provide an opportunity for them to scrutinise and improve policy choices. This link between rulemaking and information also fulfils an important accountability function. Counter-majoritarian forces can use the information generated to hold the legislature and the executive responsible for their policy choices. Moreover, acting upon a reliable empirical basis enables the policymakers to counter populist narratives.

Yet, the current integration of information leaves a lot to be desired in most jurisdictions. Legislatures and rulemaking agencies often fail to elucidate their epistemological interest, their underlying assumptions, their data-generation process, and the influence of different pieces of information. While lawmaking is – and needs to remain – an inherently political task, and democratic decision-making is not very conducive to a strict implementation of knowledge, the legislature and the executive sometimes commit themselves to explicitly rest their lawmaking efforts on an empirical basis. In the following part, I first suggest deepening these efforts by adding the instrument of legislative experimentation to the toolbox (A.). Due to the benefits and potential of legislative experimentation, I also predict a rise of such forms of rulemaking in the upcoming decade. A second and complementary strategy addresses the availability of information. Digital technology simplifies the collection, storage, and distribution of large amounts of data. This potential will likely only increase throughout the next decade. Legally establishing a resilient public information infrastructure could be a crucial step towards safeguarding the publicity of government data necessary for addressing upcoming challenges, such as climate change, and for holding public actors accountable (B.). Third, the technological transformation provides an opportunity for policymaking bodies to become more responsive to its citizens. Digital technology can provide the necessary infrastructure for creating a communicative

[79] Merkel and Lührmann (n 76) 827, 874 (taking a functionalist perspective).

[80] C Möllers, 'Separation of Powers' in R Masterman and R Schütze (eds), *The Cambridge Companion to Comparative Constitutional Law* (2019) 253–54 (stressing the importance of context-specificity and modesty).

space that allows citizens to interact and deliberate.[81] Generally, the democratic importance of citizen participation is well-recognised and studied.[82] However, legal studies on the design of participatory instruments often lack a behavioural perspective, which could make an important contribution to creating a productive and pro-social participatory online environment (C.). Ultimately, it is in these three directions that I see potential for reform that uses the insights created by the study of (comparative) constitutionalism.

A. Legislative Experimentation

The call for legislative experimentalism is not new,[83] although it has not gained much traction over the last few years. In light of the aforementioned challenges, this potent tool of policymaking should gain new momentum going forward, and I predict that it will.[84] The technological transformation will both facilitate legislative experiments and create a demand for them. Experiments are valuable for providing information in situations of high uncertainty. The current push towards the use of sandbox regulation as an instrument to identify effective regulatory policies, particularly in the realm of the fintech industry, could spark a renewed interest in the potential of legislative experimentation.[85] Moreover, the COVID-19 pandemic painfully illustrates the pitfalls of iterative policymaking without sufficient empirical knowledge.

When legislatures face new crises under high uncertainty, where no tried-and-tested policy approach exists, they compare different possible strategies in order to find a response that promises to manage the situation successfully and complies with the policy preferences of the governing parties.[86] If the politically preferred approach fails to deliver the desired results, public decision-makers often update their evaluation and proceed to the next strategy.

[81] See J Habermas, 'Überlegungen und Hypothesen zu einem erneuten Strukturwandel der politischen Öffentlichkeit' in M Seeliger and S Sevignani (eds), *Ein neuer Strukturwandel der Öffentlichkeit? (Leviathan Sonderband 37)* (Baden-Baden, Nomos, 2021) 487–99.

[82] See generally H Landemore, *Open Democracy. Reinventing Popular Rule for the Twenty-First Century* (Princeton, Princeton University Press, 2020).

[83] See especially M Abramowicz, I Ayres and Y Listokin, 'Randomizing Law' (2011) 159 *University of Pennsylvania Law Review* 929; S Ranchordás, 'The Whys and Woes of Experimental Legislation' (2013) 1 *The Theory and Practice of Legislation* 415; CV Chien, 'Rigorous Policy Pilots: Experimentation in the Administration of the Law' (2019) 104 *Iowa Law Review* 2313 (arguing in favour of increased experimentation); LL Ouellette, 'Patent Experimentalism' (2015) 101 *Virginia Law Review* 65 (arguing for experimentation in patent law).

[84] See JJ Rachlinski, 'Evidence-Based Law' (2011) 96 *Cornell Law Review* 901 (making a comparable, albeit more general prediction a decade ago).

[85] See generally S Ranchordás, 'Experimental Regulations for AI: Sandboxes for Morals and Mores' (2021) 1 *Morals and Machines* 1.

[86] C Coglianese and J D'Ambrosio, 'Policymaking Under Pressure: The Perils of Incremental Responses to Climate Change' (2008) 40 *Connecticut Law Review* 1411 (criticising experimentalism on the basis of likening it with incremental change).

An obvious illustration is the COVID-19 pandemic, where this consecutive approach became the standard operating procedure globally, first on an executive and later on a legislative level.[87] The successes and failures of different COVID-19 policies ignited a learning process that lasted probably throughout the first year of the pandemic – exemplified by frequent updates of legislative measures.[88] However, this method can only generate limited insight as to the comparative advantages of each policy, because the outcome of policies might depend on their particular context or their ordering, and any counterfactual argument remains speculative.

In general, legislatures have tried to overcome these obstacles through so-called experimental legislation. Experimental laws aim at assessing one particular legal strategy and typically display two features.[89] They enact a set of rules for a specific amount of time, often enforced through a sunset clause that automatically reverts the law back to its former status quo unless the legislature actively decides to make the rules permanent (or to extend the sunset period).[90] In addition to the limited time frame, the experimental law usually contains an evaluation mandate, which outlines when and how to assess the performance of that law.[91] However, experimental legislation – as the term is commonly used – usually fails to apply experimental methodology in a stricter empirical sense.[92] Therefore, the empirical insights generated suffer from similar limitations to those in regular lawmaking, even though a sunset clause can be a suitable enforcement mechanism and an evaluation clause demands an explicit assessment according to a predetermined goal.

An empirical method well-suited to finding answers to the pertinent questions is experimentation stricto sensu. Legislatures can resort to experimental methods, when appropriate, in order to strengthen the effectiveness of lawmaking and to increase accountability.[93] Experimentation in the formal sense is different from the trial-and-error strategy of policymaking, highlighted above. Instead of enacting laws and evaluating them in consecutive steps, experimental methods

[87] See R Cormacain and I Bar-Siman-Tov (eds), 'Global Legislative Responses to Coronavirus' (2020) 8 *The Theory and Practice of Legislation Issue* 3 (detailing the legislative measures); see R Cormacain, 'Keeping Covid-19 Emergency Legislation Socially Distant from Ordinary Legislation: Principles for the Structure of Emergency Legislation' (2020) 8 *The Theory and Practice of Legislation* 245, 252–55, 260–62 (emphasising the necessity of a temporary emergency legislation).

[88] See, eg, E Griglio, 'Parliamentary Oversight under the Covid-19 Emergency: Striving against Executive Dominance' (2020) 8 *The Theory and Practice of Legislation* 49, 53–55.

[89] See, eg, L Mader, 'Evaluating the Effects: A Contribution to the Quality of Legislation' (2001) 22 *Statute Law Review* 119, 125; ZJ Gubler, 'Experimental Rules' (2014) 55 *Boston College Law Review* 129, 141.

[90] S Ranchordás, *Constitutional Sunset and Experimental Legislation. A Comparative Perspective* (Cheltenham, Edward Elgar, 2014) 7–9, 17–77.

[91] See Mader (n 89) (discussing the role of evaluation in legislation).

[92] Abramowicz, Ayres and Listokin (n 83) 938–39.

[93] See Abramowicz, Ayres and Listokin (n 83) (making a strong argument for randomised experiments in law); see also Chien (n 83) (referring to experimental methods as 'rigorous policy pilots').

require the legislature to create a treatment and a control group (ideally through random draw), and to enact a specific legal rule only applicable to the former.[94] There are two main ways in which a legislature can set up such an experiment in a separation of powers system.[95] The legislature can experiment through self-enforcing laws and it can delegate the (limited) power to experiment in a given policy area to certain executive agencies.[96] The allocation of powers between states in a federalist system, or between municipalities more generally, creates further opportunities for experimentation. However, it is not enough merely to rely on the fact that states or municipalities will often choose different policy responses to similar problems because the underlying self-selection of these policies prevents the necessary randomisation.[97] Instead, the states or municipalities could commit themselves to becoming actual laboratories by mutually agreeing to participate in a legal experiment and enact certain rules when randomly selected for the treatment group.[98]

The most straightforward way of experimentally testing a legal instrument is to apply it randomly only to a subset of the entire population of cases and to leave the rest as an untreated control group. A new traffic rule could, for instance, apply only to a few randomly chosen areas or highways – the rulemaking body could then evaluate the effects of such a rule through a comparison to the non-treated areas or highways amounting to the control group.[99] Again, sunset clauses could help enforce this strategy in that the policy change would revert back to the former status quo after a certain period of time has elapsed, and the rulemaking body could decide anew whether to implement a broad policy covering all potential cases, or enter into a second phase of testing a modified policy.[100] One of the main prerequisites of this experimentation is also of legal value as it increases legal certainty and encourages deliberation: it is crucial that the experiment pursues a specific goal that guides the hypothesis to be tested and provides the basis for the subsequent evaluation.

Many concerns have been raised against randomising laws.[101] The most fundamental objection concerns the position of humans affected by the experiments of state actors. When public institutions rely on their authority to conduct the experiment, the affected people have not explicitly consented to their participation, either in the treatment or the control group. This could both violate their

[94] Abramowicz, Ayres and Listokin (n 83) 934–46 (explaining the power of randomisation).

[95] cp DJ Greiner and A Matthews, 'Randomized Control Trials in the United States Legal Profession' (2016) 12 *Annual Review of Law and Social Science* 295 (analysing random control trials of decisions by lawyers and judges).

[96] Abramowicz, Ayres and Listokin (n 83) 933–34, 979–87.

[97] ibid 947.

[98] ibid 948.

[99] Speed limits are an often-used example for a feasible experiment: see, eg, ibid 951, 955, 960, 961–62, 967, 976–77; Gubler (n 83) 136–137; Ranchordás (n 83) 418–419.

[100] cp Gubler (n 83) 130–131 (emphasising the value of sunset clauses for experimental laws).

[101] See Abramowicz, Ayres and Listokin (n 83) 948–60 (discussing statistical limitations).

right to equal treatment and objectify the involuntary human participants.[102] The principle of equality generally demands that like cases be treated alike unless there is a sufficient justification for a differentiation. Judicial scrutiny is generally stricter when the legislative experiment limits the exercise of fundamental rights. Even though the experiment is supposed to bring informational benefits, it offers no substantive reason for treating the treatment group worse than the control group due to its random design. Therefore, it will be difficult to justify randomly subjecting individuals to an intervention that burdens their rights.[103] Nevertheless, there remains sufficient room for experimentation. First, the legislature could award people with a favourable treatment, eg, by randomly selecting individuals for a more lenient instead of a more stringent application of the law (eg, lowering the administrative burden on companies or easing the tax filing requirements for citizens) or by distributing scarce resources to a randomly selected group.[104] Then, the informational benefits of the policy experiment offer a rational basis to justify why some individuals do not receive the benefits because randomisation is an important feature to produce the relevant information.[105] Second, a policy experiment could require prior consent of individuals to participate in the random draw and its consequences.[106] Third, experimentation remains possible in areas unprotected by fundamental rights, such as policy changes to internal rules governing administrative (or judicial) organisation or procedure.[107] Fourth, informational interventions that do not restrict the exercise of rights, such as varying the order of paragraphs in letters accompanying individual administrative decisions, do not violate the equal protection principle.[108] No unequal treatment even exists in the first place, when the treatment and the control group consist of the constituents of different lawmaking entities (in particular of different states). When different state legislatures coordinate so that both agree to be randomly assigned to the treatment or control group, the legal intervention can even fulfil the condition of randomness (albeit with a small sample size).

Another legal requirement lies in the principle of proportionality (where applicable). An intervention complies with the principle of proportionality, even if later evidence proves the earlier assumptions to be factually wrong.

[102] ibid 963–74; Ranchordás (n 83) 437–38 (discussing the principle of equal treatment).

[103] But see Chien (n 83) 2327–28 (providing an overview of US court cases upholding experimental rules challenged on equal protection grounds).

[104] See Abramowicz, Ayres and Listokin (n 83) 987–1001 (providing examples of actual and potential experiments).

[105] See ibid 968, 973–74.

[106] Chien (n 83) 2324–25; Abramowicz, Ayres and Listokin (n 83) 966–67.

[107] See Chien (n 83) 2323–24; see Ranchordás (n 83) 438 (discussing a case of the Portuguese Constitutional Court on judicial procedure).

[108] cp T Kosonen and O Ropponen, 'The Role of Information in Tax Compliance: Evidence from a Natural Field Experiment' (2015) 129 *Economics Letters* 18 (undertaking a field experiment in behavioural economics in which tax authorities send letters with varying information); cp also KM Bott et al, 'You've Got Mail: A Randomized Field Experiment on Tax Evasion' (2020) 66 *Management Science* 2801.

A temporary legislative inaction regarding the control group could only be disproportionate if there existed a corresponding public duty to act – in which case an experiment would not be appropriate. However, most often, the legislative margin of discretion also covers the legislative decision to invest the time to collect data on the proportionality of a specific legal instrument. The availability of the instrument of legal experimentation could then also impact the standard of judicial review for courts testing the proportionality of legal interventions that would be suitable for experimentation. Having the tool of legislative experimentalism more readily available would mean that the legislature (and the courts in their review) could rely on the data generated to justify retaining, abandoning, or modifying a particular rule. While some emphasise that this should increase deference towards experimental rules,[109] it could simultaneously intensify the burden of substantiation for some non-experimental rules, because the legislature would need to explain why it decided against a possible experimentation.[110]

Ultimately, legal systems leave room for experimentation (absent specific prohibitions). Despite a general hesitancy toward legal experimentation of rule-makers and legal scholars alike, successful cases exist that have not raised serious constitutional opposition. For instance, the German state of Bavaria wanted to test whether limiting the citizens' option to seek inner administrative review before going to court would be efficient. Therefore, the Bavarian legislature largely abolished the inner-administrative review procedure in only one of its seven districts in order to compare the outcomes (albeit without a random selection), which was upheld by the Bavarian Constitutional Court.[111] The legislatively guided rollout of vaccines in response to the COVID-19 pandemic would have been an ideal candidate for experimental interventions making use of the plethora of insights into effective instruments provided by the behavioural sciences.[112] Moreover, when limited funds are distributed with an element of chance, this randomisation could be exploited to test the effects of that funding (or its conditions). Experimental legislation could be a useful tool to tackle pressing challenges, such as identifying effective instruments for reducing CO_2 emissions to combat climate change. Companies might even be willing to participate voluntarily in legislative programmes in exchange for the positive publicity that such participation could entail.[113]

[109] Gubler (n 83) 163–65, 173–78.

[110] See Ouellette (n 83) 110–11 with fn 180; see also Chien (n 83) 2328, 2332.

[111] Bayerischer Verfassungsgerichtshof [Bavarian Constitutional Court], Decision of 15 November 2006, 6-VII-05, 12-VII-05.

[112] M Patel, 'Test Behavioural Nudges to Boost COVID Immunization' (2021) 590 *Nature* 185; R Schmidt and K Stenger, 'Behavioral Brittleness: The Case for Strategic Behavioral Public Policy' [2021] *Behavioural Public Policy* 1; see NT Brewer et al, 'Increasing Vaccination: Putting Psychological Science Into Action' (2017) 18 *Psychological Science in the Public Interest* 149 (writing prior to the COVID-19 pandemic).

[113] See Abramowicz, Ayres and Listokin (n 83) 1003–04 (proposing that US Congress create an 'opt-in' system for companies to commit to fair employment).

The legislature could use experimentalism as a commitment to empirical knowledge and demonstrate the courage of publicly trying to find the right policy solution, thereby making the cost and benefit assessments much more salient. The responses to the coronavirus pandemic could have benefitted much from such an approach. Instead, the main data points came from country-to-country comparisons, where so many variables were different that it was hard actually to evaluate the comparative effectiveness of the policy interventions. In cases like this, experimental proposals could actively take advantage of the characteristics of federalism and local governance and promote cooperative public policymaking. Moreover, experimentation provides the opportunity to bridge ideological disagreement and counter populist narratives by creating an empirical basis for policy initiatives.[114] Lastly, the empirical value of legislative experimentation and the required ex ante commitment have the potential to help overcome the intertemporal divide often complicating the present solution of future problems. Overall, carefully implemented, legislative experimentation could ultimately make legislative and administrative policymaking more resilient.

B. Publicity of Data

Institutions show their resilience in being responsive and accountable to their citizens. Moreover, a democracy relies upon the ability of its citizens to access the necessary information to hold public institutions accountable. One important element to promote these goals is the publicity of governmental data. Citizens, as well as the media, need to be able to access data about the behaviour of public actors, their decisions, but also the empirical bases for their actions.[115] Therefore, the central postulation is transparency, which includes making data and information readily available and accessible.[116] Public communication, ie, 'the intentional release of information' and its mediation, should only supplement, not substitute the immediate access to information.[117] Otherwise, accountability will always be limited to the narrative that the public institutions themselves provide.[118] Ultimately, public actors, in particular the legislature and the executive, have to find ways to guarantee transparency.

The first step in creating a system equipped to ensure transparency consists of making data available and granting access to it. Constitutional law does not

[114] Ranchordás (n 83) 434.

[115] N Cortez, 'Information Mischief Under the Trump Administration' (2019) 94 *Chicago-Kent Law Review* 315, 318.

[116] ibid 318–19.

[117] D Curtin, '"Accountable Independence" of the European Central Bank: Seeing the Logics of Transparency' (2017) 23 *European Law Journal* 28, 32–34, 43; see Cortez (n 115) 319–21 (distinguishing between information and messaging).

[118] Curtin (n 117) 32.

offer much guidance as to how to collect and handle information within state organisations. The relevant statutes in different jurisdictions seem to assume the existence of data as a side product of policymaking and fail to address the pertinent questions raised by the ongoing technological transformation.[119] If at all, it is administrative rules that govern the details of the accumulation and archival of data; often, however, there is little more than inner-administrative practice guiding the process.[120] Recently, the Trump presidency brought attention to the constitutional importance of these inner-administrative processes of data generation, storage, and access. Shortly after US President Donald Trump took office in 2016, several executive agencies removed politically unfeasible information, both governmental and scientific data, from the public sphere by deleting the corresponding content from public websites.[121] In particular, the administration removed an entire section with information about the scientific background of climate change from the Environmental Protection Agency's website.[122] Moreover, the Trump administration reduced the amount of data it provided in some cases. For instance, the FBI's Crime in the United States report, published in 2017, omitted previously published 'homicide data on the relationship between victims and offenders; the age, sex, and race of victims and offenders; and what types of weapons were used in the crimes'.[123]

A related question pertains to the storage of digital data, in particular the data generated through the government's presence on social media, such as Donald Trump's then-infamous Twitter account. The applicable rules for data preservation often still rely on the now antiquated model of physically filing paper products and saving them from destruction, which does not translate well to the transient nature of digital information.[124] The social media presence of government officials creates substantive content alongside a continuous stream of metadata on user activity and engagement.[125] Developing a reliable way to store this data must take into account the technical capacities and limitations of the different platforms, as well as their respective terms of service.[126] I predict that

[119] The US legislation is rather extensive in comparison, see M Fenster, 'Populism and Transparency: The Political Core of an Administrative Norm' (2021) 89 *University of Cincinnati Law Review* 236, 301–02 (providing an overview of US laws governing information policy); see also Cortez (n 115) 319, 339–45.

[120] See, eg, Cortez (n 115) 322–24 (discussing the regulation via executive memoranda during the Obama administration in the US).

[121] ibid 326–30 (listing several of such removal initiatives); RL Glicksman, 'Shuttered Government' (2020) 62 *Arizona Law Review* 573, 601.

[122] Cortez (n 115) 332–35.

[123] KA Flynn and CJ Hartnett, 'Cutting through the Fog. Government Information, Librarians, and the Forty-Fifth Presidency' (2018) 57 *Reference & User Services Quarterly* 208, 210–11.

[124] KB Cornelius and IV Pasquetto, '"What Data?" Records and Data Policy Coordination During Presidential Transitions', in G Chowdhury et al (eds), *Transforming Digital Worlds* (Cham, Springer, 2018) 160–61.

[125] A Acker and A Kriesberg, 'Tweets May Be Archived: Civic Engagement, Digital Preservation and Obama White House Social Media Data' (2017) 54 *Proceedings of the Association for Information Science and Technology* 1.

[126] See ibid (discussing the problems of a digital preservation of social media data).

we will see various technical initiatives to find ways of preserving this type of data accompanied by new legal frameworks in the near future. In reaction to the incidences described above, a countermovement has already emerged, in which civil-society activists get involved in downloading and storing governmental data to secure future public access and remove the existing data from the mercy of the officials in charge.[127] A growing number of private entities collect and publish the information on their own websites and become a valuable source of information.[128] Despite the US-centric nature of these examples, the underlying challenges are not specific to US public law, but arise in a similar fashion in other jurisdictions.[129]

Protecting information for the future should be viewed as a constitutional issue of resilient democracy. Creating a reliable information infrastructure that protects data from the interference of future governments is a crucial undertaking that has to be based on the constitutional guarantee of democracy. It requires a formalisation of core archival rules and practices to create a resilient legal information framework that transcends political change.[130] Potentially, an independent fourth-branch actor could serve as a guardian.[131]

Moreover, public institutions will need to find better ways to provide access to trustworthy information to the public and communicate with citizens. This could compensate the growing tendency of media companies to provide content that gathers attention rather than giving information.[132] However, transparency legislation is often deficient, mostly because it includes loopholes that secretive governments could exploit. Thus, freedom-of-information laws need to be strengthened and a comparative analysis provides a rich portfolio of potential instruments. In particular, freedom-of-information laws should assume that (at least newer) data is stored digitally, so that the agency cannot deny access to information requests of citizens on technical grounds. Moreover, these laws should emphasise the democratic nature of the requests for access to data. For instance, one promising element that might be adopted transnationally is the 'rule of three' included in the US Freedom of Information Act (FOIA).[133] It states that any time an executive agency is asked thrice to disclose certain information,

[127] Cortez (n 115) 346–48; Cornelius and Pasquetto (n 124) 158; M Manoff, 'Archival Silence in the Age of Trump' (2017) *Keynote presentation at ARCHIVE Symposium* 7–11.

[128] See, eg, the 'FOIA project' in the US context: www.foiaproject.org (accessed 20 October 2021).

[129] See DE Pozen, 'Freedom of Information Beyond the Freedom of Information Act' (2017) 165 *University of Pennsylvania Law Review* 1097, 1105–06 (describing the character of FOIA as a role-model).

[130] Flynn and Hartnett (n 123).

[131] See M Karanicolas and MB Kwoka, 'Overseeing Oversight' (2021) *SSRN Electronic Journal* 26–35 (providing an international comparison of oversight models); see also D Thaw, 'Administrative Truth: Comments on Cortez's *Information Mischief*' (2019) 94 *Chicago-Kent Law Review* 607, 613.

[132] Lewandowsky et al (n 23) 27–29.

[133] Freedom of Information Act of 5 July 1967, Public Law 89-487, Statutes at Large 80 Stat. 250.

it must do so publicly.[134] Furthermore, when enforcing freedom-of-information provisions, courts should be allowed and encouraged to inspect the relevant data *in camera*.[135] Beyond concrete judicial disputes, an independent fourth-branch actor could oversee the potential declassification and publication of data in general, especially since the character of information can change and its value decrease over time, which calls for periodic reviews.[136] Additionally, the respective laws could shift the costs of providing information onto the public agencies and limit their option to refuse access to information because of an undue burden on them,[137] thereby creating an incentive for better data storage and a more proactive approach to transparency.[138] Lastly, creating meta transparency, ie, publishing details about the data and documents that exist within the state, could be an important mechanism that is so far rarely utilised. Meta transparency can equip citizens with sufficient knowledge to ask for specific information that they would like to access. Without an idea of which documents to demand, making freedom-of-information requests can be a Sisyphean undertaking. For instance, the executive can commission expert studies on a specific subject, but only publish the analyses arriving at the preferred conclusion. Unless the citizens know that other studies exist, they might not think to include them in their freedom-of-information request. An open index of information would prevent the executive from hiding unfavourable evidence (unless the mere existence of an index posed a relevant threat to a protected interest in specific areas).[139] Comparative constitutionalism could create the necessary insights to sharpen these strategies and strengthen executive resilience.

[134] 5 U.S.C. § 552(a)(2)(D)(ii)(II); see Center for Biological Diversity, press release of 23 March 2017, Scientists Use 'Beetlejuice Provision' to Protect Data From Trump, available at www.biologicaldiversity.org/news/press_releases/2017/publc-records-03-23-2017.php (last accessed 20 October 2021) (discussing its use in practice); see also MA Pustay, 'Memorandums to Messages: The Evolution of FOIA in the Age of the Internet' (2016) 126 *Yale Law Journal Forum* 252, 261–62 (detailing the US Government's 'Release to One Is a Release to All' program).

[135] See M Fuchs, 'Judging Secrets: The Role Courts Should Play in Preventing Unnecessary Secrecy' (2006) 58 *Administrative Law Review* 131, 173–74 (examining the US FOIA).

[136] Karanicolas and Kwoka (n 131) 36–43 (arguing in favour of establishing an independent oversight body); cp Fuchs (n 135) 174–75 (discussing the position of a special master that can review FOIA requests subject to judicial proceedings)]; cp D Curtin, 'Overseeing Secrets in the EU: A Democratic Perspective' (2014) 52 *Journal of Common Market Studies* 684 (stating the need for parliamentary oversight of the executive classification of information).

[137] See Pozen (n 129) 1112–17 (suggesting the need for exceptions for the large number of commercially motivated requests); see also MB Kwoka, 'FOIA, Inc.' (2016) 65 *Duke Law Journal* 1361.

[138] See, eg, S Alvarez-Jones, '"Too Big To FOIA": How Agencies Avoid Compliance With the Freedom of Information Act' (2018) 39 *Cardozo Law Review* 1055, 1059, 1072–73 (arguing for a push in favour of digital record-keeping); see also AJ Wagner, '"Longstanding, Systemic Weaknesses": Hillary Clinton's Emails, FOIA's Defects and Affirmative Disclosure' (2019) 29 *University of Florida Journal of Law and Public Policy* 359 (supporting affirmative disclosure).

[139] See Wagner (n 138) 402–05 (detailing international efforts in this direction); see also NF Wessler, '"[We] Can Neither Confirm Nor Deny The Existence Or Nonexistence of Records Responsive To Your Request": Reforming the Glomar Response Under FOIA' (2010) 85 *New York University Law Review* 1381 (analysing the so-called Glomar response under the US FOIA, with which the agency refuses to even deny or confirm the existence of information).

C. Pro-Social Participatory Design

Citizen input can play an important role for public institutions in gathering relevant information, crowd-sourcing potential solutions, and raising awareness of issues that are important to citizens, but that are neglected politically.[140] Public actors can also use participatory instruments to generate consensus, to increase public support for certain policies, and to give citizens a forum to voice frustrations or concerns.[141] Especially in highly politicised decisions or even crises, using participatory tools can counteract populism and a declining interest in democratic processes.[142] The public responses to these situations need a particularly strong basis within the citizenry. Behaviourally, having the feeling of being heard can enhance the acceptance of the ultimate decision, even if it goes against the preferences expressed in the hearing.

Participation is most suitable to address well-defined singular issues. Therefore, local or area-specific rulemaking often incorporates citizen feedback. For instance, many jurisdictions include participatory instruments in the areas of zoning law and land use, partly to create the necessary knowledge, and partly to counter a development of 'Not In My Backyard' (NIMBY) movements.[143] Frequently, as in the US, the procedural rules of administrative lawmaking already contain a certain mandate to incorporate citizen input, such as the notice-and-comment procedure laid out in the US Administrative Procedure Act, which even allows for online participation.[144] Moreover, in some countries citizens can initiate referenda in order to realise a certain substantive policy goal. At times, public participation can also play a role in legislation and even constitution-making. The most prominent case is Iceland's attempt to use public participation to crowd-source a constitution in 2011, responding to the aftermath of the financial crisis.[145]

Against this backdrop, there is an emerging trend of public actors to create platforms that give citizens the opportunity to participate and engage in policymaking.[146] One of these tools are petition platforms that are designed to

[140] The following section relies on the following co-authored report, Lewandowsky et al (n 23) 73–84.

[141] See V Alsina and JL Martí, 'The Birth of the CrowdLaw Movement: Tech-Based Citizen Participation, Legitimacy and the Quality of Lawmaking' (2018) 40 *Analyse & Kritik* 337 (outlining the current crowdlaw movement).

[142] Commission, '2021 Strategic Foresight Report', COM (2021) 750 final 20 (detailing the need for participatory governance).

[143] See, eg, S Rose-Ackerman, S Egidy and J Fowkes, *Due Process of Lawmaking. The United States, South Africa, Germany, and the European Union* (Cambridge, Cambridge University Press 2015) 214–15 (addressing German law).

[144] See 5 U.S. Code § 533; ibid 79–81 (detailing the procedure set out in the Administrative Procedure Act); see also the internet portal www.regulations.gov.

[145] A Hudson, 'When Does Public Participation Make a Difference? Evidence From Iceland's Crowdsourced Constitution' (2018) 10 *Policy & Internet* 185.

[146] See BS Noveck, 'Crowdlaw: Collective Intelligence and Lawmaking' (2018) 40 *Analyse & Kritik* 359, 364–65.

bring certain issues to the attention of rulemakers. Through them, the citizens can prompt the executive to engage with a certain issue. Moreover, some cities or even countries have experimented with deliberation platforms that allow the executive to interact with citizens in order collectively to find policy solutions to specific problems and move toward a consensus. These instances are mostly local initiatives,[147] but in Taiwan, for example, the Taiwanese Government cooperates with an online deliberation platform 'vTaiwan' to allow citizens to discuss policy issues of national relevance, such as the regulation of Uber and AirBNB.[148] Recently, the EU has started a comparable enterprise with the 'Conference on the Future of Europe'.[149] Most of the current initiatives produce output that is merely advisory or informative, but which can still exercise visible political influence. So far, participation on the platforms is unincentivised, but it would be possible to create competitions and award prizes for (successfully) partaking in these projects. However, the public deliberation platforms created up to now have also illustrated the drawbacks of such online processes, including unequal access due to a lack of sufficient internet coverage, limited language abilities and literacy, as well as possible privacy concerns and potential misuse of capture.[150]

In order to fulfil their promises, participatory instruments need to be carefully designed.[151] Here, behavioural insights can offer a crucial contribution that has so far not received the necessary attention in legal analysis.[152] The starting point is the awareness that there exists no such thing as a 'neutral' design of participatory instruments.[153] Insights from behavioural sciences on information-processing and cognitive biases show in general how platform design can shape the behaviour and decision-making processes of its users.[154] Thus, the design of platforms that accommodate political behaviour can impact whether and how citizens engage

[147] See RB Bravo, J Balcells and A Padró-Solanet, 'A Model for the Analysis of Online Citizen Deliberation: Barcelona Case Study' (2019) 13 *International Journal of Communication* 5671 (analysing the government of Barcelona's use of the 'Decidim' system); P Aragón et al, 'Deliberative Platform Design: The Case Study of the Online Discussions in Decidim Barcelona', in GL Ciampaglia, A Mashhadi and T Yasseri (eds), *Social Informatics*, vol 10540 (2017).

[148] YT Hsiao et al, 'VTaiwan: An Empirical Study of Open Consultation Process in Taiwan' (SocArXiv, 2018) preprint; Noveck (n 146) 368; see also I Mitozo and FP J Marques, 'Context Matters! Looking Beyond Platform Structure to Understand Citizen Deliberation on Brazil's *Portal E-Democracia*' (2019) 11 *Policy & Internet* 370 (examining the Brazilian Portal e-Democracia designed for citizens to deliberate legislative policy reform).

[149] See S Pätsch, 'European institutions use Decidim to enable the Conference on the Future of Europe' (*Open Source Observatory*, 23 June 2021) www.joinup.ec.europa.eu/collection/open-source-observatory-osor/news/participatory-democracy-through-collaboration accessed 20 October 2021 (stating that the EU decided to use the Decidim software, already employed by Barcelona).

[150] Lewandowsky et al (n 23) 80.

[151] See Noveck (n 146) 374–77 (emphasising the need for evaluation).

[152] See WB Towne and JD Herbsleb, 'Design Considerations for Online Deliberation Systems' (2012) 9 *Journal of Information Technology & Politics* 97, 100–12 (providing a list of relevant design factors for deliberation platforms).

[153] See Lewandowsky et al (n 23) 105–06.

[154] Kozyreva, Lewandowsky and Hertwig (n 60) 109–27.

politically.[155] For instance, empirical research indicates that the features of the social media platform TikTok, in particular its interactive duet function, encourage political communication that crosses partisan lines between Democrats and Republicans (in a US context).[156] Public platforms could take advantage of such features. An additional parameter addresses their connection to private social-media platforms, which play a dual role. On the one hand, they themselves offer a platform for discussion, for sharing political advertisement, and for soliciting donations. On the other hand, they act as intermediaries between citizens and public actors, for instance when they direct users to political participatory platforms (such as petition platforms or voting guides). Accordingly, a study investigating the use of a UK Government petition platform indicates that social-media websites are important avenues for guiding their users to the platform, as 40 per cent of its traffic came via Facebook and 10 per cent via Twitter.[157]

The same study of the UK Government petition platform also reveals the substantial influence of platform design.[158] The platform introduced a new feature on its main interface, which informed visitors about trending petitions – thereby revealing social information about the behaviour of other petitioners to each user. This feature increased the support for the trending petitions depending on their exact physical position on the screen – which is in line with psychological eye-tracking evidence about the importance of the location of information on the screen.[159] Since the design, and changes to it, impact how people act on deliberative platforms, the specific features of a public participation platform need to align with the underlying goals. Then, public institutions will have to consider carefully the behavioural effects of these design elements to foster public-private interaction.[160] Some studies of deliberation platforms reveal their potential. They show the power of certain design features to foster a debate, to create a constructive environment, and to configure a process that merges different ideas to a coherent proposal. Since the output of these processes is supposed to enhance the decision-making of public actors, the common good should provide the focal point of design. There is a growing emphasis on the 'pro-social design'[161] of platforms and digital tools in general, which could prove to be very useful in the context of resilient institutional design.

[155] HS Christensen, 'A Conjoint Experiment of How Design Features Affect Evaluations of Participatory Platforms' (2021) 38 *Government Information Quarterly* 101538 (exploring the connection between design features and citizen attitudes); see Aragón et al (n 147) 282–84 (showing the stimulating effects of negative comments on deliberation).

[156] JCM Serrano, O Papakyriakopoulos and S Hegelich, 'Dancing to the Partisan Beat: A First Analysis of Political Communication on TikTok', *12th ACM Conference on Web Science* (ACM 2020).

[157] SA Hale et al, 'How Digital Design Shapes Political Participation: A Natural Experiment with Social Information' (2018) 13 *PLoS ONE* e0196068, 14.

[158] ibid.

[159] JL Orquin and S Mueller Loose, 'Attention and Choice A Review on Eye Movements in Decision Making' (2013) 144 *Acta Psychologica* 190, 195 (explaining eye-tracking research on position effects).

[160] See G Capone et al, 'Crowdlaw. Online Public Participation in Lawmaking' (The GovLab, 2017) 44–61 (providing a case study to support the design of a participation platform in Madrid).

[161] See the initiative promoting pro-social design, www.prosocialdesign.org.

V. Conclusion

This chapter takes on the challenge of envisioning the development of institutions in the upcoming decade. It uses foresight studies as a starting point to identify the challenges that are most likely to demand and prompt institutional adaptation. All three global challenges chosen for further analysis, namely climate change, the technological transformation, and democratic decline, are already well underway, and institutions around the world have already designed various policy roadmaps to tackle them. Instead of delving deeper into an evaluation of substantive measures, I argue that the policymaking actors, in particular the legislature and the executive, need to develop and adopt institutional mechanisms in order to manage and overcome the impending crises effectively.

Even though this chapter does not try to predict the state of constitutionalism in 2030, it hypothesises that the resilience of institutions will become an important factor over the course of the next eight years. I develop three potential design features that could strengthen the resilience of institutions vis-à-vis the impending challenges. All of the strategies suggested are based on the fundamental role of information for policymaking institutions. The first instrument that should be added to the rulemaking toolbox, I argue, is legislative experimentation. When faced with the challenges described, rulemaking bodies could commit themselves to a more empirical approach to policymaking in order to bridge ideological disagreement and overcome the intertemporal divide often complicating the present solution of future problems. Second, institutions have already realised the deficits of the current information infrastructure and will likely push towards creating a legal framework that can safeguard the availability of and access to data generated and used by public institutions. This would enable civil society actors both to make use of the information themselves and to hold public actors accountable for their policy choices in addressing upcoming challenges. A third strategy addresses participatory tools of public governance. The growing technological capacities will allow for an increased reliance on citizen participation. In order to realise the benefits of these tools and avoid their pitfalls, participatory platforms need to be carefully designed. Whether their use will prove successful in the future will, in part, depend on whether public institutions take into account a behavioural perspective and align their design choices with the public interest. Even though not all of these instruments will have been implemented transnationally by 2030, they might illustrate the potential strength of constitutionalism in dealing with seemingly insurmountable challenges.

8

Political Parties in 2030

PAULINA STARSKI

I. Introduction: 'Crisis of Constitutionalism' and Political Parties – An Antagonistic Approach

The agenda of this book focuses on the phenomenon of a 'crisis of constitutionalism' and makes the attempt to predict the state of 'constitutionalism' in 2030 with a view to a matrix of areas, aspects and actors.

This requires us to, first, set the record straight on the concepts of 'constitutionalism'[1] and 'crisis',[2] the latter having become a frequent 'buzz word' in constitutionalist discourse: many voices have in recent years invoked a '[d]emise of [l]iberal [c]onstitutionalism'[3] and identified processes of 'democratic backsliding'.[4]

There are a variety of 'constitutionalism' concepts.[5] To depict them goes beyond the scope of this chapter. For the purpose of this contribution 'constitutionalism' shall be understood as an umbrella term for key features of constitutional architectures following a 'modern' liberal-democratic model[6]

[1] On the concept of 'constitutionalism' with view to the international legal order M Koskenniemi, 'Constitutionalism as Mindset: Reflections on Kantian Themes About International Law and Globalization' (2007) 8 *Theoretical Inquiry Law* 9; T Kleinlein, 'Between Myths and Norms: Constructivist Constitutionalism and the Potential of Constitutional Principles in International Law' (2012) 81 *Nordic Journal of International Law* 79; J Klabbers, 'Constitutionalism and the Making of International Law' [2008] *No Foundations* 84.

[2] Cp MJ Gerhardt, 'Crisis and Constitutionalism' (2002) 63 *Montana Law Review* 277.

[3] T Ginsburg, AZ Huq and M Versteeg, 'The Coming Demise of Liberal Constitutionalism?' (2018) 85 *The University of Chicago Law Review* 239. See also P Carrozza, 'Constitutionalism's Post-Modern Opening', in M Loughlin and N Walker (eds), *The Paradox of Constitutionalism* (Oxford, OUP, 2008) 169, 171.

[4] N Bermeo, 'On Democratic Backsliding' (2016) 27 *Journal of Democracy* 5. See with regard to political parties as a cause F Wolkenstein 'European political parties' complicity in democratic backsliding' [2021] *Global Constitutionalism* 1.

[5] A Godden and J Morison, 'Constitutionalism', in *Max Planck Encyclopedia of Comparative Constitutional Law [MPECCoL]* (May 2017) para 1 et seq. Generally D Grimm, *Constitutionalism: Past, Present, and Future* (Oxford, OUP, 2016).

[6] Cp the understanding purported by Ginsburg, Huq and Versteeg (n 3) 239.

based on the idea of distribution of power and installing a 'protection of liberty mediated by democracy'.[7] What does it mean that 'constitutionalism' is in 'crisis';[8] an observation which indicates that we have reached a crucial turning point? One understanding could purport that modern constitutional architectures are inept to channel and resolve pressing conflicts of our time.[9] Another would focus on a deficient real-world effect of constitutionalist normative demands: they are ignored or generally put into question – a 'crisis of constitutional fidelity' occurs.[10] A different understanding could focus on the failure of common concepts, institutions and actors of constitutional law to generate outcomes that they have been designed to achieve.

The latter understanding appears to be particularly apt when reflecting on political parties:[11] when assessing the role of parties in the context of 'constitutionalism in crisis'[12] we think of them as actors who possibly pose an impediment to the whole constitutional project. It is within this tension that we must approach the task to make predictions about the state of constitutionalism in 2030. Here, we are required to take the frequently invoked 'crisis of representation'[13] and the 'legitimacy crisis experienced by parties' in view whose cause is purportedly the unfitness of political parties 'for the demands of postmodern society'.[14]

In detail: for the purpose of predicting the state and function of political parties as actors of constitutionalism in 2030 it is sensible to approach them in terms of three antagonisms.

The first antagonism concerns the role played by political parties within constitutional frameworks. They might operate as stabilisers of a constitutional system or function as forces contesting and destabilising the system (system stabilisation v system contestation – antagonism I).

The second relevant antagonism circles around the autonomy of political parties as safeguarded by constitutional law versus the necessity to regulate or

[7] Grimm (n 5) 252.

[8] Generally on the term 'crisis' see A Schwerdtfeger, *Krisengesetzgebung* (Tübingen, Mohr Siebeck, 2018) 6 et seq.

[9] Cp with regard to the concept of a 'constitutional crisis' JM Balkin, 'Constitutional Crisis and Constitutional Rot', in MA Graber, S Levinson and M Tushnet (eds), *Constitutional Democracy in Crisis?* (New York, OUP, 2018) 13; KE Whittington, 'Yet Another Constitutional Crisis' (2002) 43 *William and Mary Law Review* 2093, 2101; A Ristroph, 'Is Law – Constitutional Crisis and Existential Anxiety' (2009) 25 *Constitutional Comment* 431, 432.

[10] Cp Whittington (n 9) 2109 et seq.

[11] Generally C Skach, 'Political Parties and the Constitution', in M Rosenfeld and A Sajó (eds), *The Oxford Handbook of Comparative Constitutional Law* (Oxford, OUP, 2012) 874.

[12] T Khaitan, 'Political Parties in Constitutional Theory' (2020) 73 *Current Legal Problems* 89, 89.

[13] E Laclau, *On Populist Reason* (London, Verso, 2005) 137; S Hutter, H Kriesi and J Lorenzini, 'Social movements interactions with political parties', in DA Snow, SA Soule, H Kriesi and H McCammon (eds), *The Blackwell Companion to Social Movements* (Hoboken, NJ, Wiley, 2019) 322, 331. See K Heidar and B Wauters (eds), *Do Parties Still Represent? An Analysis of the Representativeness of Political Parties in Western Democracies* 2nd edn (London, Routledge, 2019).

[14] P Ignazi, 'The four knights of intra-party democracy: A rescue for party delegitimation' (2020) 26 *Party Politics* 9, 16.

restrict both governance within parties as well external activities of parties (party autonomy v party regulation – antagonism II).

The third antagonism tackles political parties as national actors and political parties as actors beyond the state (national actors v actors beyond the state – antagonism III). Here some light shall be shed on both the 'Europeanisation' of party families[15] as well as the role that political parties play in the global polity.

Obviously, various caveats are to be mentioned here:

First, the constitutional status of political parties varies across different constitutional orders. While commonalities exist, differences and peculiarities remain strong. Each constitutional system is, to a certain extent, a unicum which relativises any identification of trends.

Second, a prediction of the state of constitutionalism in 2030 regarding political parties can only be tentative and necessarily speculative. It is to be expected that some of the predictions presented here will be proven wrong upon reassessment.

Third, the assertion of trends will necessarily be schematic and ignore nuances.

II. Antagonisms

Let us take a closer look at the antagonisms identified above – parties as system stabilisers v system contesters (antagonism I), political parties as autonomous actors v regulated actors (antagonism II) and political parties as national actors v European or global actors (antagonism III).

A. Antagonism I: System Stabilisation v System Contestation

Political parties may serve as stabilisers of a constitutional system (i.) or operate as its main contesting force in extreme constellations even posing a threat to a constitutional system (ii.).

i. System Stabilisation

In terms of the system stabilising function of political parties we can contrast the 'traditional narrative' (a.) with contemporary trends (b.).

[15] On the concept of party families see P Mair and C Mudde, 'The Party Family and its Study' [1998] *Annual Review of Political Science* 211.

a. 'Transmission Belts' between Civil Society and the State – The 'Traditional Narrative'

Political parties constitute key actors within various constitutional systems,[16] particularly within systems of representative democracy[17] being for some the 'life-blood of representative democracy'.[18] In modern constitutional orders political parties are democratic institutions organising political will. Some would even argue that the very idea of democracy and political parties is essentially intertwined:[19] Elmer Schattschneider has purported the thesis that 'political parties created democracy and that modern democracy is unthinkable save in terms of the parties.'[20] Arguing in a similar vein the European Court of Human Rights [ECtHR] has posited that 'political parties are a form of association essential to the proper functioning of democracy'.[21] Political parties as institutions of representative democracy are meant to stabilise the constitutional system by channelling the political discourse, reducing information and transaction costs coming along with political will formation,[22] bundling interests

[16] Generally G Sartori, *Parties and Party Systems: A Framework For Analysis* Vol I (Cambridge, CUP, 1976). While in the US-American and British context constitutional law remains rather silent in terms of political parties (while they are regulated within statutes) (see Khaitan (n 12) 89 et seq.), the contrary is true for the continental European tradition.

[17] Z Lefkofridi and A Katsanidou, 'Step Closer to a Transnational Party System? Competition and Coherence in the 2009 and 2014 European Parliament' (2013) 56 *Journal of Common Market Studies* 1462, 1463. On 'representative democracy' in general J Locke, *Two Treatises on Government* (Clark: Lawbook Exchange reprint 2010, first published 1689), Essay Two, XII. (The Legislative, Executive, and Federative Power of the Commonwealth) § 140; JS Mill, *Considerations On Representative Government* (Cambridge, CUP, 2010; printed version of 1st edn 1861); G Frankenberg, 'Democracy', in M Rosenfeld and A Sajó (eds), *The Oxford Handbook of Comparative Constitutional Law* (Oxford, OUP, 2012) 250, 253 et seq.; A Kulick, 'Representative Democracy' in *Max Planck Encyclopedia of Comparative Constitutional Law [MPECCoL]* (May 2020) para 1 et seq.; OW Lembcke, 'Theorie demokratischer Repräsentation', in OW Lembcke, C Ritzi and GS Schaal (eds), *Zeitgenössische Demokratietheorie II* (Wiesbaden, Springer, 2016) 23; S Alonso, J Keane and W Merkel (eds), *The Future of Representative Democracy* (Cambridge, CUP, 2011).

[18] Khaitan (n 12) 125.

[19] See FCC, Judgment of the Second Senate of 27 February 2018, 2 BvE 1/16, para. 41 (non-authoritative English translation): 'In modern parliamentary democracy, political parties are of vital importance in this process […]. Art. 21 GG expresses this by acknowledging parties as institutions that are necessary under constitutional law for the formation of the political will of the people, and by elevating them to the rank of constitutional institutions. […]. They have a specific function as mediators between state and society. They are units of political action that democracy needs for organising voters in groups capable of acting politically, and thereby enabling them to effectively influence state matters […].' See even more far-reaching FCC, Judgment of the Second Senate of 9 April 1992, 2 BvE 2/89, para 85; Judgment of the Second Senate of 5 April 1952, 2 BvH 1/52, para 52.

[20] EE Schattschneider, *Party Government* (New York, Rinhart & Company, 1942) 1; T Poguntke, N Aylott, R Ladrech and KR Luther, 'The Europeanisation of national party organisations: A conceptual analysis' (2007) 46 *European Journal of Political Research* 747, 747. See EV Towfigh, *Das Parteien-Paradox* (Tübingen, Mohr Siebeck, 2015) 77. Furthermore P Mair and J Thomassen, 'Political representation and government in the European Union' (2010) 17 *Journal of European Public Policy* 20, 23 et seq.

[21] ECtHR [GC], Judgment of 30 January 1998, 19392/92, para 25 – *United Communist Party of Turkey and Others v Turkey*.

[22] See Towfigh (n 20) 81 et seq.; Khaitan (n 12) 125.

of the electorate, safeguarding the translation of popular will[23] into political policy, expediting participation,[24] facilitating elections and allowing majorities to be built.[25] According to the 'traditional narrative' political parties function as connectors, intermediaries[26] or 'transmission belts'[27] between the state, its organs and civil society[28] displaying a hybrid, public-private character. The dogma of the 'essential role' of political parties for the democratic-representative process has, however, never remained unquestioned: some scholars have elaborately established a vision of democratic rule without parties.[29] While these alternative visions for the organisation of democratic systems have merit, it is a fact that political parties persist in constitutional orders and have to a large extent been 'constitutionalised' therein: a multitude of European[30] (see, eg, Article 4 of the French Constitution,[31] Article 36, paragraph 2 Constitution of Ukraine[32]) and non-European democracies (see, eg, Article 38, paragraph 1 Constitution of Argentina,[33] Article 41(I) Constitution of Mexico,[34] Article 74, paragraph 1 Constitution of Mozambique[35]) has acknowledged political parties (and their systemic importance) on the constitutional level.

b. Loss of Significance of the 'Transmission Belt' Function and the 'Crisis of Representation'

Nevertheless, in 2013 Peter Mair asserted that '[t]he age of party democracy has passed':[36] and indeed, the 'traditional narrative' of political parties as the key 'transmission belts' between the state and society is challenged from various angles while scholarship is not unanimous on the effects of particular occurrences on the actual role played by political parties.

What are the key moments putting the significance of political parties as 'transmission belts' in doubt?

23 See H Kelsen, *Vom Wesen und Wert der Demokratie* (Tübingen, J.C.B. Mohr, 1920) 20.

24 Ginsburg, Huq and Versteeg (n 3) 246.

25 Cp SL Mudge and AS Chen, 'Political Parties and the Sociological Imagination: Past, Present, and Future Directions' (2014) 40 *Annual Review of Sociology* 305.

26 See M Weber, *Politik als Beruf* 2nd edn (München, Duncker & Humblot, 1926).

27 'Transmissionsriemen' see D Grimm, 'Politische Parteien', in E Benda, W Maihofer und H-J Vogel (eds), *Handbuch des Verfassungsrechts der Bundesrepublik Deutschland* (Berlin, De Gruyter, 1994) § 14 para 16.

28 Cp S Neumann, 'Toward a Comparative Study of Political Parties', in J Blondel (ed), *Comparative Government* (London, Palgrave, 1969) 69, 73.

29 Towfigh (n 20) 187 et seq.

30 I van Biezen, 'The Constitutionalization of Political Parties in Post-war Europe', in I van Biezen and H-M ten Napel (eds), *Regulating Political Parties* (Leiden, Leiden University Press, 2014) 93, 95.

31 *Constitution du 4 octobre 1958* (1958, with amendments through 2009).

32 Конституція України (1996, with amendments through 2019).

33 *Constitución de la Nación Argentina* (1853, with amendments through 1994).

34 *Constitución Política de los Estados Unidos Mexicanos* (1917, with amendments through 2021).

35 *Constituição da República de Moçambique* (2004, with amendments through 2018).

36 P Mair, *Ruling the void: The hollowing of western democracy* (London, Verso, 2013) 1.

First, political parties appear detached from the *demos*[37] leading to a 'crisis of representation':[38] while parties still exist, 'they have become so disconnected from the wider society, and pursue a form of competition that is so lacking in meaning, that they no longer seem capable of sustaining democracy in its present form'.[39] One of the main factors fostering this disconnection lies in the 'individualisation' that defines postmodern society.[40]

Second, whilst not being a coherent phenomenon, in certain constitutional contexts the significance of political parties is reduced by competing pathways of and venues for popular will formation and articulation: popular political will is formed, for example, within social movements[41] (eg *Fridays for Future*).[42] These are 'networks of relations between a plurality of actors' characterised by 'collective identity' and by 'conflictual issues'.[43] Yet, there exist wide interactions between political parties and social movements[44] and the rise of the latter has not eradicated the intermediary function of political parties in its entirety. Social movements are rather to be seen as complementary actors of representation impacting and potentially serving as a corrective to party politics. While they do still challenge the prerogative of political parties in the realm of democratic participation, social movements can lead to the emergence of issue-specific parties and vice versa. Beyond that, there are various competing platforms within the digital space which provide different channels allowing the popular voice to form and to be heard. Social media plays a significant role in this regard.[45]

Third, there is an increasing pressure to integrate (yet more) elements of direct democracy to constitutional architectures[46] which might have a detrimental effect on the significance of political parties.[47] The latter point remains, however, questionable. According to various authors 'there is simply no evidence for direct democracy weakening parties'.[48]

[37] Ignazi (n 14) 10.

[38] Cp Laclau (n 13) 137.

[39] Mair (n 36) 1.

[40] Ignazi (n 14) 10.

[41] On the concept of 'social movement' M Diani, 'The Concept of Social Movement' (1992) 40 *The Sociological Review* 1.

[42] A-B Kaiser, 'Die Organisation politischer Willensbildung: Parteien', presentation during the *Staatsrechtslehrertagung* in Mainz 6 to 9 November 2021 (on file with the author) 5. On social movements H Kitschelt, 'Social Movements, Political Parties, and Democratic Theory' (1993) *The ANNALS of the American Academy of Political and Social Science* 13; Hutter, Kriesi and Lorenzini (n 13) 322 et seq.

[43] Diani (n 41) 17.

[44] Hutter, Kriesi and Lorenzini (n 13) 333.

[45] Cp H Gil de Zúñiga, L Molyneux and P Zheng, 'Social Media, Political Expression, and Political Participation: Panel Analysis of Lagged and Concurrent Relationships' (2014) 64 *Journal of Communication* 612.

[46] On trends of 'direct democracy' A Gamper, 'Direct Democracy' in *Max Planck Encyclopedia of Comparative Constitutional Law [MPECCoL]* (February 2019) para 21.

[47] For a differentiated view A Ladner and M Brändle, 'Does Direct Democracy Matter for Political Parties? An Empirical Test in the Swiss Cantons' (1999) 5 *Party Politics* 283.

[48] I Budge, 'Direct Democracy', in SA Binder, RAW Rhodes and BA Rockman (eds), *The Oxford Handbook of Political Institutions* (Oxford, OUP, 2008), 595, 602 referring to M Mendelsohn and A Parkin, 'Introduction', in M Mendelsohn and A Parkin (eds), *Referendum Democracy: Citizens, Elites and*

ii. System Contestation

Political parties might have also a destabilising effect on democracy (a.) or even become focal points of a general contestation of constitutional systems (b.).

a. Pluralism and Factionalisation

Mainstream parties tend to lose significance in many political systems and various small, interest group parties[49] and 'movement parties'[50] – like *MoVimento 5 Stelle* (Italy), *Synaspismos Rizospastikis Aristeras (SYRIZA)* (Greece) and *Podemos* (Spain) – are on the rise (obvious exceptions being one-party systems like, eg, China, see Article 1, paragraph 2 second sentence of the Constitution of the People's Republic of China[51] or North Korea, see the Preamble and Article 11 of the Constitution of the Democratic People's Republic of Korea[52] – examples which do, however, fall outside the discussion of liberal-democratic constitutional models per se). A factionalisation and fragmentation[53] of the party system and a multitude of (even) democratic parties constitute potential dangers to the vitality of a democratic system as history teaches us (see the Weimar experience[54]):[55] 'even democratic political parties can, when faced with the incentives of certain constitutions, contribute to democracy's collapse'.[56]

b. Political Parties and Populism

Political parties can become the centre point of populism[57] which is characterised by its (conventionally) proclaimed anti-elitism[58] and its 'anti-establishment

Deliberation in Referendum Campaigns (London, Palgrave, 2001) 1, 7 et seq. See also W-C Chang, 'Direct Democracy and Party Membership: Testing the Role of Political Efficacy' [2021] *Political Studies Review* 1.

[49] See also K Deschouwer, 'New Parties and the Crisis of Representation: Between Indicator and Solution', in P Harfst, I Kubbe and T Poguntke (eds), *Parties, Governments and Elites* (Wiesbaden, Springer, 2017) 73.

[50] See H Kitschelt, 'Movement Parties', in R S Katz and W J Crotty (eds), *Handbook of Party Politics* (London, SAGE, 2014) 278.

[51] Constitution of the People's Republic of China (1982, with amendments through 2018).

[52] Constitution of the Democratic People's Republic of Korea (1972, with amendments through 2019).

[53] R Grote, 'Parliamentary Systems', in *Max Planck Encyclopedia of Comparative Constitutional Law [MPECCoL]* (September 2016) para 4.

[54] M Stibbe, 'Coalition-Building and Political Fragmentation, 1924–1930', in N Rossol and B Ziemann (eds), *The Oxford Handbook of the Weimar Republic* (Oxford, OUP, 2020) (online publication).

[55] Cp Khaitan (n 12) 120 et seq.

[56] Skach (n 11) 887.

[57] Cp on the concept of populism E Laclau, 'Populism: What's in a name?', in F Panizza (ed), *Populism and the Mirror of Democracy* (London, Verso, 2005) 32; R Brubaker, 'Why populism?' (2017) 46 *Theory and Society* 357; H Kriesi, 'The populist challenge' (2014) 37 *West European Politics* 361; C Mudde, 'Populism: An Ideational Approach', in CR Kaltwasser, P Taggart, P Ochoa Espejo and P Ostiguy (eds), *The Oxford Handbook of Populism* (Oxford, OUP, 2017) 27 et seq.; M Caiani and P Graziano, 'Understanding varieties of populism in times of crises' (2019) 42 *West European Politics* 1141. On the rise of populist parties Kaiser (n 42) 4 et seq.

[58] JM Balkin, 'Populism and progressivism as constitutional categories' (1995) 104 *Yale Law Journal* 1935, 1945.

appeal to mass constituencies'.[59] One of the key reasons for a rise of populism is the already stressed 'crisis or representation':[60] 'populism is what happens when political parties lose control'[61] and voters lose faith in mainstream parties – the 'establishment'.[62] As Kenneth Roberts puts it:

> 'populism thrives in contexts of representational failures or deficiencies, when mainstream political parties have lost control of the electoral marketplace due to the mobilization of previously unincorporated mass constituencies, organizational cartelization, performance failures, or programmatic convergence and electoral outflanking'.[63]

As contemporary political history has taught us, the electorate tends to look for answers outside the established party system often taking recourse to the 'post-factual' and 'post-truth' populism.[64]

This brings us to two paradoxes:[65] first, while being 'anti-establishment', 'anti-pluralism'[66] and 'anti-technocracies',[67] populists operate frequently through their own 'anti-system parties'[68] themselves taking advantage of this institutional pathway of democratic participation that constitutional systems offer.[69] The comparative picture is of course more complex: first, looking to Latin America we find, for example, that populism is rather organised in movements with charismatic leaders than within robust parties (see, eg, Bolsonaro and the instrumentalisation of the *Partido Social Liberal* until 2019; now Bolsonaro has joined the *Partido Liberal*;[70] Bukele and the party *Nuevas Ideas* in El Salvador).[71] Second, populist movements occasionally emerge out of mainstream parties (see, eg, the *Tea Party movement* which draws supporters mainly from conservative

[59] KM Roberts, 'Populism and Political Parties', in CR Kaltwasser, P Taggart, P Ochoa Espejo and P Ostiguy (eds), *The Oxford Handbook of Populism* (Oxford, OUP, 2017) 287, 288. Cp also P Mair, 'Populist Democracy vs Party Democracy', in Y Mény and Y Surel (eds), *Democracies and the Populist Challenge* (Basingstoke, Palgrave Macmillan, 2002) 81.

[60] Laclau (n 13) 137; Roberts (n 59) 289.

[61] M Bogaards, 'Lessons from Brexit and Trump: populism is what happens when political parties lose control' (2017) 11 *Zeitschrift für Vergleichende Politikwissenschaft* 513.

[62] Roberts (n 59) 287.

[63] ibid 295.

[64] Cp T Ylä-Anttila, 'Populist knowledge: "Post-truth" repertoires of contesting epistemic authorities' (2018) 5 *European Journal of Cultural and Political Sociology* 356.

[65] But see J-W Müller, 'Populism and Constitutionalism', in CR Kaltwasser, P Taggart, P Ochoa Espejo, and P Ostiguy (eds), *The Oxford Handbook of Populism* (Oxford, OUP, 2017) 590, 595.

[66] Müller (n 65) 591 et seq.

[67] See C Pinelli, 'The populist challenge to constitutional democracy' (2011) 7 *European Constitutional Law Review* 5, 14.

[68] G Capoccia, 'Anti-system Parties: A Conceptual Reassessment' (2002) 14 *Journal of Theoretical Politics* 9.

[69] For some recent empirical research on populism within political parties MJ Meijers and A Zaslove, 'Measuring Populism in Political Parties: Appraisal of a New Approach' (2021) 54 *Comparative Political Studies* 372.

[70] See 'Brazil: Bolsonaro joins Liberal Party ahead of 2022 election' (DW 11 November 2021) www.dw.com/en/brazil-bolsonaro-joins-liberal-party-ahead-of-2022-election/a-59783836.

[71] K Weyland, 'How Populism Corrodes Latin American Parties' (2021) 32 *Journal of Democracy* 42, 45 et seq.

Republicans[72]).[73] Both points do, however, not contradict the fact that robust populist parties exist.

Second, populist parties – perceiving themselves as a 'counter-hegemonic force'[74] – are characterised by their 'anti-positioning' employing an antithesis within their communicative strategies – the juxtaposition of the 'people' (understood in a nationalist and exclusionary manner)[75] in the sense of the general population on the one hand and the 'elites' on the other hand. In that regard populist parties do, however, employ constitutionalist terms and concepts – as we shall see in more depth in a moment – which leads some to perceive populism to a certain extent as a 'constitutional project'.[76] And indeed populist parties integrate a distorted version of constitutional concepts into their rhetoric.[77]

What effects do populist parties have on systems of democratic rule?

It would be ill-guided to perceive populism institutionalised within parties solely as a danger to a democratic system. The picture is more complex: on the one hand (from an optimistic perspective) the rise of populism and populist parties may have a cathartic effect[78] on mainstream parties and engender a change of their course. On the other hand, in systems which follow the proportional representation rule, anti-system parties might finally cooperate with mainstream parties.[79] The latter can have to effects: it may render mainstream parties more populist or contain the anti-system agitation of populist parties. To the least it is safe to say that the rise of populist parties has a re-configurative effect on mainstream parties.[80]

In that regard it appears feasible to draw a more differentiated picture:

We find populism at both ends of the political spectrum – the right and the left.[81] While some scholars raise doubts as to the sensibility to distinguish

[72] V Williamson, T Skocpol and J Coggin, 'The Tea Party and the Remaking of Republican Conservatism' (2011) 9 *Perspectives on Politics* 25, 27.

[73] Roberts 289.

[74] ibid 297.

[75] ibid 299.

[76] P Blokker, 'Populism as a constitutional project' (2019) 17 *I•CON* 535–553. See also Müller (n 65) 590 (also referred to by Blokker). Furthermore RD Parker, 'Here, the People Rule: A Constitutional Populist Manifesto' (1993) 27 *Valparaiso University Law Review* 531. On populism as a 'distinctive pattern of constitutionalism' from a different angle (reflecting on the essential flaws of constitutionalism) C Thornhill, 'Constitutionalism and populism: national political integration and global legal integration' (2020) 12 *International Theory* (2020) 1, 32.

[77] See T Fournier, 'From rhetoric to action, a constitutional analysis of populism' (2019) 20 *German Law Journal* 362, 365 et seq.

[78] Cp Roberts (n 59) 300.

[79] Ginsburg, Huq and Versteeg (n 3) 250. They refer to RW Jackman and K Volpert, 'Conditions Favouring Parties of the Extreme Right in Western Europe' (1996) 26 *British Journal of Political Science* 501, 517 (arguing that proportional representation-systems foster the rise of anti-system parties).

[80] Roberts (n 59) 300: 'populist mobilization has repeatedly reconstituted national party systems and reconfigured their cleavage alignments in Latin America'.

[81] See M Tushnet, 'Varieties of populism' (2019) 20 *German Law Journal* 382, 387 et seq.; id., 'Comparing Right-Wing and Left-Wing Populism', in MA Graber, S Levinson and M Tushnet (eds), *Constitutional Democracy in Crisis?* (New York, OUP, 2018) 639.

between 'right' and 'left' in terms of grasping 'populism',[82] this dichotomic scheme works to the least for some preliminary findings.

Right-wing populist parties – like *Fidesz* in Hungary or *Prawo i Sprawiedliwość (Law and Justice)* in Poland – stress the importance of majority rule and popular sovereignty facilitating a majoritarian concept of democracy. The constituent power is regarded as the centre and any protection of minorities fades. Particularly right-wing populist parties claim to speak for a fictious mass being the 'real people'[83] – which is not employed in populist discourse as 'a primary datum but a construct' and is opposed to 'the others' (which are rarely defined),[84] while aspects like pluralism and inclusiveness are disregarded and law is perceived in an instrumentalist manner.[85] This perversion and instrumentalisation of constitutional concepts is particularly dangerous: if populist parties gain power and attain governmental status, their distorted account of constitutional concepts[86] potentially paves the way to a dismantlement of the constitutional order as the example of *Prawo i Sprawiedliwość* (*Law and Justice*) shows.[87] A particularly severe danger is posed by '"far-right lite" parties' which partially succeed in rendering their radicalism 'mainstream compatible'.[88] Examples might include the *Lega* in Italy or the *Alternative für Deutschland* (AfD) in Germany.[89] Subversive efforts of such parties have a greater chance of success than those of openly extremist and violence propagating right-wing parties.

Within numerous constitutional orders left-wing populist parties – like *Podemos* in Spain, *SYRIZA* in Greece or *Partido Socialista Unido de Venezuela* – are also on the rise.[90] Left-wing populist parties oppose neoliberalism and put an emphasis on socio-economic questions[91] echoing the idea of 'international proletarian solidarity'.[92] The latter – the general claim of left-wing populists suggests – would

[82] G Halmai, 'Populism, authoritarianism and constitutionalism' (2019) 20 *German Law Journal* 296, 298 referring to KL Scheppele, 'Party's Over', in MA Graber, S Levinson and M Tushnet (eds), *Constitutional Democracy in Crisis?* (New York, OUP, 2018) 495, 496.

[83] Müller (n 65) 594.

[84] Laclau (n 57) 48; Tushnet (n 81) 388.

[85] Here and before Blokker (n 76) 536.

[86] See also G Skąpska, 'Abuse of the Constitution as a Means of Political Change: Sociological Reflections on the Crisis of Constitutionalism in Poland' (2019) 4 *Polish Sociological Review* 421.

[87] See generally W Sadurski, *Poland's Constitutional Breakdown* (Oxford, OUP, 2019); P Starski, M Szwast and M Szwed, 'The 'Gestalt' of the Polish Constitution', in A von Bogdandy, P Huber and S Ragone (eds), *Ius Publicum Europaeum* (Oxford, OUP 2022) (forthcoming).

[88] Cp TG Daly and BC Jones, 'Parties versus democracy: Addressing today's political party threats to democratic rule' (2020) 18 *I•CON* 509, 523 et seq.

[89] ibid.

[90] See, eg, G Katsambekis and A Kioupkiolis (eds), *The Populist Radical Left in Europe* (Oxford, Routledge/Taylor and Francis, 2019); C de la Torre, 'Left-Wing Populism: Inclusion and Authoritarianism in Venezuela, Bolivia, and Ecuador' (2016) 23 *Brown Journal of World Affairs* 61.

[91] S Otjes and T Louwerse, 'Populists in Parliament: Comparing Left-Wing and Right-Wing Populism in the Netherlands' (2015) 63 *Political Studies* 60, 61.

[92] Tushnet (n 81) 387.

not be addressed by the political elites which merely serve the interest of the economically powerful and foreign powers.[93] In terms of their anti-elitist stance left-wing populists do correspond with their right-wing counterparts. There are, however, also considerable differences. As Mark Tushnet stresses, left-wing populism propagating a nationalist agenda is not necessarily 'ethnocentric [...] in principle' – contrary to right-wing populism.[94] Furthermore, left-wing populism stands out due to a 'direct engagement with genuinely participatory projects of constitutionalism'.[95] Yet, also left-wing populism might have a destabilising effect on the fundaments of modern constitutionalism, since it denies – just as right-wing populism – 'a strong separation between politics and law'[96] which might ultimately lead to the eradication of the separation of powers.

iii. Tentative Outlook

Considering the first antagonism the following trends are to be expected with view to the state of constitutionalism in 2030 and political parties:

The 'crisis of representation'[97] is here to stay. Mainstream parties will modernise their internal governance structure and make the attempt to adapt to contemporary forms of political will formation. Alternative models to organise political will formation and participation will be more intensely debated, while an eradication of political parties will continue to be seen as an endangerment of democracy: 'A party-less democracy, unless really small, is unlikely to remain democratic for very long.'[98] Hence 'the Party's not over'.[99] Nevertheless, popular will is going to find ways to form outside of political parties which will lose significance in that regard. In this technological innovation – see some examples further below[100] – will probably play a major role. Anti-system parties will prevail and their rise will not be halted until 2030. Populist parties will not merely be a phenomenon of the opposition but remain in or attain governmental power[101] and potentially excel in rendering their radical positions 'mainstream compatible'. The fate of the constitutional state depends to a large extent on a societal rejection of the distorted concept of constitutionalism propagated by populist parties.

[93] See ibid 389.
[94] ibid 388.
[95] Blokker, 'Populism' (n 76) 537 fn 4.
[96] ibid.
[97] See n 13 and accompanying text.
[98] Khaitan (n 12) 125.
[99] A slight alteration of Scheppele (n 82) 495.
[100] See n 124 et seq. and accompanying text.
[101] See Müller (n 65) 602 et seq.

B. Antagonism II: Autonomy v Regulation

Constitutional architectures safeguard on the one hand the autonomy of political parties (i.), on the other hand debates continue on intensifying the regulation of political parties[102] and the installation of effective mechanisms against parties which are hostile to the constitutional order (ii.).

i. Autonomy and Governance Structures

While the autonomy of political parties is conventionally regulated within constitutional orders, regulation does, however, manifest in varying degrees (a.). A particularly intrusive tool to define the 'party space'[103] are instruments of 'militant democracy' (b.).

a. 'Regulated Autonomy' as *Conditio sine qua non* of a Viable Party System

The autonomy of parties is generally considered as an indicator for the state that a constitutional democracy is in.[104] Autonomy encompasses the freedom to regulate internal matters independently. Yet, since political parties are perceived not purely as private organisations but as 'public utilities'[105] and constitutional actors within various constitutional architectures, their autonomy is guaranteed only within certain constraints. The relevant regulative limits are to be found directly within constitutional texts and/or are provided for in 'party laws' in various democracies.[106]

A general requirement which limits the sphere of autonomy concerns internal democratic structures (see, eg, Article 21, paragraph 1, third sentence Basic Law[107]).[108] Comparable provisions requiring 'intra-party democracy' (sometimes

[102] Venice Commission, Guidelines on Political Party Regulation, 2nd edn (14 December 2020).

[103] See for the term, eg, M Gilljam and H Oscarsson, 'Mapping the Nordic Party Space' (1996) 19 *Scandinavian Political Studies* 25.

[104] Khaitan (n 12) 90.

[105] I van Biezen, 'Political Parties as Public Utilities' (2004) 10 *Party Politics* 701.

[106] F Casal-Bértoa, D Romée Piccio and E Rashkova, 'Party Laws in Comparative Perspective', in I van Biezen and H-M ten Napel (eds), *Regulating Political Parties* (Leiden, Leiden University Press, 2014) 119. On the trend to regulate in Latin America J Gerardo Flores-Díaz, 'The legal regulation of political parties in latin america: public funding and internal democracy' (2020) 26 *Comparative Law Review* 155, 167.

[107] Basic Law (1949) (C Tomuschat and D Kommers (transl.), includes amendments of 23 December 2014 (Federal Law Gazette I 2438) www.gesetze-im-internet.de/englisch_gg/englisch_gg.html#p0017.

[108] See on the 'internal democracy' requirement Y Mersel, 'The dissolution of political parties: The problem of internal democracy' (2006) 4 *I·CON* 84.

abbreviated as IPD)[109] are identifiable for example in Article 51, paragraph 5 of the Constitution of Portugal,[110] Article 6, third sentence of the Spanish Constitution,[111] Article 108, paragraph 1 of the Constitution of Ecuador,[112] Article 41(I) of the Constitution of Mexico,[113] Article 216, sentence 2 of the Constitution of the Dominican Republic[114] or Article 98, paragraph 2 of the Constitution of Costa Rica.[115] There exists a wide range of regulative invasiveness – the regulation of parties within statutes covering various dimensions being a general trend[116] – across different constitutional orders[117] with the US constitutional system being one of the least invasive ones.[118] Austria is another example of a constitutional order hesitant to put limits to autonomy with respect to the inner architecture of parties: While Article 1, paragraph 1 of the Austrian Statute on Political Parties,[119] which enjoys constitutional nature, acknowledges the constitutional status of political parties within the Austrian constitutional order,[120] neither it nor the Constitution entail provisions which would require a political party to adhere to democratic principles in terms of its internal governance structure. This is seen as a major deficit in the Austrian system of democracy and has paved the way to phenomena like the *Team Stronach*[121] – a party founded and centred around Frank Stronach, a Canadian-Austrian citizen and entrepreneur – or the *Liste Sebastian Kurz – Die neue Volkspartei* – a candidate list set up for the elections to the *Nationalrat* – the Austrian parliament – including a 'rebranding' of the *Österreichische Volkspartei* (ÖVP) initiated by Sebastian Kurz in 2017. Kurz assumed as the *Bundesparteiobmann* and later new leader of the ÖVP the prerogative to determine the candidates of the ÖVP for the elections to the *Nationalrat* largely by himself.[122]

[109] F García Lupato and M Meloni 'Digital Intra-Party Democracy: An Exploratory Analysis of Podemos and the Labour Party' [2021] *Parliamentary Affairs* 1.

[110] *Constituição da República Portuguesa* (1976, with amendments through 2005): 'Os partidos políticos devem reger-se pelos princípios da transparência, da organização e da gestão democráticas e da participação de todos os seus membros'.

[111] 'Su estructura interna y funcionamiento deberán ser democráticos.' *Constitución Española* (1978, with amendments through 2011).

[112] *Constitución Política de la República del Ecuador* (2008, with amendments through 2021).

[113] See n 34.

[114] *Constitución de la República Dominicana* (2015).

[115] *Constitución Política de la República de Costa Rica* (1949, with amendments through 2020).

[116] I van Biezen and H-M ten Napel, 'Regulating Political Parties: European Democracies in Comparative Perspective', in I van Biezen and H-M ten Napel (eds), *Regulating Political Parties* (Leiden, Leiden University Press, 2014) 7 et seq.; Casal-Bértoa, Piccio and Rashkova (n 106) 139 et seq.

[117] See generally G Borz, 'Justifying the constitutional regulation of political parties: A framework for analysis' (2017) 38 *International Political Science Review* 99.

[118] R Pildes, 'Political Parties and Constitutionalism', New York University Public Law and Legal Theory Working Papers Paper 179 (2010) 15 et seq. See also Scheppele (n 82) 511.

[119] BGBl. I Nr. 56/2012.

[120] See W Berka, *Verfassungsrecht* 4th edn (Springer, Wien, 2012) 223.

[121] www.teamstronach.at/.

[122] See only S Lenzhofer, '"Liste Sebastian Kurz": ein Auswuchs eines gravierenden Mangels im österreichischen Parteienrecht,' VerfBlog, 2017/5/30 verfassungsblog.de/liste-sebastian-kurz-ein-auswuchs-eines-gravierenden-mangels-im-oesterreichischen-parteienrecht/.

b. Internal Governance

In terms of their internal governance structures (whose design falls within the sphere of party autonomy which – as just seen – is within various constitutional orders not unlimited), political parties – also mainstream parties – tend to implement direct democratic elements,[123] also making use of digital technologies[124] in order to open up their decision processes and to reduce 'membership barriers'.[125] This turn to technological innovations includes the employment of digital platforms – see in the case of *Podemos*, for example, the platform *Participa*[126] – for the elections of party representatives, consultations with citizens, the gathering of input for party programs, organising member voting on coalition agreements[127] or the involvement of volunteers.[128] This 'bottom-up' approach and 'plebiscitary turn'[129] can be seen as a reaction to a dissatisfaction of party members with staffing policies and a general professionalisation of political representatives[130] as well as a detachment of party leadership from the 'people'.[131] Whilst plebiscitarian elements are still fairly symbolic within the German party system,[132] also here they appear on the rise;[133] their effects are, however, contested.[134]

[123] Cp G Borz and K Janda 'Contemporary trends in party organization: Revisiting intra-party democracy' (2020) 26 *Party Politics* 3; Ignazi (n 14) 11 et seq.; K-R Korte, D Michels, J Schoofs, N Switek and K Weissenbach, *Parteiendemokratie in Bewegung* (Baden-Baden, Nomos 2018) 61 et seq. Furthermore R Steinberg, 'Direkte Demokratie in Politischen Parteien – Überlegungen anlässlich des Mitgliederentscheids der SPD' (2014) 45 *Zeitschrift Für Parlamentsfragen* 402.

[124] F García Lupato and M Meloni, 'Digital Intra-Party Democracy: An Exploratory Analysis of Podemos and the Labour Party' [2021] *Parliamentary Affairs* 1; M Deseriis and D Vittori, 'The Impact of Online Participation Platforms on the Internal Democracy of Two Southern European Parties: Podemos and the Five Star Movement' (2019) 13 *International Journal of Communication* 5696; A Lioy, M Esteve Del Valle and J Gottlieb, 'Platform politics: Party organisation in the digital age' (2019) 24 *Information Polity* 41.

[125] SE Scarrow, 'New Challenges of Intra-Party Democracy: Grassroots Activists, Instant Members, and Cyber-Militants', in E Avril and C Zumello (eds), *New Technology, Organizational Change and Governance* (New York, Palgrave Macmillan, 2013) 85, 88.

[126] participa.podemos.info/es; Lupato and Meloni (n 124) 10 et seq.

[127] This is, eg, the case regarding the participation of the German *Greens* in the 'traffic light coalition' which has formed after the elections to the German *Bundestag* in 2021, see DW, 'Grüne starten Urabstimmung über Koalitionsvertrag' (25 November 2021) www.dw.com/de/gr%C3%BCne-starten-urabstimmung-%C3%BCber-koalitionsvertrag/a-59926420.

[128] See for the organization of the participation of volunteers, eg, www.voltdeutschland.org/mitmachen/anmelden.

[129] Ignazi (n 14) 16.

[130] Cp C Close, C Kelbel and E van Haute, 'What Citizens Want in Terms of Intra-Party Democracy: Popular Attitudes towards Alternative Candidate Selection Procedures' (2017) 65 *Political Studies* 646.

[131] Cp Ignazi (n 14) 10, 17.

[132] See U von Alemann, P Erbentraut and J Walther, *Das Parteiensystem der Bundesrepublik Deutschland – Eine Einführung* 5th edn (Wiesbaden, Springer 2018) 260.

[133] Two other models for party reform that are currently discussed are including the electorate in party decision making or strengthening the role of experts, see von Alemann, Erbentraut and Walther (n 132) 260 et seq.

[134] Kaiser (n 42) 3.

ii. Definition of the 'Party Space' and Instruments of 'Militant Democracy'

Regulation of political parties does not only focus on their internal governance structures, but aims also to define the general 'party space'[135] within constitutional orders. In this context constraints on the political agenda of political parties gain relevance as part of the attempt to install a 'resilient' regulation of parties.[136]

A particularly invasive regulative scheme is the concept of a 'militant democracy'[137] (or 'defensive'/'fighting democracy'[138] – 'wehrhafte Demokratie')[139] as for example enshrined in German constitutional law – see Article 21, paragraphs 2 and 3 of the Basic Law.[140] It entails the option to ban parties which fight the fundaments of the constitutional order. This manifestation of a 'militant democracy' is not a singularity of German constitutional law: around one third of constitutional courts worldwide are endowed with the competence to ban parties.[141] Several prominent cases of party bans and dissolutions have been recently discussed (see, eg, the dissolution of the *Unified Progressive Party* in South Korea, the ban against the *Hong Kong National Party*[142] and the dissolution of the *Cambodia National Rescue Party* in Cambodia) – all examples hinting at the abusive potential of party ban competences.[143] Constitutional manifestations of the idea of a 'militant democracy' can, for example, be found in Articles 68, paragraph 4 and 69, paragraph 4 of the Turkish Constitution,[144] Article 46, paragraph 4 of the Armenian Constitution,[145]

[135] JO Frosini and S Pennicino, 'Ban on Political Parties', in *Max Planck Encyclopedia of Comparative Constitutional Law [MPECCoL]* (January 2017) para 2.

[136] Kaiser (n 42) 13.

[137] This term has been coined by K Loewenstein, 'Militant Democracy and Fundamental Rights, I' (1937) 31 *American Political Science Review* 417. See generally J-W Müller, 'Militant Democracy', in M Rosenfeld and A Sajó (eds), *The Oxford Handbook of Comparative Constitutional Law* (Oxford, OUP, 2012) 1253.

[138] Frosini and Pennicino (n 135) para 3.

[139] ibid.

[140] In terms of party bans in Europe from 1945-2015 and a comparative perspective see F Casal Bértoa and A Bourne, 'Prescribing democracy? Party proscription and party system stability in Germany, Spain and Turkey' (2017) 56 *European Journal of Political Research* 440, 443; A K Bourne and F Casal Bértoa, 'Mapping "Militant Democracy": Variation in Party Ban Practices in European Democracies' (1945-2015) (2017) 13 *European Constitutional Law Review* 221.

[141] T Ginsburg, AZ Huq and D Landau, 'The Law of Democratic Disqualification' (2021) 25 (pre-print SSRN) referring to T Ginsburg and Z Elkins, 'Ancillary Powers of Constitutional Courts' (2008) 87 *Texas Law Review* 1431, 1443 (table 1).

[142] BBC, 'Hong Kong government bans pro-independence party' (24 September 2018) www.bbc.com/news/world-asia-45623556; CJ Petersen, 'Prohibiting the Hong Kong National Party: Has Hong Kong Violated the International Covenant on Civil and Political Rights' (2018) 48 *Hong Kong Law Journal 789.*

[143] See with regard to the *Unified Progressive Party* in South Korea J Kim, 'Dissolution of the Unified Progressive Party Case in Korea' (2017) 10 *Journal of East Asia and International Law*. 139. In terms of the *Cambodia National Rescue Party* see UN Human Rights, Office of the High Commissioner, 'UN human rights chief voices concern about Cambodia election after opposition ban' (17 November 2017) www.ohchr.org/en/NewsEvents/Pages/DisplayNews.aspx?NewsID=22406&LangID=E.

[144] *Türkiye Cumhuriyeti Anayasası* (1982, with amendments through 2017).

[145] Constitution of the Republic of Armenia (1995, with amendments through 2015, 2020).

Article 15, paragraph 11 of the Constitution of Bhutan[146] or Article 8, paragraph 4 of the Constitution of the Republic of Korea.[147]

As seen, there exists the obvious danger that party bans are instrumentalised politically: this instrument designed to stabilise democracy has – if abused – the potential to undermine its very basis[148] (see, eg, the case of the *Cambodia National Rescue Party*).[149] Furthermore, party bans raise crucial human rights issues if seen through the prism of the freedom of association (see, eg, Article 22 International Covenant on Civil and Political Rights,[150] Article 16 American Convention on Human Rights[151]).[152] Scholarship has widely evidenced that party bans might become a slippery slope towards an 'intolerant'[153] and autocratic state. In light of this the ECtHR has established – arguing from a human rights perspective – restrictive limits to party bans based on Article 11 of the European Convention on Human Rights (ECHR).[154]

Within the German constitutional order the prerogative to ban parties rests with the Federal Constitutional Court (FCC). Whilst being a sharp sword, the Court has rarely used its competence to ban parties. More interesting and practically relevant appears the competence of the FCC to exclude parties from state funding[155] and from a preferential tax treatment of contributions made to the respective party (Article 21, paragraph 3 Basic Law). This competence – introduced in 2017 – applies to parties that 'are oriented towards an undermining or abolition of the free democratic basic order or an endangerment of the existence of the Federal Republic of Germany' (Article 21, paragraph 3 Basic Law). This constitutional amendment is to be seen as a direct legislative reaction to the ruling of the FCC in the second NPD (*Nationaldemokratische Partei Deutschlands*) case[156] which established the threshold of 'potentiality' as a prerequisite for declaring a

[146] Constitution of the Kingdom of Bhutan (2008).

[147] Constitution of the Republic of Korea (1948, with amendments through 1987).

[148] Cp Wolkenstein (n 4) 20; Frosini and Pennicino (n 135) para 24; Bértoa and Bourne (n 140) 440 et seq.

[149] See n 143.

[150] 999 UNTS 171.

[151] 1144 UNTS 123.

[152] See S Tyulkina, 'Fragmentation in International Human Rights Law: Political Parties and Freedom of Association in the Practice of the UN Human Rights Committee, European Court of Human Rights and Inter-American Court of Human Rights' (2014) 32 *Nordic Journal of Human Rights* 157.

[153] GH Fox and G Nolte (1995) 36 *Harvard International Law Journal* 1.

[154] See ECtHR [GC], Judgment of 13 February 2003, 41340/98, 41342/98, 41343/98 et al., para 190 et seq. – *Refah Partisi (the Welfare Party) and Others v Turkey.*

[155] See Art 21, para 3: 'Parties that, by reason of their aims or the behaviour of their adherents, are oriented towards an undermining or abolition of the free democratic basic order or an endangerment of the existence of the Federal Republic of Germany shall be excluded from state financing. If such exclusion is determined, any favourable fiscal treatment of these parties and of payments made to those parties shall cease.'

[156] See generally U Backes, 'Banning political parties in a democratic constitutional state: the second NPD ban proceedings in a comparative perspective' (2019) 53 *Patterns of Prejudice* 136.

party ban[157] – a restrictive reading of Article 21, paragraph 2 Basic Law which in its result implements the proportionality requirement established by the ECtHR:[158] A party may only be banned if it has the potential to actually endanger the free democratic order,[159] while a lower threshold applies to the exclusion of a party from state funding. Similar provisions are to be found in other constitutional orders: Belgium, for example, does exclude political parties which agitate against human rights as enshrined in the ECHR from state subsidies.[160] While being less invasive than a general ban, the exclusion from state funding weakens political parties significantly. Since party bans and banning procedures might have – besides general doubts with regard to the instrument as such when seen from the stance of constitutional law and democracy theory – several negative side-effects (eg, inadvertently strengthening and putting the spotlight on an 'anti-system party'), it appears that cutting off extremist parties from state funding might prove to be a more effective means in combatting their agitation than their prohibition and dissolution. Such 'minus measures' seem to be easier accommodatable with the jurisprudence of the ECtHR and general human rights standards.

iii. Tentative Outlook

The trend to regulate political parties will not come to an end – particularly considering the rise of 'anti-system parties'. In terms of their internal architectures, it is to be assumed that parties will both expand direct democratic elements within their governance structures as well as take recourse to information technologies to render their decision-making procedures more inclusive, whilst it remains doubtful whether this will halt their 'legitimacy crisis' considering also the pitfalls of plebiscitary elements.[161] Democracies will continue to ban parties, while the idea to merely cut off particular parties from state funding might gain appeal.

[157] FCC, Judgment of 17 January 2017, 2 BvB 1/13 – *National Democratic Party II*. See G Molier and B Rijpkema, 'Germany's New Militant Democracy Regime: National Democratic Party II and the German Federal Constitutional Court's 'Potentiality' Criterion for Party Bans' (2018) 14 *European Constitutional Law Review* 394.

[158] M Hailbronner, 'Combatting malfunction or optimizing democracy? Lessons from Germany for a comparative political process theory' (2021) 19 *I•CON* 495, 510. On proportionality see also Venice Commission, Guidelines (n 102) para 110.

[159] FCC, Judgment of 17 January 2017, 2 BvB 1/13, para 585 et seq. – *National Democratic Party II*.

[160] B Low, 'The Centre Cannot Hold: Reflections on Militant Democracy in Germany' (2018) 21 *Trinity CL Rev* 136, 157. See M Bogaards, 'Militant Consociational Democracy: The Political Exclusion of the Extreme-Right in Belgium', in S Baume and S Novak (eds), *Compromises in Democracy* (Cham, Palgrave Macmillan, 2020) 175, 180 et seq.; T Bale, 'Are Bans on Political Parties Bound to Turn Out Badly? A Comparative Investigation of Three 'Intolerant' Democracies: Turkey, Spain, and Belgium' (2007) 5 *Comparative European Politics* 141.

[161] See Ignazi (n 14) 17.

C. Antagonism III: Political Parties as National Actors v European and International Actors

Coming now to the third antagonism: typically, political parties are perceived as national actors. Since political parties serve as 'transmission belts' – see above – between society and the state, they are national constitutional actors in the first place. In various dimensions the activities of political parties do, however, extend beyond the national realm. Here we can particularly take both the 'Europeanisation'[162] of party families (i.) as well as the 'internationalisation' and 'globalisation' of the 'party space' in view (ii.).

i. Europeanisation of Party Families

Since the emergence of the supranational entity EU[163] – neither fitting into the logic of national nor international law, neither being a confederation nor a federal state – we could witness an incremental Europeanisation of party families.[164] After some general remarks on this process (a.) we will turn to a close-up on different manifestations of Europeanisation ex ante and ex post the elections to the European Parliament (EP) in 2019 (b.) which some have termed 'as the first genuine European elections in the history of the Union'.[165] This will allow us to draw some conclusions on possible future developments.

But at first, some general remarks are in place: The process of European integration has had an extensive effect on the policies, policy-making, activities and organisational logic of party families within the European 'political space'. 'Europeanisation' understood as 'an incremental process reorienting the direction and shape of politics to the degree that EC political and economic dynamics become part of the organizational logic of national politics and policy-making'[166] occurred in various manifestations. '[N]ew patterns of behaviour and decision making among political actors and institutions resulting from the impact of European integration'[167] extended also to political parties.

[162] See generally P Mair, 'Political Parties and Party Systems', in P Graziano and MP Vink (eds), *Europeanization* (Basingstoke, Palgrave Macmillian, 2008) 154.

[163] Generally A von Bogdandy, *Supranationaler Föderalismus als Wirklichkeit und Idee einer neuen Herrschaftsform* (Baden-Baden, Nomos, 1999).

[164] See on Europeanisation of political parties R Ladrech, 'Europeanization and Political Parties' (2002) 8 *Party Politics* 389.

[165] A Hoppe and J Schmälter, 'What's New in the EP? EU-issue Parties and the Europeanization of National Party Systems', in M Kaeding, M Müller and J Schmälter (eds), *Die Europawahl 2019* (Wiesbaden, Springer, 2020) 143, 151.

[166] R Ladrech, 'Europeanization of Domestic Politics and Institutions: The Case of France' (1994) 32 *Journal of Common Market Studies* (1994) 69, 69. See also Ladrech (n 164) 391.

[167] T Poguntke, N Aylott, R Ladrech and KR Luther, 'The Europeanisation of national party organisations: A conceptual analysis' (2007) 46 *European Journal of Political Research* 747, 748.

A transnational cooperation and a closer entanglement of national parties started with the first direct elections to the EP in 1979.[168] This entanglement took a more institutionalised shape in the course of time. Members of the EP (MEPs) – who are acting together with the Council as co-legislators[169] being also responsible for the election of the Commission and its President[170] – are elected by EU citizens.[171] However, EU law establishes only some requirements for the election of MEPs,[172] which follow national rules constrained by some EU law requirements.[173] Until now none of the MEPs are elected in a transnational constituency across the EU. Therefore, during elections to the EP we, in fact, become witnesses to now 27 national elections.[174] Within this electoral process national parties play a key role. Yet, triggered by the European dimension of the elections to the EP, formal transnational associations allowing the exchange of views along party lines first emerged in the course of the 1970s[175] ultimately finding a basis in EU primary law.[176] According to Article 10, paragraph 4 TEU[177] 'Political parties at European level contribute to forming European political awareness and to expressing the will of citizens of the Union.'[178] Currently ten 'Political Parties at European Level' – 'European party federations'[179] or colloquially 'Europarties' – are registered.[180]

[168] Cp E Liedtke, '40 Jahre Europawahlen – und noch immer kein europäisches Parteiensystem?', in M Kaeding, M Müller and J Schmälter (eds), *Die Europawahl 2019* (Wiesbaden, Springer, 2020) 105, 110 et seq.

[169] Art 14 para 1 TEU.

[170] Art 17 para 7 TEU.

[171] Arts 10 para 2, 14 para 2 TEU.

[172] Art 14 para 2 TEU.

[173] See Council Decision (EU, Euratom) 2018/994 of 13 July 2018; L Cicchi, 'Europeanising the elections of the European Parliament', Outlook on the implementation of Council Decision 2018/994 and harmonisation of national rules on European elections, STUDY Requested by the AFCO committee (2021); R Hrbek, 'The Arduous Way Towards a Uniform Electoral System for the European Parliament', in O Costa (ed), *The European Parliament in Times of EU Crisis. European Administrative Governance* (Cham, Palgrave Macmillan, 2019) 255.

[174] Cp K Reif and H Schmitt, 'Nine second-order national elections – A Conceptual Framework for the Analysis of European Election Results' (1980) 8 *European Journal of Political Research* 3; J Pollex, 'Deutsche und europäische Programme zur Europawahl – Europäisierung und nationale Profilierung im europäischen Mehrebenen-Wahlsystem', in M Kaeding, M Müller and J Schmälter (eds), *Die Europawahl 2019* (Wiesbaden, Springer, 2020) 119, 120.

[175] See S Hix, 'Parties at the European Level', in P Webb, D Farrell and I Holliday (eds), *Political Parties in Advanced Industrial Democracies* (Oxford, OUP, 2002) 280, 280 et seq.

[176] Europarties are also regulated by EU secondary law: Art 3 para 1 EU Regulation No 1141/2014 provides for the registration of Europarties and employs a transnational Europarty concept.

[177] See also Art 224 TFEU and Art 12 para 2 EU Charter of Fundamental Freedoms.

[178] See Art 2 para 3 EU Regulation No 1141/2014 (regulating funding of inter alia political parties): '"European political party" means a political alliance which pursues political objectives and is registered with the Authority for European political parties and foundations established in Article 6, in accordance with the conditions and procedures laid down in this Regulation; […].'

[179] M Bogaards, 'The European Union: Consociational Past, Centripetal Future?' [2021] *Representation* 1, 3.

[180] See Authority for European Political Parties and European Political Foundations, www.appf.europa.eu/appf/en/parties-and-foundations/registered-parties. Amongst these are the *European People's Party*

While Europarties are designed to serve as 'transmission belts'[181] between the EU governance structure and the European *demos*, they have fulfilled this role imperfectly until now. This 'failure' is essentially linked to the peculiarities of the elections to the EP: considering the lack of a transnational constituency, elections to the EP have often been termed as 'second-order elections'[182] since governing parties are usually punished by the voters,[183] parties fight campaigns on national issues[184] and candidates operate within national 'monologue-bubbles'.[185]

a. Europeanisation Processes in the Course of Elections to the European Parliament in 2019

The EP parliamentary election in 2019 formed an important moment for both further Europeanisation of political parties in some dimensions and its reversion in others displaying a complex picture: here it is sensible to distinguish Europeanisation processes ex ante and ex post the EP elections 2019.

Ex ante: in terms of the phase before the election, Europeanisation occurred in various dimensions of which only three shall be addressed here: Europeanisation via content and service, Europeanisation via personalisation and Europeanisation 'at the fringes'.[186]

Europarties – as in previous election campaigns[187] – have adopted common manifestos which have tackled European topics.[188] Not all national member

(EPP); *Party of European Socialists* (PES), *Alliance of Liberals and Democrats for Europe* (ALDE); *European Democratic Party* (PDE EDP); *European Green Party* (European Greens), *European Free Alliance, Identité et Démocratie Parti* (ID), *European Conservatives and Reformists Party* (ECR), *Party of the European Left, European Christian and Political Movement*. Parliamentary groups ('European party groups' see Bogaards (n 179) 3) – not allowed to campaign during the EP elections – form within the EP along party lines which is a further institutional scheme to foster the entanglement of party families. Generally, G McElroy and K Benoit, 'Party Policy and Group Affiliation in the European Parliament' (2010) 40 *British Journal of Political Science* 377.

[181] On this concept see already above n 27 and accompanying text.

[182] Reif and Schmitt (n 174) 3; P Mair and J Thomassen, 'Political representation and government in the European Union' (2010) 17 *Journal of European Public Policy* 20, 28 et seq.

[183] Reif and Schmitt (n 174) 10. Cp P Ehin and L Talving, 'Still second-order? European elections in the era of populism, extremism, and Euroscepticism' (2021) 41 *Politics* 467, 482.

[184] Cp Reif and Schmitt (n 174) 3; SB Hobolt and J Wittrock, 'The second-order election model revisited: An experimental test of vote choices in EP elections' (2011) 30 *Electoral Studies*, 29, 39.

[185] K Hoffmeister, 'Transnational Lists in European Parliamentary Elections – a Fresh Proposal for European Democracy' [2020] *ZeuS* 129, 137.

[186] A Alemanno, 'Towards Transnational European Democracy? The New Battles Lines of the 2019 European Parliament Election' HEC Paris Research Paper No LAW-2018-1287 (2018) 4.

[187] See I Hertner, 'Are European election campaigns Europeanized? The case of the party of European socialists in 2009' (2011) 46 *Government and Opposition* 321, 333 et seq.

[188] See, eg, manifesto of the European Greens 'EGP Priorities for 2019: What European Greens Fight For' (adopted 23 to 25 November 2018) europeangreens.eu/sites/europeangreens.eu/files/Adopted%20EGP%20priorities%20for%202019_EN.pdf; manifesto of ALDE, 'Freedom, opportunity, prosperity: the Liberal vision for the future of Europe' (adopted 10 November 2018); d3n8a8pro7vhmx.cloudfront.net/aldeparty/pages/1590/attachments/original/1594139136/2019_freedom_opportunity_prosperity_the_liberal_vision_for_the_future_of_europe_0_%281%29.pdf?1594139136.

parties made use of these manifestos,[189] which have remained rather general,[190] in their own campaign however, they influenced national manifestos.[191] At the very least, an alignment of Europarty manifestos and national party positions occurred.[192] Europarties have generated campaign material[193] and implemented digital campaigns.[194] They functioned as 'service providers'[195] sharing expertise in campaigning, organising campaign workshops and discussing campaign strategies with national member parties.[196] European issues have played a central role in the campaign of national parties,[197] which marks a departure from the traditional narrative of EP elections as 'second-order elections'[198] (see above).[199] Candidates to the EP engaged – although to a limited extent – in 'transnational campaign interactions'.[200]

Europeanisation has also occurred via personalisation and its most evident manifestations have been the '*Spitzenkandidaten* process'[201] – applied for the first time when Jean-Claude Juncker was elected[202] – and the 'Team Europe strategy'.[203] The '*Spitzenkandidaten* process' is based on a specific reading of Article 17, paragraph 7 TEU focussing on the phrase 'taking into account'.[204]

[189] E Novelli and B Johansson (eds), *European Elections Campaign* (Report by the European Elections Monitoring Center, 2019) 15.

[190] Pollex (n 174) 129.

[191] Cp P Clasen, 'Does the Europarty Still not Matter? European Elections 2019 and the Party of European Socialists', in M Kaeding, M Müller and J Schmälter (eds) *Die Europawahl 2019* (Wiesbaden, Springer, 2020) 39, 42. But see Novelli and Johansson (n 189) 15.

[192] N Switek and K Weissenbach, 'An Ever-Closer Party? The Institutionalization of the European Green Party After the 2019 European Election', in M Kaeding, M Müller and J Schmälter (eds), *Die Europawahl 2019* (Wiesbaden, Springer, 2020) 63, 72.

[193] See, eg, vote.europeangreens.eu/de.

[194] See, eg, vote.europeangreens.eu/volunteer. See Edoardo Novelli and Johansson (n 191) 15.

[195] See on this term W Gagatek, *European Political Parties as Campaign Organisations* (Centre for European Studies, 2009) 37.

[196] A Groen, *With a little help from our friends* (Maastricht 2020) 170 et seq.

[197] See on the centrality of European topics E Novelli and B Johansson (n 191) 20; Pollex (n 174) 119 et seq.

[198] Reif and Schmitt (n 174) 3.

[199] C Galpin and J Renz, 'In the Shadow of Brexit: The 2019 European Parliament Elections as First-Order Polity Elections?' (2019) 90 *The Political Quarterly* 664, 665 et seq.; Hoppe and Schmälter (n 165) 143. But see more cautionary Ehin and Talving (n 183) 482 et seq. For a nuanced view S Stier, C Froio and WJ Schünemann, 'Going transnational? Candidates' transnational linkages on Twitter during the 2019 European Parliament elections' (2021) 44 *West European Politics* 1455, 1473.

[200] Stier, Froio and Schünemann (n 199) 1456.

[201] See already H Schmitt, S Hobolt and SA Popa, 'Does Personalization Increase Turnout? Spitzenkandidaten in the 2014 European Parliament Elections' [2015] *European Union Politics* 347.

[202] L Tilindyte, European Parliamentary Research Service, Briefing: Election of the President of the European Commission (2019) 4.

[203] teameurope.eu/. See W Wolfs, G-J Put and S van Hecke, 'The Second Time Around: Status Quo and Reform of the Europarties' Selection Procedures for Spitzenkandidaten in 2019', in M Kaeding, M Müller and J Schmälter (eds), *Die Europawahl 2019* (Wiesbaden, Springer, 2020) 157, 161.

[204] Critically T Holzner, 'Das Europäische Parliament im Institutionengefüge der EU – Verschiebung der Kräfteverhältnisse infolge der Durchsetzung eines "Spitzenkandidaten" als Kommissionspräsident?' [2015] *EuR* 525, 537.

With its implementation the EU took 'a decisive step in a particular direction – namely, towards a parliamentary, party-based democracy':[205] Europarties appoint a *Spitzenkandidat* before the election,[206] the Council proposes a candidate for the presidency of the Commission of the political party capable of gathering sufficient support within the parliament. The '*Spitzenkandidaten* procedure' was designed to make EP elections more similar to national parliamentary elections: in the case of national parliamentary elections voters cast votes for a particular party by supporting a specific candidate. The ultimate purpose was hence to strengthen the chain of legitimation between the elections to the EP and the Commission. The *Alliance of Liberals and Democrats for Europe* (ALDE) refrained from designating a lead candidate but opted for a 'Team Europe Strategy' proposing a list of seven nominees for the key positions within the EU governance structure.[207]

The third dimension of Europeanisation occurred within a cluster of right-wing populists[208] and Euro-sceptical movements[209] which united: *Identity and Democracy* as a 'political party on the European level' emerged.[210] Here we come across a paradox: parties which oppose cosmopolitanism taking a nationalist stance have become facilitators and beneficiaries of Europeanisation.[211]

The evolution of a European *demos* took a major blow when the '*Spitzenkandidaten* procedure' imploded in the aftermath of the elections.[212] While the *European People's Party* (EPP) came out of the elections as the strongest party, its lead candidate Manfred Weber was not proposed by the European Council.[213] The reasons for this are manifold: the Council opposed the automatism of the

[205] M Westlake, 'Possible Future European Union Party Political Systems', in O Costa (ed), *The European Parliament in Times of EU Crisis. European Administrative Governance* (Cham, Palgrave Macmillan, 2019) 321, 337.

[206] SB Hobolt, 'A vote for the President? The role of *Spitzenkandidaten* in the 2014 European Parliament elections' (2014) 21 *Journal of European Public Policy* 1528, 1529.

[207] See teameurope.eu/.

[208] See M Golder, 'Far Right Parties in Europe' (2016) 19 *Annual Review of Political Science* 477; S van Hauwaert, 'On Far Right Parties, Master Frames and Trans-National Diffusion: Understanding Far Right Party Development in Western Europe' (2019) 17 *Comparative European Politics* 132. Cp A Pirro, P Taggart and S van Kessel, 'The Populist Politics of Euroscepticism in Times of Crisis: Comparative Conclusions' (2018) 38 *Politics* 378.

[209] On 'eurosceptisism' see O Treib, 'Euroscepticism is here to stay: what cleavage theory can teach us about the 2019 European Parliament elections' (2021) 28 *Journal of European Public Policy* 174, 176 et seq.

[210] See generally J Rettig, 'Zur Politikfähigkeit der extremen Rechten im Europäischen Parlament', in M Kaeding, M Müller and J Schmälter (eds), *Die Europawahl 2019* (Wiesbaden, Springer, 2020) 91.

[211] Cp also n 219 and accompanying text.

[212] P de Wilde, 'The Fall of the Spitzenkandidaten: Political Parties and Conflict in the 2019 European Elections', in S Kritzinger, C Plescia, K Raube, J Wilhelm and J Wouters (eds), *Assessing the 2019 European Parliament Elections* (London, Routledge, 2020) 37.

[213] S Stolton with A Brzozowski, 'Weber forced to stand aside as EU leaders bypass Spitzenkandidaten' *Euractiv* (2 July 2019) www.euractiv.com/section/eu-elections-2019/news/weber-forced-to-stand-aside-as-eu-leaders-bypass-spitzenkandidaten/. See on the role of Emanuel Macron M Kaeding, M Müller and J Schmälter, 'Die Europawahl 2019: Ringen um die Zukunft Europas', in M Kaeding, M Müller and J Schmälter (eds), *Die Europawahl 2019* (Wiesbaden, Springer, 2020) 9, 18 et seq.; de Wilde (n 212) 37, see figure 3.2.

'*Spitzenkandidaten* process'. No clear majorities existed in the EP and Weber was unable to find sufficient support amongst the other groupings in the EP.[214]

This failure shaped the discourse within party families and led in the end to a re-invigoration of the debate on further steps that were to be taken to foster the birth of a 'European polity'.[215] Here different propositions were discussed: the implementation of a compulsory '*Spitzenkandidaten* process',[216] a direct election of the President of the European Commission[217] or the election of some MEPs via transnational lists.[218] The latter proposition has faced severe opposition: while transnational lists would foster the establishment of a pan-European constituency, they would create different categories of MEPs as their key opponents stress.[219] Important steps taken towards allocating some seats in the EP via transnational lists have hence ultimately failed.[220]

ii. Internationalisation of Political Parties and Global Polity

Political parties are also to be seen in the context of the 'global political space' – and here we can identify four important phenomena:

On the one hand, a backlash against international norms,[221] particularly international human rights law[222] and international institutions[223] can be witnessed.

[214] Here and before A Gray, J Barigazzi and M de la Baume, 'Who killed the Spitzenkandidat?' *Politico* (5 July 2019) www.politico.eu/article/who-killed-the-spitzenkandidat-european-parliament-election-2019-transition/.

[215] Generally on the problem of a transnationalisation of the party system Z Lefkofridi and A Katsanidou, 'Step Closer to a Transnational Party System? Competition and Coherence in the 2009 and 2014 European Parliament' (2018) 56 *Journal of Common Market Studies* 1462.

[216] Cp J Edthofer and P Schmidt, 'The future of the EU`s Spitzenkandidaten procedure', ÖGfE Policy Brief 04a'2021 (2021) 9 (Conclusion).

[217] On this issue see already F Decker and J Sonnicksen, 'An Alternative Approach to European Union Democratization: Re-Examining the Direct Election of the Commission President' (2011) 46 *Government and Opposition* 168.

[218] See M Diaz Crego, EPRS (European Parliamentary Research Service), *Transnational Electoral Lists* (February 2021).

[219] A Alemanno, 'Why transnational lists matter for EU democracy' *Euractiv* (7 February 2018) www.euractiv.com/section/elections/opinion/why-transnational-lists-matter-for-eu-democracy/; also referred to by M Bartl, 'Hayek Upside-Down: On the Democratic Effects of Transnational Lists' (2020) 21 *German Law Journal* 57, 60; Hoffmeister (n 185) 136.

[220] See Report on the composition of the European Parliament, Motion for a EP Resolution (rapporteurs Danuta Maria Hübner and Pedro Silva Pereira) – (2017/2054(INL) – 2017/0900(NLE). On transnational lists see already S van Hecke et al, 'Reconnecting European Political Parties with European Union Citizens', International IDEA Discussion Paper 6/2018; Bartl (n 219) 60 et seq.; Hoffmeister (n 185) 129 et seq.

[221] See on a general 'withdrawal trend' J Crawford, 'The Current Political Discourse Concerning International Law' (2018) 81 *Modern Law Review* 1.

[222] P Alston, 'The Populist Challenge to Human Rights' (2017) 9 *Journal of Human Rights Practice* 1; J Hartmann and S White, in K McCall-Smith, A Birdsall and E Casanas Adam (eds), *Human Rights in Times of Transition: Liberal Democracies and Challenges of National Security* (Cheltenham, Edward Elgar Publishing, 2020) 139; E Posner, 'Liberal Internationalism and the Populist Backlash', University of Chicago Public Law & Legal Theory Paper Series, No 606 (2017).

[223] H Krieger, 'Populist Governments and International Law' (2019) 30 *European Journal of International Law* 971, 980 et seq.; M Rask Madsen, 'Two-level politics and the backlash against

Within the national political discourse, parties – mostly populist parties of the far right – take an anti-cosmopolitan stance being united therein. They fight 'the global technocratic elite',[224] propagate a '[p]rincipled opposition'[225] and at times even an 'open defiance' to international law in its post 1945 guise challenging global constitutionalism.[226] Whilst international issues are on the agenda of such parties, they take an opposite position.

On the other hand, the 'parliamentarisation' of foreign affairs[227] might foster a global focus of political parties in a way which enhances legitimacy processes within the global realm in a productive way. Within the international legal order various actors exert 'international public authority'[228] which is only deficiently legitimised. Considering the imperfect chain of legitimation down to the individual in the international sphere the idea of 'compensatory constitutionalism' gains track: democratic deficits on the international plane can be compensated by processes of democratic participation on the national level and vice versa.[229] In that regard political parties might play a role which should not be underestimated: First, national parties tackle international political issues – here are just two examples: the *Freie Demokraten* (FDP), the German liberals, have addressed questions of UN reform and a strengthening of the 'responsibility to protect'[230] concept in their manifesto for the *Bundestag* elections in 2021.[231] The idea of Spain as a promotor of 'international democracy' and a democratisation of the UN is

international courts: Evidence from the politicisation of the European court of human rights' (2020) 22 *The British Journal of Politics and International Relations* 728, Ø Stiansen and E Voeten, 'Backlash and Judicial Restraint: Evidence from the European Court of Human Rights' (2020) 64 *International Studies Quarterly* 770.

[224] Krieger (n 223) 976.

[225] ibid 996.

[226] CM Koch, 'Varieties of populism and the challenges to Global Constitutionalism: Dangers, promises and implications' [2020] *Global Constitutionalism* 1.

[227] See in the context of the conclusion of treaties P-H Verdier and M Versteeg, 'Separation of Powers, Treaty-Making, and Treaty Withdrawal: A Global Survey', in C Bradley (ed), *The Oxford Handbook of Comparative Foreign Relations Law* (Oxford, OUP, 2019) 135, 149. Generally B Ehrenzeller, *Legislative Gewalt und Außenpolitik* (Basel, Helbing und Lichtenhahn, 1993); U Fastenrath, *Kompetenzverteilung im Bereich der auswärtigen Gewalt* (München, Beck, 1986); R Wolfrum, 'Kontrolle der auswärtigen Gewalt' (1997) 56 *Veröffentlichungen der Vereinigung der Deutschen Staatsrechtslehrer* 38.

[228] M Goldmann, *Internationale Öffentliche Gewalt* (Berlin, Springer, 2015); A von Bogdandy, P Dann and M Goldmann, 'Developing the Publicness of Public International Law: Towards a Legal Framework for Global Governance Activities' (2008) 9 *German Law Journal* 1375; A von Bogdandy, 'General Principles of International Public Authority: Sketching a Research Field' (2008) 9 *German Law Journal* 1909.

[229] Cp A Peters, 'Compensatory Constitutionalism: The Function and Potential of Fundamental International Norms and Structures' (2006) 19 *Leiden Journal of International Law* 579 (who focusses on compensatory mechanisms for national de-constitutionalisation processes on the international plane).

[230] See only UNSG, Report of the Secretary-General, 'Responsibility to protect: from early warning to early action' (1 June 2018) (UN Doc. A/72/884–S/2018/525) and World Summit Outcome Document (UNGA A/RES/60/1), para 138, 139.

[231] 'Nie gab es mehr zu tun', Das Programm der Freien Demokraten (2021) 54 www.fdp.de/sites/default/files/2021-08/FDP_BTW2021_Wahlprogramm_1.pdf.

an element of the *Podemos* party program.[232] Second, parliaments are required in various constitutional orders to approve international treaties if they display a certain quality.[233] Since international treaties become issues of parliamentary factions they necessarily become part of party policy considerations which evolve ideally within a dialogue with society.

Beyond that, national parties tend to have branches abroad or to the least extend their activities abroad, which is a reaction to the mobility of citizens[234] and voting rights of non-resident citizens within 'diasporas'. Activities of national parties abroad display different degrees of formalisation.[235] Examples include the activities of *Adalet ve Kalkınma Partisi* (AKP – *Justice and Development Party*) in Germany,[236] the operations of *World Likud* which is 'the Likud Party's wing for global communication and networking'[237] or formalised (also in varying degrees) branches like the *Democrats Abroad* – the 'Democratic Party arm' abroad – which are allocated eight voting members on the National Democratic Committee[238] or the *CDU Brussels*.[239] Whilst this externalisation of party activities is mainly directed towards representation of non-residents within the 'home land', it naturally requires parties to take foreign issues into account in terms of their policies.

Furthermore, there exist structures within which parties cooperate globally[240] beyond the 'European political space'. In terms of global party bonds also beyond left-wing populism[241] the 'Socialist International' is to be mentioned: the 'Socialist International' is 'the worldwide organisation of social democratic, socialist and labour parties'.[242] It is more than an artefact of past times and continues to engender some effects on its members: one of its full members is, for example, the Argentine party *Unión Cívica Radical* (UCR). The latter stresses in its *Carta ética*

[232] Programa de PODEMOS, 'Las razones siguen intactas' (2016) para 117 podemos.info/wp-content/uploads/2019/10/Podemos_programa_generales_10N.pdf.

[233] Verdier and Versteeg (n 227) 139 et seq.; P Starski, 'Parlamentarische Mitwirkungsbefugnisse bei der Kündigung völkerrechtlicher Verträge – eine rechtsvergleichende Betrachtung' (2020; on file with the author).

[234] T Kernalegenn and E von Haute (eds), *Political Parties Abroad* (Milton, Routledge, 2020); ER Rashkova and S van der Staak, 'The Party Abroad and Its Role for National Party Politics' [2019] *Security and Human Rights* 108; A Friedman and O Kenig, 'Parties beyond national borders: exploring the activities of Israeli political parties abroad' (2021) 9 *Comparative Migration Studies* 23. See on the question of representation E Østergaard-Nielsen and I Ciornei, 'Making the absent present: Political parties and emigrant issues in country of origin parliaments' (2019) 25 *Party Politics* 153.

[235] Rashkova and van der Staak (n 234) 115 et seq.

[236] S Adar, 'Rethinking Political Attitudes of Migrants from Turkey and Their Germany-Born Children', SWP Research Paper 7 (June 2019).

[237] See www.worldlikud.org.il/en/about-us.

[238] www.democratsabroad.org/.

[239] www.cdu-bruessel.org/index.html. On the latter two see also Rashkova and van der Staak (n 234) 122 et seq.; 126 et seq.

[240] See H Patomäki, 'Towards global political parties' (2011) 4 *Ethics & Global Politics* 81, 88 et seq.; J Smith, 'Political Parties in a Global Age', in D Josselin and W Wallace (eds), *Non-state Actors in World Politics* (London, Palgrave Macmillian, 2001) 59.

[241] Cp Tushnet (n 81) 389.

[242] www.socialistinternational.org/about-us/.

the significance of a cooperation with other parties within the 'Socialist International'.[243] But also beyond that, propositions to establish a 'world political party', which would facilitate the emergence of a global *demos*, can be heard.[244] Whilst it might be questioned whether a 'party' in its conventional understanding is the right institutional actor to facilitate the formation of a global popular will within global governance structures, arguing for the emergence of a global *demos* appears consequential in light of the global dimension and origin of societal problems as well as different, largely untamed instances of 'international public authority'[245] determining the reality of each national citizen.

iii. Tentative Outlook

It is very likely that we will identify contradicting strands of development in the future with view to the supranational and international realm in terms of the state of constitutionalism in 2030 and political parties.

While the Europeanisation of party families will progress, so will the transnationalisation of a backlash against the EU and its normative fundaments continue to unfold. Euroscepticism – both right and left – will prevail.[246] As it is already the case, specific EU-issue parties will continue to emerge in some national orders.[247] The debates on the creation of a truly 'European polity' and a 'European consciousness that one might call the beginning of a European demos'[248] – as it is already commanded by Article 10, paragraph 4 TEU – will continue and the pressure to part with EP elections as 'second-order elections'[249] will rise. In terms of the 'European political space' it is to be expected that 'established' Europarties will continue to be confronted with competitors as contemporary developments suggest: during the 2019 EP elections the grassroot, pan-European movement and party *VOLT* emerged[250] which has registered the same symbol in all Member States and operates with one single political programme. The pan-European movement *DiEM25* (*Democracy in Europe Movement 2025*) can also be mentioned in this context.[251] Movements 'from below' might become important actors in creating a European *demos*. The EP elections in 2024 will be a crucial moment for the European 'political space' particularly with view to a possible reactivation of the '*Spitzenkandidaten* procedure'.

[243] ucr.org.ar/lo-que-somos/carta-etica.

[244] H Patomäki, 'A World Political Party: The Time Has Come', GTI Essay, February 2019; see also www.opendemocracy.net/en/can-europe-make-it/time-for-world-political-party-has-come/.

[245] von Bogdandy, Dann and Goldmann (n 228) 1375; Goldmann (n 228).

[246] Treib (n 209) 184.

[247] Hoppe and Schmälter (n 165) 147: *Forum voor Democratie* (Netherlands), *Svoboda a prímá demokracie* (Czech Republic), Brexit Party (UK) and *Fratelli d'Italia* (Italy).

[248] Hoffmeister (n 185) 140.

[249] Reif and Schmitt (n 174) 3.

[250] www.volteuropa.org.

[251] diem25.org/en/.

Contradicting strands of development are also to be expected in terms of the international realm: cosmopolitanism will continue to be attacked by some political parties and their transnational bonds might tighten over their opposition, while global issues will be addressed by national parties more intensely.

III. Conclusion: Political Parties and Constitutionalism in 2030

What general conclusions allows this exercise of antagonisms to draw with a view to the state of constitutionalism in 2030 and political parties?

By 2030 neither will political parties have disappeared nor will the 'crisis of representation'[252] and the 'legitimacy crisis' of political parties be over. Popular will is going to find ways to form outside of political parties which will become players among others. The fate of the constitutional state will depend on the containment of anti-system forces (antagonism I). Mainstream political parties will adapt their international governance structures in order to render decision-making processes more inclusive and strengthen elements of direct democracy. Anti-system parties will continue to exist and this will put instruments of 'constitutional self-defence' like party bans to a test (antagonism II). Processes of Europeanisation and internationalisation of political parties will continue to occur with various back-and-forth steps (antagonism III). Within this matrix of antagonisms the resilience of the constitutional state and key concepts of constitutionalism will be tested.

[252] See n 13 and accompanying text.

9

Popular Movements in 2030

TOMAS DUMBROVSKY

I. Introduction: Constitutional Identity or Identity Constitutionalism

In the upcoming decade the ability of constitutionalism to streamline societal development will further weaken. The reason, I will argue, is that the concept of universal rights, which has been the main constructive element of constitutionalism for the past decades, seems unable to react to the demand for a local (as opposed to global) collective identity. Populist movements are striving on this demand and offer extra-constitutional solutions by resurrecting nationalism, sovereigntism, and sectarianism as alternative bases for collective identity formation. The solution, I aim to propose, is to reconceptualise constitutionalism in such a way that responses to these identity demands and as a result strengthens the role of constitutionalism in our political communities.

The empirical evidence from the United States and Germany shows that constitutionalism can stimulate centripetal forces within society that can be directed towards making the constitution the primary source of a political community's identity (call it a community-building function). In this respect, constitutionalism can replace other concepts that have been employed to this end, while eliminating the excessive side effects which the application of these alternative concepts has historically produced. The failure of the Arab Spring revolutions to constitutionalise freedom in the Arab world and the rise of conservative populism in the Euro-Atlantic world strongly suggest that the potential of post-war, rights-based constitutionalism has been exhausted. The constitutional-identity jurisprudence can be understood as an attempt at judicialisation of the issues of collective identity vis-à-vis individual entitlements in response to these broader political processes. This ongoing reconfiguration of the legal-political discourse, however, provide populist movements and established regimes with new tools for undermining their regional and international commitments to rule of law, human rights, and (liberal) democracy.[1]

[1] See Hungarian Constitutional Court, Decision No 22/2016 (XII. 5.), ABH (*Journal of Constitutional Court decisions*) 2016, 1418; Polish Constitutional Tribunal, Decision No K 3/21, judgment of 7 October

Retaining the social function of constitutionalism in face of these challenges requires a substantial shift in focus, while responding to societal demands for reassessing collective political identity. Identity constitutionalism, rather than constitutional-identity jurisprudence, might be a response. In this chapter, I will outline my idea of such a conceptual framework.

For starters, a constitution's community-building capacity depends on it becoming pivotal in peoples' judgments about the legitimate use of power, which requires it to achieve centrality in political discourse. Such centrality depends, in my view, on three conditions. First, citizens must consider the constitution to be an authentic expression of their will. Second, the constitution must ensure compatibility between co-existing normative systems (the domestic legal order, morality, and international law). This compatibility condition ensures an openness of the political community to international and regional cooperation. Third, the constitution must create an adversarial institutional setting which stimulates officials to prefer constitutional arguments over other types of communication in public discourse.

The first part of this chapter addresses the specific methodological challenges that the aim of this book presents. The second part explains what I mean by the crisis of rights-based constitutionalism. The third part looks at a possible response to such crisis through re-politicising constitutionalism by shifting the focus to collective identity. The fourth part unwraps in detail the conditions of the constitution's centrality in post-rights constitutionalism (constitutional authenticity, normative compatibility, and institutional adversariality). The final part proposes a methodology for researching these conditions.

II. Methodological Challenges

The face of constitutionalism has been changing for the last two decades, offering us a glimpse into its future. Its deep entrenchment in western political organisation has provided us with a mistaken feeling that it is here to stay indefinitely. The success of constitutionalism in the last 50 years has been, to a great extent, due to its marriage with the idea of fundamental rights, which has supplied constitutionalism with moral authority, and due to the seemingly apolitical conflict-resolution mechanism (judicial review and balancing) that has enhanced this authority. This version of constitutionalism – rights-based constitutionalism – seems to be in crisis. The rights-based constitutionalism removed questions most significant for the identity of political communities from politics, while courts, on the other hand,

2021. For an analysis of creative (ab)use of German Constitutional Court's identity based ultra-vires case law in case of Hungary see B Bakó, 'The Zauberlehrling Unchained? The Recycling of the German Federal Constitutional Court's Case Law on Identity: Ultra Vires and Fundamental Rights Review in Hungary' (2018) 78 *ZaöRV* 863.

have been increasingly failing to provide answers – be it the War on Terror, the Great Recession and growing material inequality, or governing under the pandemic emergency. The growing discontent caused partly by this tacit suppression of political identity discourse was exploited by political movements that were willing to challenge the post-war consensus in the West. Their combination of old recipes (nationalism, Christianity, sovereignty, concealed or not so concealed bigotry) with modern political marketing is, unfortunately, working quite well. Outside the West, rights-based constitutionalism has failed spectacularly in the aftermath of the Arab Spring. It has been questioned in Latin America for its collusion with neoliberalism. Its embedded individualism has been seen as foreign to Asian values. The geopolitical decline of traditional exporters of rights-based constitutionalism adds to that.

These challenges, in the West and East, the North and South, suggest the need for reconsidering the rights-based approach based on the pretences of eternal and universal values and neutral adjudication of fundamental political conflicts in favour of an openly political approach where constitutionalism provides a discursive platform for the formation of collective identity. Call it identity constitutionalism.

Before unwrapping this idea, allow me to address methodological difficulties that structured my contribution and helped to clarify its purpose. When preparing it, images from two series of Star Trek – the Original Series and the Next Generation – were constantly coming into my mind and what I found striking was how much the visual representation of the same future as well as issues that mankind would face changed in the two decades that separated the two series. That makes me put forward two methodological limitations: the first limitation is that we cannot but imagine the future through concepts we have. The second limitation is that in addressing the future we use narratives that are comprehensible to the participants in today's discourse (ie narratives that relate to their experience).

The other challenges relate more directly to the method employed. On the one hand, the only method we can legitimately use is to research the past and identify causes of current problems. But sometimes, it might be too late. On the other hand, pointing out problems that have not yet fully materialised, weakens the impact of such analysis. Here comes the advantage of this project. Setting the mark for 2030 allows me to assess the problems in their maturity if no action is taken. This, however, brings an additional problem – mixing up the normative and the descriptive (since the facts are yet to happen). We tend to exaggerate the gravity of immediate events and oscillate between dystopia and utopia, between projecting our fears and our hopes.

Still, I will do my best not to be carried away with this unusual freedom and stick to the projection of long-term trends beyond the present. The normative-descriptive problem works also to my advantage. While I focus on projecting trends beyond the present, my prediction is based on that alternative vision of a 2030 in which we will have taken a corrective action.

III. The Crisis of Rights-Based Constitutionalism

I see four interrelated reasons for the decline of rights-based constitutionalism. First, material inequality (and the publicity of this phenomenon) reaches a critical point. The partnership of convenience neoliberalism (with its conceptually embedded indifference to material inequality) and (human) rights forged in the 1970s starts to undermine the legitimacy of rights-based constitutionalism.[2] Rising material inequality has also highlighted other dimensions of structural injustices in our systems against certain groups (such as non-Caucasian minorities or women) that rights-based constitutionalism, despite all its effort, failed to rectify.[3]

The second reason is related to the disintegration of post-war Christian-social-democratic consensus. It was this consensus that catalysed rights-based constitutionalism in the West and its global export. At the core of this consensus was a common solution to social tensions caused primarily by industrialisation and accompanying phenomena that directly led to the success of populist movements combining socialism and nationalism in the interwar period. Part of this consensus was the removal of fundamental political questions from politics[4] and their fortification through the dubious deployment of legalist constitutionalism (eternity clauses being the example here). This consensus was the result of the ascendancy of Christian democratic and socialist (or social democratic) parties in the post-war period. Their evident decline in the aftermath of the Great Recession leads to the disintegration of this consensus.

The third reason for the crisis of rights-based constitutionalism is the success of non-liberal/non-democratic regimes in providing security, stability, and growth (and correlative failure of number of liberal-democratic attempts in Russia, Latin America, South-East Asia, or the Arab world to do the same, Europe not excluded). This has two facets. First, the emergence of these alternatives undermines the idea of liberal democracy as the ultimate regime, a matter of human progress, and as such morally superior. Second, the alternatives force rights-based constitutionalism to compromise on liberal premises, which undermines its coherence (such as freedom of speech and political competition limitations).[5]

[2] S Moyn, *The Last Utopia: Human Rights in History* (Cambridge, Harvard University Press, 2010); S Moyn, *Christian Human Rights* (Philadelphia, University of Pennsylvania Press, 2015).

[3] See, eg, IM Young, *Justice and the politics of difference* (Princeton, Princeton University Press, 1990) (introducing the concept of structural injustice); IM Young, *Responsibility for Justice* (Oxford, Oxford University Press, 2011).

[4] Hans Kelsen's ascendancy over Carl Schmitt has largely defined the post-war positivist turn.

[5] See, eg, the deployment of the concept of militant democracy against the left-wing assaults on German political establishment in the 1970s as well as against Holocaust denial. For the intellectual origins see K Loewenstein, 'Militant Democracy and Fundamental Rights, I' (1937) 31 *American Political Science Review* 417; K Loewenstein, 'Militant democracy and fundamental rights II' (1937) 31 *American Political Science Review* 638.

Finally, the central importance of courts in this version of constitutionalism has changed from being the solution to being part of the problem. The pretence that (civil) rights adjudication does not have distributional effects is untenable. When it comes to more overt distributional questions, the courts have proved, with minor exceptions, unable or unwilling to address socio-economic injustices and reframing these problems as civil rights issues has not worked fast or well enough to prevent escalating societal tensions as the rise of the 'Me Too' and the 'Black Lives Matter' movements indicates.

Furthermore, the Great Recession and the pandemic revealed how much courts have trapped themselves in their own doctrines developed in and for different times. They are expected to challenge trillion euro political decisions or pandemic lockdowns using their existing tools. In the face of the impact of things like the fiscal constitution, Draghi's whatever-it-takes policy or unprecedented economic recovery packages, courts' reactions such as the *OMT* or *PSPP* judgments[6] look parochial and increasingly detached from reality.

IV. Re-politicising constitutionalism: From Rights to Identity

The solution in my view is to re-politicise constitutionalism while preserving the major achievements of the rights era. The Derek Chauvin trial in 2021 saw the Black Lives Matter movement demanding the court to convict Chauvin of second-degree murder (the gravest of the three chargers against Chauvin) and threatened directly or indirectly civil unrest in case of acquittal. Given the historical track record of courts on these matters, the movement was determined to force the result.[7] This has been the strategy of conservative populist movements in the US and Europe in their quest to bypass parliaments and courts and appeal directly to the people – undermining the idea of rule of law, separation of powers and neutrality of judicial decision-making. Rights and courts have become their targets. Once they gain control over them, they use constitutionalism for power consolidation. In a stark contrast to that, progressive liberal movements have always relied on the power of rights in societal imagination and rights adjudication. Frustration with regime resilience as well as competitive disadvantage vis-à-vis the populists it creates, has been changing this asymmetry.

The strong appeal of populist movements comes from their resurrection of identity politics offering a sense of fraternity and privilege (in various

[6] German Federal Constitutional Court, *Gauweiler and Others v German Bundestag (Outright Monetary Transactions)*, 2 BvR 2728/13 [2016] BVerfGE 142, 123; German Federal Constitutional Court, *Public Sector Purchase Programme*, 2 BvR 859/15 and others [2020].

[7] State of Minnesota District Court, *State v Derek Chauvin*, 27-CR-20-12646 [2021]. See, eg, Black Lives Matter, Derek Chauvin Verdict, April 20, 2021, at www.blacklivesmatter.com/derek-chauvin-verdict/ (last accessed 8 Nov 2021).

forms – nation, white, Christian, etc). It attracts the younger generation, in particular, which seems frustrated from the burden of individual responsibility, which underpins both liberalism and capitalism, and seeks refuge in a collective (real or virtual). The societal demands for collective identity can be seized by progressive movements too. Compare the 'Me Too' and the 'Black Lives Matter' movements with, for instance, the 'Occupy Wall Street' movement. The 'Occupy Wall Street' movement failed to achieve meaningful change. The regulatory responses in the US and Europe were not answering to the distributional demands of the movement, but to macroeconomic instability, further entrenching the inequality trajectory. The 'Black Lives Matter' and the 'Me Too' movements have shown more potential in this regard and part of their success is their identity component.

These are not particularly favourable developments for constitutionalism whose projections forward would mean further deterioration of the rule of law and the capacity of courts to participate in public discourse and checking executive power alongside parliaments. The adaptation of constitutionalism will require to intertwine the advantages manifested by constitutionalism so far with a more political and communal focus. What are these advantages? First, it is constitutionalism's ability to ensure that political discourse is focused on fundamentals by way of a single document listing the main substantive and organisational principles of the given community. Second, constitutionalism has manifested the ability to rationalise political discourse through legal reasoning. And third, it has shown that it can itself create a genuinely new political identity. How different this process can be is well visible when we compare various 'We the People' theories in the US on the one hand[8] and, say, constitutional patriotism in Germany on the other.[9] While the specific contexts are perhaps irreplicable, I believe the key lies in certain general conditions under which constitutionalism can serve a community-building function in different cultural environments and thus regain its universal potential.

V. Conditions of Constitution's Centrality in Post-Rights Constitutionalism

Can a constitution in a broader sense (the constitutional text, its interpretation, practices, and experiences) be the primary source of political

[8] Eg, B Ackerman, *We the people. Vol 1: Foundations* (Cambridge, Belknap Press of Harvard University Press, 1991); L Kramer, *The People Themselves: Popular Constitutionalism and Judicial Review* (Oxford, Oxford University Press, 2004); R Post and R Siegel, 'Roe Rage: Democratic Constitutionalism and Backlash' (2007) 42 *Harvard Civil Rights–Civil Liberties Law Review* 373.

[9] For a superb overview of the conceptual foundations of constitutional patriotism see JW Müller, 'On the Origins of Constitutional Patriotism' (2006) 5 *Contemporary Political Theory* 278. See also JW Müller, *Constitutional Patriotism* (Princeton, Princeton University Press, 2007).

identity?[10] The experiences of the US and post-war Germany suggest that a political community can be built primarily around the constitution and that constitutional discourse can significantly shape what it means to be an American (individualism and equality) or German (social welfare and human dignity). These two examples also indicate the diverse paths these processes can take. What they share is the discursive approach to democracy.[11] Discursive democracy differs from traditional democratic theory in the emphasis it puts on deliberation preceding a political choice. Deliberation is expected to produce (more) authentic choices, and in turn to increase the legitimacy of such choices.

From this point of view, the constitution 'belongs' to all members of the political community, the people, if you like. It constructs equality. This equality is primarily discursive. Every member of the political community has an equal right to say what the constitution means and to use it to assess whether any exercise of power, by state officials or a neighbour, is legitimate or not. The constitution sums up basic principles that allow for such an assessment without requiring the evaluator to be a specialist. Through these multiple, overlapping, and ongoing discursive exchanges the members of the community shape the substance of the community and their understanding of themselves as its members. This is the promise of constitutionalism. The complex functionality of specific mechanisms – checks and balances, elections, judicial review, fundamental rights – should not blind us to this bigger quest of constitutionalism.

The aim is, therefore, to bring forward the discursive function of constitutionalism. If we succeed in finding and elaborating on what conditions this function, we will know how to stimulate it. Accumulated knowledge, ever more specialised and nuanced, nudges us to take many attributes of constitutionalism as axioms, such as the universalisability of Enlightenment rationality, secularism, a catalogue of indispensable human rights and Montesquieu's three-part structure of government. Empirical evidence (the rise of populism, the relative stability of illiberal and non-democratic regimes, failed regional democratic revolutions, etc) indicates that the 1990s idealism of global aspirations for constitutionalism failed. The global spread of constitutionalism was often window dressing used to legitimise authoritarian regimes south and east of Europe. The Arab Spring revealed that a rights-based constitutionalism is unable to conceptualise non-secular constitutionalism.[12] Alongside the development in post-war Iraq and Afghanistan, it became clear that the Enlightenment transplants substantially decrease, if not eliminate, the

[10] *cf* GJ Jacobsohn, *Constitutional Identity* (Cambridge, Harvard University Press, 2010); see also M Rosenfeld, *The Identity of the Constitutional Subject: Selfhood, Citizenship, Culture, and Community* (New York, Routledge, 2010).

[11] Ackerman (n 8); J Habermas, *Between Facts and Norms: Contributions to a Discourse Theory of Law and Democracy* (Cambridge, Massachusetts Institute of Technology Press, 1996); *cf* also R Levy, H Kong, G Orr and J King (eds), *The Cambridge Handbook of Deliberative Constitutionalism* (Cambridge, Cambridge University Press, 2018).

[12] AA Ninet and M Tushnet, *The Arab Spring: An Essay on Revolution and Constitutionalism* (Cheltenham, Edward Elgar Publishing, 2015).

discursive function of constitutionalism. Similarly, the overt rhetoric of illiberalism that has proliferated in eastern Europe,[13] abuse of constitutional legitimacy with the aim of capturing the state[14] and widespread populist attacks on rights-based constitutionalism in other parts of Europe indicate that the problem goes beyond exporting Enlightenment ideals to faraway places.[15] Perhaps, lowering our demands on substantive constitutional content and focusing instead on making the constitution central (or restoring its centrality) to political discourse through the three conditions of constitutional authenticity, normative compatibility and institutional adversariality will: (a) moderate religious and national extremism; (b) increase regional cooperation; and (c) gradually democratise political regimes.

This discursive reorientation of constitutionalism scholarship requires nothing less than building up a new theoretical and methodological framework. The three conditions constitute its backbone. The new framework will allow to compare constitutional regimes across socio-economic, cultural, linguistic, and religious divides. The philosophical and legal-theoretical underpinnings of the proposed framework are rooted in critical theory and communication theory with law being approached as a social system,[16] and hence primarily as an instrument of social change, the dynamics of which depends on the quality of societal deliberation.[17]

For the purposes of the theoretical framework developed in this chapter, a constitution is understood as a legal-political document that creates a bridge between the value system of a political community and its domestic legal order. Domestic law represents one of the co-existing normative systems that legitimise power, beside morality (based on religion or a secularised version of it) and international law. The other two normative systems inform a community's values. As the bridge between the political and legal realms, the constitution has the capacity to legitimise both the public power, of which the constitution is the source, and the private power, where the horizontal application of basic rights justifies inter-personal power claims. The interconnection between the political and legal realms that the constitution creates allows it to assume the centrality in political

[13] *Cf* C Tóth, Full text of Viktor Orbán's speech at Băile Tuşnad (Tusnádfürdő) of 26 July 2014 [2014] *The Budapest Beacon*.

[14] Müller (n 9); L Pech and KL Scheppele, 'Illiberalism Within: Rule of Law Backsliding in the EU' (2017) 19 *Cambridge Yearbook of European Legal Studies* 3.

[15] T Ginsburg, AZ Huq and M Versteeg, 'The Coming Demise of Liberal Constitutionalism?' (2018) 85 *University of Chicago Law Review* 239.

[16] N Luhmann, *Law as a Social System* (Oxford, Oxford University Press, 2004); G Teubner, *Constitutional Fragments: Societal Constitutionalism and Globalization* (Oxford, Oxford University Press, 2012); C Thornhill, *A Sociology of Transnational Constitutions* (Cambridge, Cambridge University Press, 2016).

[17] Habermas, *Between Facts and Norms*; Ackerman (n 8); S Tierney, *Constitutional Referendums: The Theory and Practice of Republican Deliberation* (Oxford, Oxford University Press, 2012); R Levy, H Kong, G Orr and J King (eds), *The Cambridge Handbook of Deliberative Constitutionalism* (Cambridge, Cambridge University Press, 2018); A Bächtiger, JS Dryzek, J Mansbridge and M Warren, *The Oxford Handbook of Deliberative Democracy* (Oxford, Oxford University Press, 2018).

community and to become the primary source of collective identity for such community. At the same time, the role the constitution plays in integrating the three co-existing normative systems ensures that collective identity is conceptually compatible with regional and international cooperation.

A. Constitutional Authenticity Condition: Revolutionary and Non-revolutionary Constitutionalism

The first condition for a constitution's centrality in political discourse is its acceptance by the members of the political community as the ultimate source of authority. Several constitutional paths may lead to this result. Bruce Ackerman's categorisation provides a suitable starting point for this endeavour.[18] Ackerman's revolutionary path constructs a dualistic model of political legitimacy distinguishing the super-legitimacy of the rare decisions made by mobilised society that command constitutional authority from the lesser legitimacy of political decisions made during periods of 'normal politics'. The people can seriously consider the constitution as higher law of their own making. To sustain this original connection between the citizens and the constitution (which might be renewed from time to time)[19] beyond the founding generation, the rules of interpretation must reflect this duality and derive the meaning of the higher law from revolutionary discourse. We must therefore focus not only on whether a revolutionary path has been taken but also on the discursive tools that officials employ in normal times to sustain the relevance of the revolutionary path.

Experience with religious texts indicates that people can also create an intimate relationship with a normative text even if they cannot claim its authorship, which creates the second of possible paths.[20] Germany's rights foundationalism[21] is a good secular example. The content of the Basic Law was dictated by the occupying forces. The alterations by the Herrenchiemsee constitutional convention and formal adoption by the Parliamentary Council did not change this fact. However, the German Federal Constitutional Court succeeded in forging a remarkable bond between German society and the Basic Law.[22]

[18] B Ackerman, *Revolutionary Constitutions. Charismatic Leadership and the Rule of Law* (Cambridge, Belknap Press of Harvard University Press, 2019).

[19] The long history of the US Constitution provides the best example. The societal consensus on the constitutional regime has been renewed three times through the Reconstruction, the New Deal, and the Civil Rights revolutions. Ackerman (n 8).

[20] See, eg, D Cohn-Sherbok, G Chryssides and U Hasan, *People of the Book: An Interfaith Dialogue about How Jews, Christians and Muslims Understand Their Sacred Scriptures* (Philadelphia, Jessica Kingsley Publishers, 2018).

[21] Ackerman (n 18).

[22] *Cf* H Vorläander, *Konsens und Verfassung* (Berlin, Duncker & Humblot, 1981); H Vorländer (ed), *Integration durch Verfassung* (Wiesbaden, Westdeutscher Verlag, 2002); D Grimm, 'Integration by constitution' (2003) 3 *International Journal of Constitutional Law* 193. See, in particular, the influence of Smend's integration theory for German Federal Constitutional Court's community-building exercise.

The third path involves elite-construction, where the old regime is repudiated but society stays on the side lines. Post-Franco Spain is Ackerman's paramount example here. Several constitutions will be on the continuum that runs from a constitution of pure revolutionary origins to a constitution of pure elite construction. As both employ rhetoric of a new beginning (portraying the new constitutional regime as the antithesis of the repudiated regime), we need to understand how elite-construction regimes compensate for the lack of empirical evidence of society's involvement. The hypothesis is that such regimes combine constitutional-moment propaganda with rights foundationalism.

Finally, an evolutionary path, experienced in its ideal form in Great Britain (at least until its recent experiment with popular mobilisation during the Brexit) and other Commonwealth countries, builds its authority on effective governance.[23] While the previous three paths tend to increase the constitution's centrality in political discourse, the evolutionary path seems to lack this effect. The Netherlands is a good example outside the Commonwealth. While the lack of institutional mechanisms stimulating the constitution's centrality (see the third condition below) plays an important role, the Dutch elite has successfully adapted the regime to new challenges and gradually incorporated new social classes into its governance.

The Ackermanian categorisation brings two important insights for the construction of constitutional authenticity. Authenticity is more persuasive if the regime is in a position to recall its revolutionary origins. The revolutionary foundations are strengthened when the regime parts away with the old regime through the use of narrative of 'new beginning'. Such narrative may also be employed in a situation of a radical departure from the old regime when the revolutionary origins, due to the lack of participation of mobilised public in the regime change, are missing. Both the German and the Spanish cases can be said to construct a 'new beginning' momentum to a varying extent (and success). The variables for assessment of the authenticity condition are therefore a revolutionary and non-revolutionary substance of constitutions and new beginning and continuity narratives. Using the examples from the EU and MENAP regions, the binary variables can be combined into the following matrix:

Table 1 Variables of Authenticity Condition

	New Beginning	**Continuity**
Revolutionary	France 1946; Italy 1947; Tunisia 2014; Czech Republic 1993; Poland 1997	France 1958;[24] Morocco 1962
Non-Revolutionary	(West) Germany 1949; Afghanistan 2004; Spain 1978	The Netherlands 1815 (1983); UAE 1971 (1996); Qatar 2004

[23] Ackerman (n 18). See also B Ackerman, 'Three Paths to Constitutionalism – and the Crisis of the European Union' (2015) 45 *British Journal of Political Science* 705.

[24] The 1971 Constitutional Council decision (71-44DC) created partial continuity by incorporating the 1789 Declaration of the Rights of Man and of the Citizen and, especially, the preamble to the 1946 Constitution, which provides a basis for a number of social rights and gender equality.

B. Normative Compatibility Condition

The second condition that affects a constitution's centrality in public discourse is how successfully it incorporates external normative systems, so that the members of political community are not forced to choose between several collective identities. The claim here is that a constitution cannot become *the* source for collective identity if there are other normative systems operating alongside the constitution. These other normative systems provide an alternative basis for collective identity and compete with the constitution as an identity source. The solution is to incorporate these external normative systems into the constitution, harmonise between them and transmit the harmonised solutions down the legal order. For the sake of simplifying the matter for the purposes of this contribution, I will group what I call 'external norms' into two big normative systems that are external to domestic legal order – morality on the one hand and international human rights on the other.

The normative compatibility condition takes non-secular constitutions seriously. The experience of many Arab states over the last two decades has shown that a harmonistic interpretation (at least at the doctrinal level) between the constitutionally incorporated external normative systems (Islam as the prevailing source of morality and international human rights) is possible.[25] Such a reconciliation increases the constitution's community-building capacity. In addition, the overt secularity of European constitutions must be taken less formalistically as the prevailing moral system might be incorporated through other means. Research on the theoretical foundations and practice of human rights in the western world has shown that they are the result of a synthesis of the Christian tradition with the Enlightenment thought.[26] The possibility to doctrinally arrive at similar outcomes using radically different underlying constitutionally incorporated frameworks (the Enlightenment-Christian synthesis and Shari'a) as indicated, for instance, by the decisions of French and Egyptian courts regarding wearing the veil in public places,[27] shows that the secular/non-secular dichotomy can be less important and can be overcome by the use of the concept of incorporated normative frameworks instead. The existence of explicit Shari'a incorporation clauses in the majority of MENAP constitutions provide a laboratory on how the two incorporated external systems interact and affect the third (ie the domestic legal order).

[25] M Baderin, *International Human Rights and Islamic Law* (Oxford, Oxford University Press, 2003); M Baderin, 'Islam and the Realization of Human Rights in Muslim World: A Reflection on Two Essential Approaches and Two Divergent Perspectives' (2007) 4 *Muslim World Journal of Human Rights* 1; MA Ramadan, 'Notes on the Shari'a: Human Rights, Democracy and European Court of Human Rights' (2007) 40 *Israel Law Review* 156.

[26] S Moyn, *The Last Utopia: Human Rights in History* (Cambridge, Harvard University Press, 2010); S Hopgood, *The Endtimes of Human Rights* (Ithaca, Cornell University Press, 2013); L Hunt, 'The Paradoxical Origins of Human Rights', in JN Wasserstrom et al (eds), *Human Rights and Revolutions*, 2nd edn (Lanham, Rowman & Littlefield Publishers, 2007).

[27] See more below.

Let me first outline the constructive variables of the normative compatibility condition. The first variable is how constitutions (understood as constitutional practice) incorporate international law. The monism-dualism binary categorisation seems insufficient and scholarship has, consequently, developed more nuanced categories based on a combination of formal clauses and judicial practice.[28] The important factors are the justiciability of international law clauses (such as that the state observes its obligations resulting from international law,[29] or that the state 'strives to implement international treaties'[30]), the position constitutions grant to international law in the hierarchy of sources of law (and which law – human rights treaties, the ECHR, ratified treaties, etc) and how the constitution deals with conflict between constitutional provisions and treaty provisions (nullity, inapplicability), the obstacles that exist in practice (eg avoidance doctrines,[31] eternity clauses[32]) and the interpretative solutions that have been developed to overcome compatibility problems (such as the principle of consistent interpretation required by Article 233 of the South African Constitution).

The second variable is how constitutions incorporate the moral normative system and how constitutional practice mediates between the two incorporated systems (international human rights and morality). This dimension of the problem is more tangible when it comes to countries where morality can be more clearly identified with religion and its constitutional incorporation takes the form of explicit incorporation of the complex system of religious norms, such as constitutional incorporation of Shari'a. In the case of self-proclaimed secular constitutions, the incorporation of a moral system is less straightforward, yet we may find several extra-legal references, such as good faith, traditions, conscience, etc, which meaning is embedded in a moral system external to the legal order. Allow me to postpone this more difficult analysis for another time and demonstrate the problem on the example of constitutional incorporation of Shari'a.

Qatar, for instance incorporates Shari'a as the 'principal source of legislation'[33] and, at the same time, incorporates international law by requiring the state to 'respect international charters and conventions'.[34] Its accession to both the

[28] E Benvenisti, 'Judicial Misgivings Regarding the Application of International Law: An Analysis of Attitudes of National Courts' (1993) 4 *European Journal of International Law* 159; E Benvenisti, 'Reclaiming Democracy: The Strategic Uses of Foreign and International Law by National Courts' (2008) 102 *American Journal of International Law* 241; T Ginsburg, S Chernykh and Z Elkins, 'Commitment and Diffusion: How and Why National Constitutions Incorporate International Law' [2008] *University of Illinois Law Review* 201; PH Verdier and M Versteeg, 'Modes of Domestic Incorporation of International Law', in W Sandholtz and CA Whytock (eds), *Handbook on the Politics of International Law* (Cheltenham, Edward Elgar, 2016).

[29] Art 1(2) of the 1993 Constitution of the Czech Republic.

[30] Art 7 of the 2004 Constitution of Qatar.

[31] E Benvenisti, 'Judicial Misgivings Regarding the Application of International Law: An Analysis of Attitudes of National Courts' (1993) 4 *European Journal of International Law* 159.

[32] Y Roznai, *Unconstitutional Constitutional Amendments: The Limits of Amendment Powers* (Oxford, Oxford University Press, 2017); A Stone, 'Unconstitutional Constitutional Amendments: Between Contradiction and Necessity' (2018) 12 *Vienna Journal on International Constitutional Law* 357.

[33] Art 1 of the 2004 Constitution of Qatar.

[34] Art 7 of the 2004 Constitution of Qatar.

International Covenant on Civil and Political Rights and the International Covenant on Economic, Social and Cultural Rights in 2018 included reservations that allows Qatar to retain the supremacy of Shari'a in practice.[35] The international pressure on the stable illiberal states of the Gulf region to adopt human rights reforms increases the complexity of the compatibility problem.

We can identify three basic types of Islamic clauses in MENAP constitutions: repugnancy clauses, supremacy clauses and source of law clauses. The constitutions of six states in the MENAP region contain a repugnancy clause.[36] Several other constitutions in the region have similar provisions that incorporate Shari'a in positive law, in particular through supremacy and source of law clauses.[37] For practical operation of repugnancy and source of law clauses, the institutional design has proven a crucial factor.[38]

By using examples of Egypt, Pakistan, Iraq and Afghanistan, let me explain how the compatibility condition is addressed in its complex practice and the variants of constitutional regimes it creates and outline my method of inquiry into the compatibility issue. The 2014 Egyptian Constitution's supremacy clause states that '[t]he principles of Islamic Shari'a are the principle source of legislation.'[39] The preamble refers to Mubarak-era jurisprudence for the purpose of interpretating Article 2. The Egyptian Supreme Constitutional Court has established two fundamental doctrines regarding the compatibility problem. In its 1985 decision, the Court limited the temporal effect of the supremacy clause to legislation adopted ex post the Constitution.[40] A decade later, the Egyptian Court adopted a more structural solution. It upheld a rule prohibiting face-veiling in public schools as compatible with Islamic law and the freedoms of expression

[35] Qatar rejected gender equality provisions on marriage, divorce and child custody on grounds that they contravene shari'a and declared that it would interpret the term 'trade unions' in accordance with its national law, limiting migrant workers' rights to form unions.

[36] The Iranian 1979 Constitution (as revised in 1989), the Iraqi 2005 Constitution, the Maldivian 2008 Constitution, the Pakistani 1973 Constitution (as revised in 2002 and 2012), and the Somalian 2012 Constitution. See a list of Islamic provisions in the constitutions of Muslim-majority countries in T Moustafa, *Constituting Religion: Islam, Liberal Rights, and the Malaysian State* (Cambridge, Cambridge University Press, 2018) 159–163.

[37] The following constitutions contain both supremacy and source of law clauses that incorporate, with various degree of intensity, Islamic law: Bahrain 2002, Comoros 2001 (rev. 2009), Egypt 2014, Iran, Iraq, Kuwait 1962 (reinstated 1992), Libya 2011, Maldives, Mauritania 1991 (rev. 2012), Oman 1995 (rev. 2011), Qatar 2003, Saudi Arabia 1992 (rev. 2005), Somalia, Sudan 2005, Syria 2012, UAE 1971 (rev. 2004) and Yemen 1991 (rev. 2001). The Constitutions of Saudi Arabia and Yemen use comparatively stronger wording in their supremacy clauses than the other constitutions.

[38] S Waheedi and K Stilt, 'Judicial review in the context of constitutional Islam', in EF Delaney and R Dixon (eds), *Comparative Judicial Review* (Cheltenham, Edward Elgar, 2018).

[39] Art 2, second sentence of the 2014 Egyptian Constitution. The original wording of the 1971 Constitution that Shari'a is *a* source of law was changed in 1981 to make Shari'a *the* source of law. DI Ahmed and M Gouda, 'Measuring Constitutional Islamization: The Islamic Constitutions Index' (2015) 38 *Hastings International and Comparative Law Review* 1.

[40] Decision 20 of 1985 of the Supreme Constitutional Court of Egypt (upholding a provision of the Civil Code permitting the taking of money interest on loans that might have been in contradiction with the Shari'a condemnation of riba).

and religion guaranteed by the Constitution.[41] By pointing out a disagreement among Islamist jurists and that different schools of jurisprudence varied in their interpretation and application of the relevant provisions of Shari'a, the Court distinguished between 'unalterable and universally binding principles, and malleable applications of those principles'.[42] Only when legislation or other regulation contravenes a strict unalterable principle recognised as such by all interpretive schools would the Court declare it unconstitutional and void. In cases where such agreement did not exist, *ijtihad* (new interpretation of Shari'a) was permitted to fill textual lacunae or interpret vague or open-ended provisions.[43]

The Pakistani Supreme Court approached the compatibility problem from a different angle. As the 1973 Constitution[44] requires that 'all existing laws shall be brought in conformity with Injunctions of Islam' and that 'no law shall be enacted which is repugnant to such injunctions', the road alongside Egypt's temporality solution was foreclosed. In *Hakim Khan v Government of Pakistan*,[45] the Court instead developed its 'harmonisation doctrine' arguing that no specific provision of the Constitution stands above any other provision.[46] By overturning its 1972 doctrine of *Asma Jilani*,[47] which had declared Islam to be the *Grundnorm* of the Pakistani legal system, the Court refused to grant supra-constitutional status to the Objectives Resolution.[48] The Resolution requires, inter alia, the principles of democracy, freedom, equality, tolerance and social justice to be interpreted as enunciated by Islam.[49] The Pakistani Supreme Court continued to play a nuanced balancing act over the next decades amid provincial and federal advances of Islamists. It established de facto appellate jurisdiction over the Federal Shari'ah Court, which is constitutionally mandated to conduct a repugnancy clause review.[50] The Supreme Court neutralised the Federal Shari'ah Court's decisions that sought to nullify certain liberalising provisions of family law and on loan interest, by requiring the

[41] Decision No 8 of 1996 of the Supreme Constitutional Court of Egypt. CB Lombardi and B Clark, 'Egypt's Supreme Constitutional Court: Managing Constitutional Conflict in an Authoritarian, Aspirationally 'Islamic' State' (2008) 3 *Journal of Comparative Law* 234.

[42] NJ Brown, 'Islamic Constitutionalism in Theory and Practice', in E Cotran and AO Sherif (eds), *Democracy, the Rule of Law and Islam* (Basel, Springer, 1999).

[43] R Hirschl, *Constitutional Theocracy* (Cambridge, Harvard University Press, 2010).

[44] As revised in 2002 and 2012. Source of English translation: www.pakistani.org/pakistan/constitution/.

[45] *Hakim Khan v Government of Pakistan*, P.L.D. 1992 S.C. 595 (the Court stated: 'It may be observed that the principles for interpreting constitutional documents as laid down by this Court are that all provisions should be read together and harmonious construction should be placed on such provisions so that no provision is rendered nugatory.').

[46] Hirschl (n 43).

[47] Decision in *Asma Jilani v The Government of the Punjab* of the Supreme Court of Pakistan (1972).

[48] The Objectives Resolution (so-called Islamisation amendment) was inserted into the Constitution via Art 2A in 1985.

[49] Point 4 of the Objectives Resolution.

[50] Art 203C of the Constitution affords the Federal Shari'ah Court a competence to 'examine and decide the question whether or not any law or provision of law is repugnant to the injunctions of Islam, as laid down in the Holy Quran and Sunnah of the Holy Prophet.'

Shari'ah Court to take a cohesive view of Pakistan's constitutional law wherever Islamic jurisprudence involves significant constitutional law aspects.[51] In addition to judicial ex-post control, Article 228 of the Constitution created the Council of Islamic Ideology, which advises the government on whether a proposed law is repugnant to the Injunctions of Islam.[52]

While the Egyptian Court has used the source of law clause to de facto assume interpretative authority over Shari'a[53] and the Pakistani Court's harmonisation doctrine laid the ground for balancing between Shari'a and human rights, the Iraqi Supreme Court has refrained from application of either the supremacy or repugnancy clauses. Article 2.1 of the 2005 Iraqi Constitution states that 'Islam … is a foundation source of legislation' and that '[n]o law may be enacted that contradicts the established provisions of Islam [or settled rulings of Islam].'[54] Article 130 of the Constitution is then interpreted as immunising laws in force at the time of adoption of the Constitution from Article 2 review (compare, for example, the Egyptian temporality solution).[55] This reluctance is caused by the problematic authority of the judiciary for such interpretation in Shia societies, where the sole institution to credibly interpret Shari'a is the Marja'iyya. During the drafting of the Constitution, the question of who would interpret what the 'established provisions of Islam' were received utmost attention. The compromise solution led to the creation of the Federal Supreme Court composed of judges, legal experts, and experts in Islamic law.[56] The appointment process was left to later legislation requiring a two-third majority to pass. As Parliament was unable to agree on the implementing legislation (mostly due to disagreements over the inclusion of Islamic jurists), the Court has operated on the basis of law that predates the Constitution.[57] In practice it means that secular judges have dominated the Court, while the Court's legitimacy to engage in serious application of the repugnancy clause has been low.[58] As a result, the Court has purposefully evaded Article 2 review, despite its bold rulings in a number of other areas, with one important exception. In 2010, the Federal Supreme Court directly interpreted Shari'a based on two Qur'anic

[51] Decision in *Muhammad Siddique et al. v Government of Pakistan* of the Supreme court of Pakistan (2004).

[52] Art 230.1.b of the Pakistani Constitution.

[53] One of the reasons was the loss of legitimacy of the Sunni clerics at the Azhar University, which were entitled to such interpretation. HA Hamoudi, 'Ornamental Repugnancy: Identitarian Islam and the Iraqi Constitution' (2010) 7 *University of St. Thomas Law Review* 692.

[54] Source of English translation: www.constituteproject.org/constitution/Iraq_2005.pdf?lang=en.

[55] HA Hamoudi, 'Repugnancy in The Arab World' (2012) 48 *Willamette Law Review* 427.

[56] Art 92 of the Iraqi Constitution.

[57] A draft law implementing Art 92 of the Constitution, which has been discussed in the Parliament recently, has caused a public controversy as it envisages four Islamic jurists in the 13-strong Court with veto power.

[58] S Choudhry and K G Bass, *Constitutional Courts after the Arab Spring: Appointment mechanisms and relative judicial independence* (Center for Constitutional Transitions at NYU Law International Institute for Democracy and Electoral Assistance 2014).

verses as recommending, if not requiring, a contract to be concluded in writing.[59] This interpretation was at odds with the view of both Grand Ayatollah Sistani and his predecessor Grand Ayatollah Khu'i.

The Afghan repugnancy clause is unique in the region due to an explicit prohibition of altering it (eternity clause). At the same time, fundamental rights are also in fact unamendable as they can only be changed to improve them.[60] The Supreme Court can be composed of lawyers as well as Islamic jurists but, unlike the Iraqi Constitution, the 2004 Afghan Constitution does not envisage any proportional distribution among them. Lower courts have extensively used the source of law clause of the Constitution (Article 130) to expand the list of crimes beyond the Penal Code through direct application of Hanafi jurisprudence.[61] In *Kambakhsh*, a case concerning blasphemy,[62] the Supreme Court upheld a harsh sentence by first applying the repugnancy clause to establish that the Penal Code was not in compliance with the 'tenets of Islam' since it failed to criminalise such behaviour and consequently applyed Article 130 to fill this 'lacuna.' Unlike its Egyptian and Pakistani counterparts, the Afghan Court not only failed to strike a balance between Shari'a and constitutionally guaranteed rights[63] but extended the reach of Shari'a through the creative use of Article 130, moreover with Shari'a interpretation often influenced by local customs.

The third variable is how the constitution transforms the value system (based on the mixture achieved through incorporation of international law and morality) into domestic law. The doctrines developed in German constitutional law and European law provides a suitable starting point for assessing the constitution's penetration of the legal order, such as the radiation effect, direct and indirect effects, and vertical and horizontal effects. For instance, the most intrusive is the radiation (*Ausstrahlung*) doctrine, which focuses on the horizontal effect of fundamental rights (*Drittwirkung*). As the intensity of these effects might be multiplied by the choice of interpretative method (eg, teleological interpretation), the variable must also include whether the constitution prescribes a certain method of interpretation or whether it is left to the discretion of the constitutional/supreme court and how the interpretative method relates to discursive context.

[59] Decision No 60 of 2010 of the Federal Supreme Court of Iraq (this interpretation allowed the Court to uphold evidentiary positive law that requires written contracts).

[60] Art 149, second sentence of the 2004 Constitution of Afghanistan.

[61] G Hashimi, 'Defending the Principle of Legality in Afghanistan: Toward a Unified Interpretation of Article 130 to the Afghan Constitution' (2017) 18 *Oregon Review of International Law* 185.

[62] The case concerned a journalist who had distributed an annotated article, which he downloaded from the internet, criticising certain Quranic verses about women. See J Witte Jr. and M C Green, 'Religious Freedom, Democracy, And International Human Rights' (2009) 23 *Emory International Law Review* 583.

[63] Strengthened further by constitutional incorporation of the Universal Declaration of Human Rights and other international treaties and conventions to which Afghanistan is a signatory. See Art 7 of the 2004 Afghan Constitution.

C. Institutional Adversariality Condition: The Positive Role of Conflict

The third condition focuses on the functioning of constitutional regimes in normal times, where constitutional discourse is driven by inter-institutional communicative exchanges. The hypothesis here is that the quality of discourse depends on the intensity of conflict and mechanisms for its de-escalation. Structured institutional conflict has significant effects on argumentative rationales. This requires communication-rationalising stimuli (such as judicial review) and a public audience, on which the legitimacy of officials depends.

The intensity of inter-institutional discourse depends on three variables: (a) the number of independent institutions with claims to constitutional interpretation (constitutional actors); (b) their ability to credibly appeal to the people for authority; and (c) their control over their agenda. Two relevant groups of institutions according to their democratic substance may be isolated: majoritarian and non-majoritarian institutions. The category of non-majoritarian institutions allows us to employ the insight of the scholarship on judicial politics to understand the operation of similar institutions such as central banks and independent agencies, and regionally relevant non-majoritarian actors such as the military and high religious institutions.

The first variable focuses on which institutions are formally entitled to constitutional interpretation: if there is a judicial review, which institution conducts the review (a court, a council, a parliamentary committee, another type institution); what types of judicial review the system sanctions (ex ante, ex post; obligatory or consultative; individual standing; civil society representatives' standing); is the review binding on the Parliament (or what other obligations arise from the review[64]) and other courts; does it have precedential force; and which parts of the decision are binding; what majority is needed to overcome the court's decision.[65]

The second variable (credibility of the appeal to the people for authority) focuses on the communicative techniques officials use to increase their independence in inter-institutional discourse by direct appeal to citizens as guardians of a constitution[66] or guarantors of regime stability (eg, the European Central Bank employed such appeals during the Euro crisis in order to broaden its competences under the EU primary law to include quasi-bail-out mechanisms

[64] *cf* the Westminster system variants. S Stephenson, *From Dialogue to Disagreement in Comparative Rights Constitutionalism* (Alexandria, Federation Press, 2016).

[65] Constitutional majority, simple majority, or none in case of unamendable provisions.

[66] On the German Federal Constitutional Court, see J Collings, *Democracy's Guardians: A History of the German Federal Constitutional Court 1951-2001* (Oxford, Oxford University Press, 2015); M Hailbronner, *Traditions and Transformations: The Rise of German Constitutionalism* (Oxford, Oxford University Press, 2015). On military see, eg, OO Varol, 'The Military as the Guardian of Constitutional Democracy' (2013) 51 *Columbia Journal of Transnational Law* 547.

(outright monetary transactions, quantitative easing, etc). This variable, therefore, focuses on what legitimising techniques majoritarian institutions use (besides the democratic mandate, the majoritarian institutions, for instance, emphasise their expertise) and what techniques non-majoritarian institutions employ (such as constructing a quasi-democratic mandate).

The third variable (agenda control) focuses on discursive constraints on constitutional actors. This is particularly relevant for non-majoritarian institutions – constitutional courts, central banks, the bureaucracy, the military, and religious institutions. The variable includes how religious institutions are involved in constitutional interpretation and what techniques they use to expand their interpretation of religious text to constitutional interpretation (through incorporation clauses, ex ante review of legislation for compatibility, etc), how central banks manage the dilemma of publicising their market-sensitive actions, what techniques courts use to increase their agenda control (case selection; overcoming limitations by the scope of pleading and the possibility of binding force of ratio decidendi). In the case of majoritarian institutions, the variable focuses on instruments constraining their agenda control (such as who has legislative initiative, what majority is needed to alter bills, etc).

VI. The Constitutional-Cycles Method

The outlined theoretical framework also requires the adaptation of a methodology in order to capture the relevant societal dynamics behind a constitution's discursive role. I suggest a modified version of Ackerman's constitutional-moment method (call it constitutional-cycles method or CCM).[67] I have used the method for researching the democratic origins of European constitutionalism.[68] Given the insight it was able to generate when applied to an environment lacking institutional structure at the start, the method has proved its independence from state-like structures, making it also suitable for political communities in transition and failed states, where state institutions do not fully control the territory. The robustness of the CCM was further vindicated by its ability to capture the dynamics of failed constitutional moments and non-revolutionary transitions and to provide important information on a constitution's role in society. The CCM takes a generational and regime perspective and can isolate normatively relevant constitutional contexts. Its major advantage lies in structuring constitutional development

[67] The modifications made to Ackerman's framework comes perhaps close to Jack Balkin's concept of constitutional decay as the driving force for renewal, however, the emphasis remains on civil society, self-conscious choice, where the circumstances of decay have psychological consequences for new movements' popular support, but no more. JM Balkin, *The Cycles of Constitutional Time* (Oxford, Oxford University Press, 2020).

[68] T Dumbrovsky, *The European Republic: The Democratic Origins of European Constitutionalism* (forthcoming 2022).

into two substantially different times and observing different phenomena in each of these times. Furthermore, the division of these times into several discursive periods (see the four stages of the constitutional cycle below) allows empirical verification of the constitutional path taken.

The CCM has its roots in the theory of constitutional moments.[69] I believe that these moments are cyclical. They come when society's frustration with a regime's inability to deliver on its original promises or to update its policies to reflect crucial socio-economic changes reaches a critical point. When a major crisis (call it triggering crisis) intervenes, the accumulated energy behind this frustration is released all at once and overwhelms the regime. As the crisis disrupts people's routines, they turn to public affairs in search of explanations. The crisis might be external (for instance the demise of an empire or a war) or internal, caused by the regime faltering (such as an economic crisis). The crisis weakens the regime's control of society making it vulnerable to challenges from political outsiders, who use the activated society to advance their constitutional vision. Although the triggering crises that opens the way for a constitutional moment are cyclical, this does not mean that they come at regular intervals or that they inevitably culminate in a constitutional moment.

The constitutional cycle proceeds through four stages. The first two stages are crucial to determine which constitutional path has been taken. In the first stage (mobilisation), scattered groups of activists arrive at a similar diagnosis of the causes of the old regime's faltering, which opens possibilities for forming a broader movement. A radical change that the movement seeks requires it to join forces with all the strands that share the underlying objective and develop the basic outlines of a common programme and strategy for mobilising the public. If the movement succeeds in rallying the public behind its ideas, it can move to the next stage. In the second stage (constitutionalisation), the movement attempts to constitutionalise the new beginning's promise. While there is overall agreement on the causes and the ultimate solution, differences in the philosophical-political underpinnings of the ultimate solution and strategy to achieve it become apparent. The movement is held together by the expectations of a mobilised society and through considerable leadership efforts that keep the movement focused on the common aim. Constitutionalisation increases internal conflicts, which weakens the movement but also clarifies which forces within the movement appeal most to the mobilised public. This leads both to a fragmentation of the movement and concentration behind the most promising visions. The consensus that is eventually reached to pass a new constitutional framework often leaves considerable space for any of the visions that formed part of the consensus to be expanded further. The constitution's text by itself cannot resolve this. It provides an initial platform for further struggles now confined to a limited number of consensus-embedded visions that are equipped with new legitimising forms (institutional and substantive) that

[69] Ackerman (n 8).

the constitution establishes. In the third stage (struggle for meaning), different revolutionary factions, now occupying institutional positions in the new regime, attempt to implement their understandings of the meaning of the constitution. In the fourth stage (consolidation), the involvement of society diminishes, and the revolutionary factions agree on a compromise.

Between the cycles, the regime relies on a constitutional canon, the fundamental principles of which were forged at its founding and developed over the years through constitutional practice and inter-institutional struggles that addressed challenges arising. Not every cycle of high-energy constitutional politics culminates in a constitutional moment but a failure of this to happen has consequences perhaps as important as a constitutional moment itself for the regime's future direction and legitimacy. Instead of a strong popular endorsement of a revolutionary change, which provides time and space for its implementation, a failed constitutional moment leaves a sharply divided society with unsolved problems. The radicalisation of society due to the high stakes involved and intense constitutional discussion during the attempt at a constitutional moment make it difficult to simply return to the last inter-cycle state. To simplify the matter, after a failed constitutional moment society is not divided into progressives who demand a change and conservatives who defend the status quo. Instead, the proposals of 'constitutional momenters' are counterbalanced by those who demand a change in roughly the opposite direction rather than defending the status quo. A mouldable mass in between is forced to choose sides. With the conclusion of the cycle, the new constitutional regime enters normal times, in which the compromised understanding of the constitution is doctrinally elaborated in inter-institutional discourse (see the third condition). Eventually, a new constitutional cycle can be triggered.

The first two stages indicate what path was taken. If the revolutionary path was not taken, the third stage will reveal which alternative legitimating narrative constitutional actors employed to construct an allegiance between society and the constitution and whether they succeeded in making the constitution central to political discourse. In normal times, the question is how this narrative is retained and how inter-institutional communication solidifies the centrality of the constitution.

VII. Conclusion

The challenge ahead for constitutionalism is not the increased role of political movements (since that is not a novelty), but the limited ability of rights-based constitutionalism to provide liberal democratic movements with an operational framework through which they can counterweight conservative movements' appeal to collective identity. The proposed reconfiguration of constitutionalism research with its accompanying methodology may lead to isolating such substantive, institutional, and legitimising solutions that could restore a constitution's centrality in public discourse. While the highest courts remain critical for rationalising the discourse, they will be, as a number of theories already claim – from constitutional pluralism (in both the Canadian and the European versions) to the backlash theory to the constitutional-moments theory – understood more as a part of the discourse than its end. In other words, they will lose their monopoly on constitutional interpretation (real or imagined). With the courts' role diminished, even if still important, the constitutionalism's re-focus from individual rights to collective identity will allow to capture the broader spectrum of relevant institutional drivers of public discourse, that would otherwise remain below constitutionalism's radar.

Moreover, we are likely to see more concentration of political movements on both the populist and progressive sides along the cultural regional lines. Continuing federalisation of the Euro-area (even if with less states) will correlatively increase the appeal for these movements to control the European Parliament (and indirectly the Commission). This tendency is likely to take place also in those parts of the world where regional identity is historical strong, such as the Arab world. There, social movements with political aspirations might take the lesson from the Arab Spring and seek better organisation and cooperation next time around.

To conclude on the theme of this book, constitutionalism might play the prime role in western political organisation in 2030 and become more acceptable elsewhere if a rights-based approach has been replaced with a more political and communal approach. It may foster universal discursive conditions while encouraging substantive differentiation between political communities at the same time.

INDEX

Lightning Source UK Ltd.
Milton Keynes UK
UKHW020154090922
408527UK00003B/37

9 781509 942701